Law and Order

An Honest Citizen's Guide to Crime and Control

Robert Reiner

polity

First published in 2007 by Polity Press

Polity Press
65 Bridge Street
Cambridge CB2 1UR, UK.

Polity Press
350 Main Street
Malden, MA 02148, USA

ISBN-13: 978-07456-2996-4
ISBN-13: 978-07456-2997-1 (pb)

A catalogue record for this book is available from the British Library.

Typeset in 10.5 on 12 pt Plantin
by SNP Best-set Typesetter Ltd., Hong Kong
Printed and bound in Great Britain
by MPG Books Ltd, Bodmin Cornwall

For further information on Polity, visit our website: www.polity.co.uk

Contents

Preface and Acknowledgements

The media are saturated with dramatic crime stories; public concern and political argument about crime and its control are more intense than ever throughout the Western world. In Britain, the government itself speaks of the criminal justice system as not fit for purpose in the twenty-first century, and pledges to 'rebalance' and modernize it – again and again. Paradoxically this comes after more than a decade of falling crime rates. This is only one of the many ways in which the febrile discourse of law and order is out of kilter with a more sober and measured analysis.

The aim of this book is to inject some of the findings of the extensive research conducted by criminologists into the public debate on crime and control. Its main thesis is likely to be controversial and disputed, however, even among criminologists. The core thread running through the book is the argument that neoliberalism, the increasing penetration of free market principles and practices into all spheres of life, is the fundamental factor underlying both the threats of crime and violence, *and* increasingly authoritarian control tactics.

The abandonment of the more regulated and welfarist mixed economy strategy that prevailed in the three decades after World War II, often looked back on now – for all its faults – as a golden age of widely shared economic progress and security, was a Faustian bargain. We are learning that there is a high price to be paid for the fantastic wealth of some and the glittering baubles enjoyed by many: growing unhappiness, family breakdown, mental illness – especially among the young – looming environmental catastrophe, financial and physical insecurities and risks of many kinds.

The crimes that are focused on by the media act as a lightning conductor for a mass of other anxieties and resentments. Nonetheless the pains inflicted by these crimes, and by the attempts to control them, are real enough, and this book aims to shed light on their sources and the prospects for effective and humane protection.

The subtitle of the book will be recognized by criminologists as homage to the classic liberal analysis of criminal justice, published in 1970 by Chicago University Press: Norval Morris and Gordon Hawkins's *The Honest Politician's Guide to Crime Control*. This was an inspiration to me and I'm sure many of my generation, although my analysis here differs in many profound ways from theirs. An obvious difference is my substitution of 'honest citizen' for 'honest politician'. Sadly the latter label would appear an impossible dream today. But the book is aimed at the many honest citizens remaining, so that they may impress on their supposed representatives smarter and more humane crime control policies. As a brief but reasonably comprehensive review of criminological literature, it is also hoped that the book will be useful as an introduction to the subject for its rapidly growing number of students.

My intellectual debts to many scholars are too many to even begin to acknowledge them all here. But the ideas in the book have been developed over many years during which I have had the privilege of teaching at the Law Department of the London School of Economics and

Political Science. The LSE Mannheim Centre for Criminology has a remarkable number of criminological giants whom I have had the benefit of learning from, at the weekly Tuesday Ph.D. seminars, and the many courses we teach jointly – though they will probably disagree with much if not all of what I say. I would like to thank its members, past and present: Stan Cohen, Rachel Condry, David Downes, Marian Fitzgerald, Janet Foster, Roger Graef, Frances Heidensohn, Mercedes Hinton, Dick Hobbs, Jon Jackson, Nicola Lacey, Leonard Leigh, Terence Morris, David Nelken, Tim Newburn, Jill Peay, Coretta Phillips, Maurice Punch, Peter Ramsay, Paddy Rawlinson, Mike Redmayne, Paul Rock, Judith Rumgay, Mike Shiner, David Smith, Anna Souhami, Janet Stockdale, Michael Zander. I would also like to add Kate Malleson and Lucia Zedner, both of whom left for other pastures some time ago, and Ben Bowling and Wayne Morrison with whom I taught joint courses on the now defunct London University intercollegiate LLM. I have also learned much from Mike Maguire and Rod Morgan during our joint editing since 1994 of the *Oxford Handbook of Criminology*, now in its fourth edition.

The burdens of this book have fallen mainly on my family. I must apologize to them for my mental absence and grumpiness while writing it. Above all I must thank my children, Toby, Charlotte and Ben, and my wife, Joanna Benjamin, for their constant and never-failing support, encouragement, and above all inspiration. I only hope I can find some way of repaying them for everything.

1

Introduction: Neoliberalism, Crime and Control

> If I am not for myself, who will be for me? And if I am only for myself, what am I?
>
> Hillel, *Ethics of the Fathers*, 1:14

Law and order has become a central issue of our times. Opinion polls show that over the last twenty-five years it has regularly been rated 'one of the most important issues facing Britain today'. This has not always been the case. Law and order emerged as a political issue in the early 1970s (following the US where it became contentious in the late 1960s). During this time there has also been a huge rise in recorded crime rates. Concern about crime is far from unwarranted, but the growing obsession with law and order can only be explained in small part by increasing risks of victimization. This book's main thesis is that the massive rise in crime of recent decades, *and* the turn to law and order, are both due to the same 'root cause': the increasing dominance of neoliberal political economy since the 1970s.

Neoliberalism: The Revolution of the Rich

Neoliberalism is the most common label for the economic theory and practice that has swept the world since the early

1970s, displacing communism in Eastern Europe and China, as well as the Keynesian, mixed economy, welfare state consensus that had prevailed in Western liberal democracies since the Second World War.[1] As an economic doctrine it postulates that free markets maximize efficiency and prosperity, by signalling consumer wants to producers, optimizing the allocation of resources and providing incentives for entrepreneurs and workers.[2] Beyond economics, however, neoliberalism has become the hegemonic discourse of our times, so deeply embedded in all corners of our culture that its nostrums, once controversial and contested, have become the commonsense, taken-for-granted orthodoxy underpinning most public policy debates.

Neoliberalism as culture and ethic

Advocates of neoliberalism see it as not only promoting economic efficiency, but also political and personal virtue.[3] To neoliberals, free markets are associated with democracy, liberty and ethics. Welfare states, they claim, have many moral hazards: they undermine personal responsibility, and meet the sectional interests of public sector workers, not public service. Neoliberals advocate market discipline, workfare and New Public Management (NPM) to counteract this.[4]

Neoliberalism has spread from the economic sphere to the social and cultural. The roots of contemporary consumer culture predate neoliberal dominance, but it has now become hegemonic. Aspirations and conceptions of the good life have become thoroughly permeated by materialist and acquisitive values.[5] Business solutions, business news and business models permeate all fields of activity from sport and entertainment, to charities, non-governmental organizations, and even crime control.[6]

'Neoliberalization has meant, in short, the financialization of everything',[7] penetrating everywhere, from the stuff of dreams to the minutiae of daily life. Money has become the measure of men and women, with the 'Rich List' and its many variations ousting all other rankings of status.

The harms of neoliberalism

The benefits of neoliberalism have been familiarized as common sense by its cheerleaders, and indeed in most public discussion Mrs Thatcher's TINA ('there is no alternative') rules. There are however many negative consequences of unbridled markets and materialism. They used to be stressed by a variety of traditions, above all the diverse forms of socialism, but also by many religions. They were well understood by classical liberal political economy, from Adam Smith to Alfred Marshall and Pigou. As with the trumpeted virtues of markets, their dysfunctions transcend the economic, and include moral, social and political harms.

In the light of the huge increases in inequality sketched below, the rise of neoliberalism can best be interpreted as a revolution of the rich. Since the 1970s the operations of capital that had been restrained in the interests of security, stability and social justice by Keynesian and social democratic leaning governments around the world after the Second World War were more or less rapidly 'unleashed'.[8] In essence neoliberalism has been a class war launched and won to devastating effect by 'capital resurgent'.[9] In the absence of countervailing interventions, markets tend to produce a variety of negative economic, ethical, and socio-political consequences:

Economic harms Free markets are prone to generate concentrations of power that undermine their freedom.

- Left to themselves markets will become increasingly dominated by monopolistic accumulations of power, as the winners use their resources to drive out competitors. 'While the virtues of competition are placed up front, the reality is the increasing consolidation of oligopolistic, monopoly, and transnational power within a few centralized multinational corporations: the world of soft-drinks competition is reduced to Coca-Cola versus Pepsi, the energy industry is reduced to five huge transnational corporations, and a few media magnates control most of the flow of news, much of which then becomes pure propaganda.'[10]
- Inequality of wealth and income become ever greater, as the winners of early competition multiply their advantages. The wealthiest 1 per cent in Britain now own more than half of all wealth, and the wealthiest half of the population own nearly all the country's wealth – 94 per cent, a considerable increase over the last three decades.[11] Neoliberal political economies such as the US and Britain have seen inequality rocketing up by contrast with those (notably in Scandinavia) that have retained more of the postwar social democratic framework. In the last twenty years, income inequality rose 28 per cent in the UK, and 24 per cent in the US. By contrast, inequality of incomes rose by only 1 per cent in Denmark, 4 per cent in Finland, 7 per cent in Norway, and 12 per cent in Sweden.[12]
- Allocation of resources increasingly reflects the consumer power of the rich, not human need, exemplified by Galbraith's juxtaposition of private affluence and public squalor.[13] The central claim made on behalf of free markets by proponents, now largely conceded even by most of the left, is that they produce economic 'efficiency', an optimal allocation of resources guided by the myriad signals of what people demand. This system is

often represented as more democratic than state planning. What is seldom pointed out is that the market is a peculiar form of democracy: not one person, one vote, but one *pound*, one vote. Demand that counts in the market is not human need but *effective* demand, demand backed by purchasing power. So celebrity chefs in Mayfair flourish, while many poor children are undernourished, or obese because of cheap junk food. Pharmaceutical corporations produce drugs to enable affluent old men to have sex, while research languishes on diseases of the poor like malaria that kill millions around the world. Measuring economic progress by national income growth based on market prices is to use an index that reflects market power not human welfare. The New Economics Foundation has produced alternative indices, incorporating estimates of the social costs of conventional economic activity (such as pollution), and of social benefits that do not command an adequate market price (for example childcare, health, security, happiness). They suggest that economic welfare has fallen back since the advent of neoliberalism.[14] Inequality itself complicates the assessment of economic efficiency and growth. How can one say that the higher gross national product of 2006 compared to 1976 represents progress in well-being when some have done very well but there are also many losers? Is this not a biased judgement that the latter are less important than the former? The conventional economic answer is that if the overall cake is bigger the gainers can overcompensate the losers and everyone is better off. But this answer is unpersuasive unless such compensatory redistribution *actually* occurs.

- Market systems are prone to macroeconomic cyclical fluctuations. The postwar dominance of Keynesianism was because it was seen as offering a set of techniques for managing these cycles, and thus hopefully averting a repetition of the 1930s Depression, with its disastrous consequences for everyone, including in part the Second World War itself.

- Insecurities caused by the adversities of ill-health, old age, etc., are widespread and hard to predict at the level of the individual. The welfare state originated in Bismarckian Germany and other countries in the late nineteenth century because of the view that these largely random vicissitudes are better protected against by collective rather than individual insurance. Although neoliberals have trumpeted the 'moral hazards' and other supposed deficiencies of state welfare and insurance it is far from clear that market solutions are preferable. The sorry sagas of private pensions 'mis-selling' and 'NHS plc'[15] illustrate this.

Ethical harms Materialistic market societies generate cultures of egoism, short-termism, *irresponsibility* towards others. They encourage lack of concern about the wider ramifications of action, in the present, but above all for posterity (as the threat of climate change shows most obviously). Bakan demonstrates that company law requires corporations to act in ways psychiatrists would diagnose as psychopathic in an individual.[16] The 'live now, pay later' mentality of consumer culture parallels the psychic structure of criminality suggested by much conservative criminology: 'impulsive, insensitive . . . risk-taking, short-sighted'.[17] The changing work patterns of 'the new capitalism', their 'flexibility' and 'dynamism' eroding the security and stability that could inculcate virtues of commitment and craftsmanship, produce a 'corrosion of character'.[18] The 'aspirational' culture, celebrated by many commentators, prioritizes the desire for individual success in the form of material accumulation.

It is the essence of the concept of 'anomie', the key explanation of crime and deviance in classical social theory.

Tawney anticipated this in his stirring statement of ethical socialism in *The Acquisitive Society*. Competitive market society

> suspends a golden prize, which not all can attain, but for which each may strive, the enchanting vision of infinite expression. It assures men that there are no ends other than their ends, no law other than their desires, no limit other than that which they think advisable. Thus it makes the individual the centre of his own universe, and dissolves moral principles into a choice of expediencies.[19]

Social/political harms Inequality and competitiveness produce many adverse social consequences, notably poor health, social conflict and violence.[20] The affinity between markets and democracy postulated by neoliberal theorists is doubtful. 'Free' markets have complex institutional, cultural and legal conditions of existence. These include state suppression of the disorder sparked by market-generated social dislocations. As Karl Polanyi forecast in 1944, the same year that Hayek published his *Road to Serfdom* warning of the perils of socialism:[21]

> The idea of freedom . . . degenerates into a mere advocacy of free enterprise . . . the fullness of freedom for those whose income, leisure, and security need no enhancing, and a mere pittance of liberty for the people, who may in vain attempt to make use of their democratic rights to gain shelter from the power of the owners of property.[22]

In Andrew Gamble's famous formulation, the 'free' market needs the 'strong state'[23] . . . and the 'strong' state may well become authoritarian. Democracy today remains threatened by wide inequality, as a wide-ranging study by the

American Political Science Association has shown.[24] Neo-liberalism supplies the 'best democracy money can buy':[25] the costs of campaigning spiral beyond the reach of all but the wealthy and their corporate interests.

'Root Causes' or 'Realism'?

'Root cause' and political economy perspectives have become deeply unfashionable in criminology. James Q. Wilson launched the attack on 'root cause' perspectives with ferocious acerbity in his 1975 book *Thinking about Crime*. 'I have yet to see a "root cause" or to encounter a government programme that has successfully attacked it.'[26] Wilson's book became the beacon of a new right-wing realist approach to crime and control. It advocated that the key to controlling crime was to increase its costs to prospective offenders, in terms of the probability and intensity of penalties. This chimed in with the resurgence of neoclassical economic perspectives more generally, and their increasing application to crime and punishment.[27] It was also congruent with the developing rational choice perspective, especially influential in the British Home Office. This saw the key to effective crime control as changing the *situations* in which offending occurs – for example by target hardening – without tackling its causes. In the 1980s these conservative and administrative perspectives were joined by a new school of 'left realists'.[28] Left realism sought practicable short-term crime reduction measures, although it never denied the significance of structural causes as well, regarding policy recommendations as transitional steps to alleviate the immediate suffering of victims.

All the varieties of the new post-1970s realism shared certain elements, despite profound differences in analysis and political commitment. The most important were a common representation (or rather, *mis*representation) of the earlier social democratic analysis of crime that they criticized, and a concomitant can-do faith in the capacity of criminal justice to reduce crime.

The shared misrepresentation of social democratic criminology attributed to it a simple association of crime and poverty. Wilson bluntly caricatured the social democratic (or in American terms 'liberal') orthodoxy he was attacking thus: 'Men steal because they are poor and deprived'.[29] Social democratic criminology did *not* see crime as a straightforward reflex of poverty, or indeed any other economic variable such as unemployment.[30] It always stressed the importance of culture and morality in shaping how economic circumstances were experienced and interpreted, and thus in mediating any link with crime. The main social democratic criminological perspectives, notably Robert Merton's formulation of anomie theory, had little difficulty understanding why crime rose as the new culture of consumerism drove up aspirations more rapidly than attainment, despite the advent of mass 'affluence' (especially in view of the extensive inequality that remained).[31]

What works? The limits of criminal justice policy

Perhaps the most significant aspect of the new realism was confidence in the capacity of appropriate criminal justice policies to deliver effective crime control. Paradoxically this can-do faith arose phoenix-like from the ashes of traditional approaches to criminal justice, previously regarded as refuted by the 'nothing works' evaluative research on punishment and policing of the 1970s. This had been symbolized by Robert Martinson's review of studies of penal treatment, as well as evaluative research on policing.[32] By the late 1980s *nothing* works had transmuted (true to Martinson's own original purpose) into the search for *what* works in policing, punishment, probation and prevention. The crime drop of the 1990s, starting in the US and then in most of the Western world, consolidated a gathering mood of can-do optimism among criminal justice elites.

The evidence that will be reviewed in chapter 5 suggests that criminal justice policy and practice can only have relatively marginal effects on crime levels, except perhaps in extreme circumstances. Short of saturation policing 24/7 throughout the year even the smartest, toughest force of Jack Bauer clones cannot provide cover for the huge array of potential crime targets in any contemporary area, urban, suburban or rural. Nor could it clear up more than a very small proportion of the crimes it knows about – which is only a tiny proportion of all the crimes that occur. The killer fact about criminal justice is that only a tiny proportion of crimes *ever* get cleared up, let alone result in anyone being formally punished. Some 2 per cent of crimes recorded in the British Crime Survey (itself only a small proportion of all crimes) end with a perpetrator being convicted (as figure 3.1 on p. 54 shows).[33]

The popular belief that (in Michael Howard's words) 'prison works' relies mainly on the commonsense view that while incarcerated people cannot victimize anyone (outside prison). But incapacitation will only lower crime rates if the prison population keeps rising (otherwise – in the absence of successful rehabilitative interventions – released convicts will commit crimes to replace those not committed by the newly incarcerated). Continuously raising imprisonment a huge amount (as the US has since the 1970s) plausibly had some incapacitative effect which contributed to its crime fall (although the extent of this is disputable).[34] But comparative analysis questions even this. Countries adjacent to, and broadly comparable with jurisdictions that saw a particularly large growth in their prison populations, notably the US and England and Wales, experienced similar crime falls without increasing imprisonment, as the cases of Canada and Scotland illustrate.[35] In any case, if falling crime in the US depends upon continuously jacking up imprisonment, the country could end up as one big prison 'from sea to shining sea'. Liberal philosophy has always agonized about the justifications for punishment – the infliction of pain by the state. Punishment in itself is an evil, even if it may be a necessary or moral response to wrongdoing. So there are both pragmatic and ethical grounds for not seeing criminal justice as central to the control of crime. Levels of crime are only partly a function of how well criminal justice institutions operate, and are primarily shaped by wider social, economic and cultural factors (as chapters 4 and 5 will show).

Criminals: the mark of Cain or the Casablanca syndrome?

The myth that offenders are a highly distinctive group, marked off from the 'normal' population, is energetically promulgated by many criminal justice professionals. Current government strategy on crime is underpinned by the belief that a small group of persistent offenders are the major problem. Tony Blair, for instance, launched the Prolific and Priority Offenders Strategy in 2004 by promising that it would target the 'hard core of prolific offenders – just 5,000 people' who were said to be responsible for '10 per cent of all crime'. At the same launch, the then Home Secretary, David Blunkett, claimed that '100,000 offenders commit half of all crime'.[36]

It is perhaps comforting for criminal justice policymakers and practitioners to think that they *know* who is responsible for crime, even if they often cannot get enough evidence to secure convictions. But the hard fact is that in view of the huge 'attrition' rate, that is, the tiny proportion of all crimes that result in a convicted offender, we do *not know* who has perpetrated the vast majority of offences. The government's confident assertions purport to be grounded in a Home Office analysis of the Offenders Index, which collates details of all people who have been convicted of a particular 'standard' set of offences since 1963.[37] This does indeed find that about two-thirds of all convictions are accounted for by a quarter of the individuals on the database. But given that at most 2 per cent of known crimes result in a conviction, these patterns cannot be extrapolated with any confidence to offenders as a whole. The Home Office study of the Offenders Index itself gives the health warning that it is impossible to know how representative their data are of all offenders. It may well be that the frequent conviction of a relatively small proportion of offenders results from the *Casablanca* syndrome – endlessly recycling 'the usual suspects'. Ministers' confident pronouncements that the crime problem is due to a small group of known hardcore offenders amounts to a huge non sequitur from the analysis of convicts.[38]

Although the risks of being convicted for any offence are tiny, repeat offenders do stack up the probability of being caught eventually. Nonetheless, field studies of active (as opposed to incarcerated) burglars, armed robbers, and other professional criminals show that a significant proportion have no criminal records, and that most have no convictions for the offence that they live by.[39] Perpetrators of the kinds of crimes that are seldom recorded in the first place, in particular 'crimes of the powerful' such as corporate or state crime, domestic violence and crimes against children, are even less likely to be apprehended or to fit the underclass profile of apprehended criminals. Convicted offenders are an unrepresentative bunch, the double losers of the lotteries of legitimate opportunity *and* criminal justice.

Neoliberalism, Anomie, Crime and Control

The main thesis of this book is that the dangerous and oppressive trends in crime and in crime control that have occurred in the last three decades are fundamentally rooted in the political economy of neoliberalism, and its cultural and social concomitants. The increasing focus on criminal justice and known offenders is itself an aspect of this new law and order complex. This does not mean, however, that criminal justice is irrelevant or indeed that it hasn't become in many ways much more effective recently. It is important to distinguish between what might be called 'normal' and 'surplus' criminality in any specific social order, adopting the terminology of Marcuse in his critical extension of Freud.[40] As many theorists have argued, some deviance is inevitable in any society[41] – wars against crime are doomed to failure. Certain levels and patterns of criminality are normal in any particular conjuncture of political economy, social relations, and culture. However, if criminal justice functions poorly, rates of crime may rise beyond that normal level – what may be called 'surplus' criminality. In such circumstances, reforms of criminal justice can bring crime levels back to the norm – perhaps even suppress them for a time, but arguably with displacement of symptoms (as the analogy with repression implies).

The evidence presented in chapters 4 and 5 suggests that neoliberalism is associated both with higher levels of serious crime than social democracies, *and* with more punitive and inhumane crime control. The reasons for this were spelled out long ago in the classics of social democratic criminology, notably the theory of anomie as developed by Robert Merton, following the trail pioneered by Durkheim.[42] The essence of this perspective was expressed by an aphorism of the Mishnaic sage Ben Zoma some 1,800 years ago. 'Who is rich? Someone who rejoices in their portion' (*Ethics of the Fathers*, 4:1).[43] Anomie broadly refers to the tension arising from unsatisfied aspirations. The key insight is that the character of the desires inculcated by different cultural conceptions of the 'good life' can generate social and individual tensions and conflicts. As spelled out by Merton, this may arise in a number of ways. One is the argument his analysis is usually reduced to: inequality of opportunities, especially in a culture that cultivates a mythology of open opportunities for all, generates strains leading to deviance and crime, in particular among those lowest in the social hierarchy. But this was never an economically reductionist theory, as it has often been (mis)represented. The crucial factor is not the structure of opportunities per se, but its social meaning in different cultures.

Disjuncture between cultural goals and structurally available opportunities is only one of the processes analysed by Merton as anomie. The very *nature* of the aspirations held out by particular cultures, their conceptions of what counts as success, are possible sources of anomie. If these values are highly materialistic, in particular if they are exclusively defined in monetary terms, then anomie is likely to result, quite apart from the issue of inequality of opportunity. This is for three reasons. A materialistic culture is likely to generate aspirations that cannot be satisfied, particularly if emphasis is placed on monetary success rather than the goods or lifestyles it buys. There is no intrinsic end-point to the pursuit of monetary success: it is always possible to chase after more. The second reason is that a culture that stresses the importance of reaching material goals generates temptations and pressures to deviate, unless there is a countervailing emphasis on the legitimacy of the means to be adopted. Thirdly, an *exclusive* valorization of material goals is in itself also prone to anomie, because those who fail in that sphere have no possibility of compensation elsewhere, unlike in cultures with multiple conceptions of the good life.

Merton's analysis of anomie was specifically designed to provide a framework for explaining variations in crime rates and patterns between societies as a whole, as well as between different groups or individuals (although in contemporary criminology it has primarily been represented as the latter). Merton's particular concern was to elucidate the high levels of serious crime in the US. He saw this as a function both of the materialistic, money-oriented culture of the US, and of the tension between the 'American Dream' of a meritocracy in which all can succeed irrespective of class origins, on the one hand, and the reality of structural inequalities of opportunity comparable to those of the disdained and supposedly rigidly hierarchical old Europe, on the other.[44]

The decades after the Second World War witnessed a growing Americanization of cultures around the world, predating the clear hegemony of the neoliberal, 'Washington consensus', free market model. It is thirty years, for example, since an influential book declared that *The Media are American*.[45] The values of a consumer culture, and subsequently the social impact of neoliberal economic policies, drove up crime rates, just as the theory of anomie would predict. Aspirations to acquire 'must have' new and exciting consumer goods outstripped the ability to acquire them legitimately, increasing temptations and pressures to cut corners at all levels of society. Conceptions of the good life and of status became increasingly materialistic.

The term 'aspirational' has been used by many analysts to celebrate contemporary culture. Anthony Giddens, for example, speaks of the 'aspirational society', in which 'people . . . are prepared to be dynamic . . . want to get on . . . to make something of their life'.[46] But the effects of the new consumerism on the cultures and aspirations of poor young men in particular have been shown to be a factor in the growth of street crime by many studies.[47] The heightened anomic pressures have been vividly described as 'social bulimia' by Jock Young: young people are sucked into the voracious appetites for fashionable stuff by the media and pop culture, but the relatively disadvantaged are expelled from the legal possibilities of attaining the objects of their desire.[48]

Ethics and Individual Responsibility

> [T]here is no such thing as society. There are individual men and women, and there are families . . . and people must look to themselves first. It's our duty to look after ourselves and then, also to look after our neighbour.
>
> (Margaret Thatcher interview, *Woman's Own*, 31 Oct. 1987)

These famous (notorious?) words are often seen as a quintessential statement of individualism, but they elide two different conceptions. The first is what social theorists call 'methodological individualism'. Usually traced back to the perspective of Max Weber,[49] there have been many intense debates about the concept, because it covers a spectrum of interpretations, from the completely uncontentious to the deeply controversial. At one level there is the unchallengeable point that Thatcher appears to begin with: only flesh and blood individuals have a physical, observable existence, and only they can be said to think or act in a straightforward sense (this applies equally to the 'families' that she credits with real 'thingness'). Nonetheless, it is common to talk of 'social collectivities, such as states, associations, business corporations, foundations, as if they were individual persons',[50] and Weber explicitly sees no objection to this, provided one bears in mind that this is an anthropomorphic usage.

The serious controversies begin when methodological individualism denies that meaningful statements can be made about collectivities, or that there are patterns and structures in collective behaviour, resulting from the complex interactions of myriad individuals, which have a considerable measure of 'reality' in the sense of stability and predictability. These patterns are robust enough for insurance companies that rely on the high probability of their continuation to normally remain profitable. But the predictions of all organizations – from Lloyds to Tesco to police chiefs deciding on patrol levels – making decisions on the basis of analysis of past patterns are always vulnerable. They are hostage to shifts in 'collective' sentiments and behaviour, resulting from a myriad of changes in individual choices, 're-fashioned by human actors who simply rewrote their narratives'.[51] Statistical correlations, however strong and long-lasting, are not sufficient to establish causation, as all methodology texts emphasize (but econometricians and many other social scientists routinely ignore). They are only plausible candidates for causal explanation at all if they are also, in Weber's words, 'adequate at the level of meaning'.[52] They have to be placed in a narrative that can interpret them as subjectively meaningful sequences of human action. But because they are patterns of meaningful human action they are always vulnerable to change stemming from human creativity and new interpretations.

A second problem with statements of methodological individualism arises if they slide from methodology to morality, as Mrs Thatcher's plainly does. That only individuals have a concrete physical existence does not entail that they should be egoistic, 'look to themselves first'. Mrs Thatcher explicitly inverts the biblical Golden Rule, 'Love your neighbour as yourself' (Leviticus 19: 18): neighbours have to wait in line while we look after ourselves first. But the Golden Rule is *not* a collectivist ethos. It clearly relates to individuals, whose interests have to be balanced on the basis of fundamentally equal concern ('as yourself').[53] This is the ethical basis of most, arguably all, forms of social democracy.[54] Although collectivities such as the state, trade unions, and social classes may be seen by social democrats as instruments for achieving justice, they are not venerated in themselves.

Contrary to what Mrs Thatcher said, there is not a simple contrast between individualism and other ethics. There are important differences between forms of individualism that she blots out. Specifically, the *egoistic individualism* that she and other neoliberals champion must be contrasted with the *reciprocal individualism* that underpins social democracy. Egoistic individualism regards individuals as responsible primarily for themselves – neighbours hold back! Reciprocal individualism sees all individuals as mutually responsible: neighbours are to be treated *as* oneself, requiring equal concern and respect. These two versions of the ethics of individualism suggest radically different notions of social policy, crime and criminal justice. It is not surprising that, as the empirical evidence reviewed in chapters 4 and 5 shows, neoliberalism with its ethic of egoistic individualism is associated with more punishment, less welfare and more violent crime than social democracies, which are underpinned by reciprocal individualism.

A related neoliberal argument is that social explanations of crime (such as anomie) overlook the individual responsibility of offenders. In this view, the prevalence of such causal explanations actually contributes to crime by undermining personal responsibility. As Thatcher's successor John Major famously put it, 'Society needs to condemn a little more and understand a little less'.[55] In recent years the idea that there is an incompatibility between understanding and condemnation has become widespread. Even some avowed progressives who feel that the majority of the left are not sufficiently concerned to distance themselves from terrorism have offered versions of this argument. They criticize what they regard as the indecent haste with which people move from condemning terrorist attacks to seeking to explain them.[56]

It is true that a completely deterministic account of crime leaves no scope at all for moral responsibility, and such a position is incompatible with any notions of just punishment (as opposed to treatment or training).[57] Most attempts to explain crime, however, are not deterministic but probabilistic. They seek to identify individual, situational, cultural, social, economic and other factors that make offending more likely, but not inevitable. Choice and responsibility – and hence the scope for condemnation and just punishment – remain. Offenders make their own histories – but not under conditions of their own choosing. *Pace* John Major, it is hard to see why condemnation should be seen as challenged by understanding. After all, generations of teachers and students have discussed the 'causes of the Second World War' in lectures and essays, without wavering for a moment in the common conviction that Hitler was the epitome of evil.

Indeed, for my own part, it is precisely my deep fear and revulsion at the harms done by crime – as well as many other practices – that makes me eager to go beyond this and understand their sources, precisely to protect potential future victims. The idea that there is a zero-sum contest between victims and offenders, causal explanation and moral responsibility, understanding and condemnation, is a key feature of the currently dominant politics of law and order. But it is not a universal feature of popular culture or political discourse.[58] Social democratic cultures of reciprocal individualism are not characterized by the zero-sum, us-or-them syndrome that is a feature of the egoistic individualism engendered by contemporary neoliberalism. Punitive obsessions are the undeclared projection, not the obverse, of the evils they condemn. Shakespeare saw this most clearly:

> Thou rascal beadle, hold thy bloody hand!
> Why dost thou lash that whore? Strip thy own back;
> Thou hotly lusts to use her in that kind
> For which thou whip'st her
>
> (*King Lear*, IV. vi. 157–60)

2

An Inspector Calls: Putting Crime in its Place

Authors usually try to magnify the significance of the topics they write about, but the aim of this chapter is precisely the opposite. It questions the coherence and importance attributed to 'crime'. This is not to deny or belittle the immense human suffering and harm endured by victims – nor to ignore the pains inflicted in punishing offenders. The mass media are saturated with news and fiction stories graphically portraying the violence and anguish suffered in the worst cases. The anxiety, loss and disruption caused by the much more widespread, *relatively* less serious offences that are casually referred to in policy documents as 'volume' crime – as well as the more ambiguous troubles conveyed by the term 'anti-social behaviour' – are unfortunately familiar to many of us (including myself, a repeat victim of burglaries and other thefts). Nonetheless the purpose of this chapter is to put crime in its place, questioning its coherence as a concept, and querying why its significance as a source of suffering and danger is so exaggerated in our culture compared to other risks.

The term 'crime' is usually tossed about as if it has a clear and unambiguous meaning, but many if not most arguments about crime involve people talking past each other, with fundamentally different issues in mind.[1] The concept of 'crime' has specific historical conditions of existence, and its emergence is related to the rise of the capitalist political economy and certain associated features of modern culture, notably its individualism.

All societies, perhaps all relationships, are characterized by deviance, for reasons that were well set out a century ago by Émile Durkheim. People will always vary somewhat in their capacity or willingness to conform to established norms. Thus even in a 'cloister of saints' there will be deviance and sanctions, even though the precise nature of the 'sins' in such an environment might not cause any concern in our own more blasé, morally insensitive cultures.[2] But while deviance and control are perennial, there are distinctive features of modern concepts of crime and the repertoire of formalized responses. It is only in relatively complex societies with a developed division of labour that specific 'legal' mechanisms for dispute resolution and order maintenance emerge. In simpler societies these functions are achieved through other institutions, notably kinship and religion. The development of specifically 'criminal' law, as distinct from other forms of adjudication and enforcement of norms, is even more clearly associated with modernism. The distinctive features of 'criminal' law are its association with the state, and the notion of individual responsibility. Criminal laws are deemed to be offences against the public realm as distinct from private interests, even if there is also harm to specific other people. The legislative and judicial arms of the state have the authority to determine what is processed as criminal, that is, subject to state-organized punishment rather than private redress or revenge.

Violators of these laws are regarded as personally responsible, and in principle there is supposed to be a fault element, 'mens rea' (literally, a guilty mind), as an ingredient of the offence. Many contemporary laws that belong to criminal law, in that their alleged breach is followed by prosecution and punishment following a verdict of guilt, are strict liability offences without a requirement of individual culpability, but these are regarded widely as problematic, and indeed treated as different from criminal law 'proper' in many jurisdictions.[3]

These two elements of the modern notion of crime are related to key characteristics of modern capitalist political economy and culture.[4] The growth of strong centralized states is clearly a precondition of the first feature, the notion of crime as a *public* offence, with harm to individuals constituting neither a necessary nor a sufficient condition of criminalization. The idea of individual moral responsibility is related to the conception of people as autonomous subjects capable (at least in principle) of rational choice. It is the criminological translation of the rational economic actor model of classical political economy, developing in the eighteenth century with the rise of capitalist industrialism.

A further aspect of the fully fledged modern idea of crime develops with the stabilization of modern capitalism during the nineteenth century:[5] 'crime' is an intermediate level of threat, attributable to individuals or at most small groups ('gangs'). Criminalizing nuisances below a certain threshold of seriousness (as has been done from the late medieval vagrancy laws to the contemporary anti-social behaviour order) is always controversial. Conversely, very great levels of violence and disorder are seen as distinct from 'ordinary' crime: 'terrorism', civil war, genocide, war – even though they involve many severe 'crimes'. When there is perceived to be a complete breakdown of order, as in 'failed' states or wars between states, it is hard to distinguish between crime and politics, the evils of war and war crimes.[6] The notion of 'crime' as an offence against a fundamentally consensual public interest, committed by individuals who are all separately culpable and subject to adjudication and punishment, presupposes a degree of settled order. This was achieved during the nineteenth century and for most of the 20th century in the liberal democracies of Europe, North America and the rest of the 'Western' world, the heyday of modern criminal justice. As we will see, the last quarter of the twentieth century saw profound changes in political economy and culture that threaten the conditions of existence of modern criminal justice.

Within these core parameters of the idea of 'crime', considerable diversity and disagreement still remain about what crime is. At least the following five different constructions of crime and the criminal can be distinguished in different aspects of contemporary discourse, each itself signifying a complex web of concepts, practices and values.

(1) Legal constructions

Probably most people if asked to define 'crime' would invoke the criminal law as its basis. 'An offence against an individual or the state which is punishable by law' is the primary definition given by the Compact Oxford English Dictionary. Yet people talk of crime in many ways that are different from, even contradictory to, criminal law perspectives. Indeed the Compact OED offers a further 'informal' definition of crime: 'something shameful or deplorable'. There is considerable variation between such social or moral constructions of crime, and legal ones.

There is also 'an enormous diversity among criminal laws: in terms of the style of their drafting; their scope; their construction of their subjects and objects; their assumptions about responsibility; their procedural requirements'.[7] Defining the scope of criminal law in substantive rather than formal or procedural ways is notoriously problematic, because of the diversity of function and character apparent in the vast, rapidly growing and shifting corpus of criminal law.[8]

There is huge cultural variation across space and time in what is counted by the law as criminal. The business of the English courts a few centuries ago would be largely unrecognizable to their contemporary counterparts, as illustrated by a historical study of felony indictments in Essex between 1559 and 1603.[9] This found a predominance of property-related offences, and a smaller proportion of violent and sex crimes, not unlike present patterns. What differentiated the Essex assizes of the first Queen Elizabeth from the Crown Courts of the second Elizabeth were the 172 cases of witchcraft tried in the former. The change in conceptions of crime is even more striking in the business of the lower courts. A study of Essex quarter sessions between 1628 and 1632 found that out of 3,514 offences prosecuted, 144 were thefts and 48 assaults. But these figures are dwarfed by the 480 prosecutions for allowing bridges or roads to fall into decay, 229 for keeping a disorderly alehouse, and – the most numerous offence category – 684 prosecutions for failing to attend church.[10] Prosecutions before ecclesiastical or manorial courts show a yet wider range of offences which are not recognized today:[11] adultery, fornication, bridal pregnancy, scolding, and disrupting the sabbath in a variety of ways such as working, drinking in an alehouse, or wearing felt hats.

It can plausibly be argued that certain core functions must be met by some form of control process if a society is to survive, for example the minimal protection of person and property, as in Hart's conception of a 'minimum content of natural law'.[12] However, the variation in how this 'minimum' is achieved, and what other activities are proscribed at different times and places, makes the content of law contingent on a host of social, political, economic and cultural circumstances that underpin the processes of criminalization.[13] Consequently, most criminal law texts define crime in a positivist, formal, essentially circular way, following the arguments advanced fifty years ago in a celebrated lecture by Glanville Williams: 'crime is an act capable of being followed by criminal proceedings having a criminal outcome, and a proceeding or its outcome is criminal if it has certain characteristics which mark it as criminal.'[14]

This formalism is confirmed by recent jurisprudence in this country and in Europe that continues to demarcate criminal law in essentially procedural terms. The European Convention for the Protection of Human Rights (ECHR), incorporated into UK law by the Human Rights Act 1998, has stimulated much case-law about what makes proceedings criminal. Article 6 of the ECHR aims to protect the right to a fair trial, setting out specific rights for those facing 'any criminal charge', notably the presumption of innocence, and adequate legal assistance. There are further due process requirements specifically for criminal cases in Article 7 and several Protocols. This has resulted in extensive ECHR jurisprudence seeking to delineate the criminal/civil borderline.[15]

The leading case is *Engel*,[16] in which the European Court of Human Rights formulated three criteria for determining whether proceedings are 'criminal'. These are: (1) the domestic classification of the offence, (2) 'the very nature of the offence', (3) the seriousness of the potential punishment. The ECHR has maintained an 'autonomous' definition of 'criminal', to ensure states cannot deny the rights necessary for a criminal trial by redefining the offence, so criterion (1) is asymmetric: an offence is criminal if it is so defined in domestic law, but it may also be held to be criminal even if not defined as such by a particular country. The second criterion, the substance of the offence, has not produced analysis of the principles characterizing behaviour as criminal. Rather it has involved a set of essentially procedural issues: Is there a punitive element to the sanction? Is the offence generally binding or restricted to a specific subgroup? Does the verdict require finding culpability? Are proceedings instituted by a public body? How are such matters defined in other jurisdictions? In most cases the third criterion, the severity of potential punishment, has proved decisive.[17] The ECHR case-law thus delineates the criminal/civil borderline in essentially formal and procedural terms, and does not offer a substantive theory of the nature of crime.

The issue of legal definitions of crime has become even more complex in the last decade with the rise of hybrid offences whereby criminal sanctions (often severe) attach to breach of orders that are initially determined by civil processes. The most significant of these is the anti-social behaviour order (ASBO) under section 1 of the Crime and Disorder Act 1998, which may be made by a magistrates court in civil proceedings.[18] Breach of this order without reasonable excuse can attract a penalty of up to five years' imprisonment on indictment. The ECHR principles seem to suggest that this potentially severe penalty makes the proceedings as a whole (including the initial imposition of the order) 'criminal', but the House of Lords has held that an ASBO is preventive not punitive in purpose.[19] The imposition of an ASBO thus represents 'a position midway between the civil and the criminal paradigms':[20] the Lords have held that it requires the criminal standard of proof because of the potentially severe penalties, but with the more relaxed civil rules of evidence, including hearsay. ASBOs have been controversial as an extension of criminal sanctions to vaguely defined behaviour, requiring judgements of value about what is 'reasonable' in specific contexts that are likely to vary according to the social position of the defendant.[21]

Andrew Ashworth has suggested recently that we *can* 'identify a principled core of criminal law . . . the criminal law should be used, and only used, to censure persons for substantial wrongdoing'.[22] This claim certainly has bite and substance: it would for example rule out the penchant of governments for hybrid offences like the ASBO, or the plethora of 'administrative offences' with diluted culpability requirements. However, it clearly raises the issue of whether there is, or can be, agreement on what constitutes culpable 'substantial wrongdoing'. Ashworth's explicit purpose is 'to re-kindle debate about the functions and characteristics that the criminal law ought to have'[23] if criminal law is to have principled coherence and integrity. As Tadros and Tierney argue, despite recent theoretical advances, 'fully coherent and well defended principles that could be used to identify and distinguish wrongs are yet to emerge, let alone principles that might govern incorporation of those distinctions into the criminal law.'[24]

This leaves to social scientists, historians, philosophers, and people on Clapham omnibuses the task of explaining and evaluating the substantive scope of criminal law. Some critical theorists of criminal law have sought to transcend this divide,[25] analysing the processes of criminalization 'as a set of interlocking practices in which the moments of "defining" and "responding to" crime can rarely be completely distinguished and in which legal and social (extra-legal) constructions of crime constantly interact'.[26] This points to the variety of alternative, often conflicting conceptions of crime apart from, and often in conflict with, the legal. What is clear is that criminal law offers a coherent definition of crime only in a formalistic way, as behaviour that is sanctioned by specific procedures. Explaining or evaluating its content requires us to look elsewhere.

(2) *Normative constructions*

Formalist legal definitions of crime open themselves to normative critique. From different moral perspectives it can be claimed that criminal law proscribes and sanctions actions that ought not to be punished, because they are acceptable or perhaps even desirable. There is a long and honourable lineage of lawbreakers who have subsequently been hailed as moral heroes, from Socrates, Spartacus and Jesus to Nelson Mandela. Even if behaviour is regarded as wrong, it can be argued that criminalization is – for a variety of possible reasons – not the most appropriate means of control. Conversely the scope of criminal law can be criticized normatively for failing to include behaviours that should be proscribed and punished: 'there ought to be a law against it' must be one of the most commonly used clichés.

There are many jurisprudential and criminological debates about the normative limits of criminal law. Perhaps the most familiar argument about alleged overreach of criminal law is the claim from liberal political philosophy that 'private (im)moral behaviour' should not be subject to criminal law, for both principled and pragmatic reasons. This was the subject of the famous 'debates' between John Stuart Mill and Fitzjames Stephen in the nineteenth century, and Hart and Lord Devlin in the 1960s.[27] On the other hand, critical criminologists have frequently argued that criminal law fails to define or enforce as criminal serious and wilful harms that are committed by the powerful, in particular by states and corporations.[28] This has developed into the recent claim that criminology should be replaced by 'zemiology', the study of serious culpable harms, rendering as problematic whether or not they are proscribed by criminal law.[29] The definition of 'harms' is, of course, as socially contentious as notions of 'crime', but it explicitly involves normative evaluation not authoritative declaration. It opens up questions about what should be sanctioned, rather than foreclosing them by a mask of objectivity that shields the value judgements and biases of law and its enforcement from critical examination.

Critical criminologists have demonstrated that the monetary and human value of the harms inflicted by the crimes of the powerful are immensely greater than those caused by the routine thefts and offences against the person that are the predominant business of the criminal justice system. 'The collapse of the savings and loan institutions (similar to what in Britain are described as building societies) in the United States in the late 1980s, may end up costing a trillion dollars.'[30] The 2001 collapse of Enron following the revelation of its fraudulent activities cost nearly 20,000 innocent employees their jobs, savings and pensions, and huge losses to many small investors and creditors ('Enron', *Guardian Unlimited*, 6 July 2006).

Nor is corporate crime just about property. Many well-known cases have involved colossal loss of life: the 1988 Alpha oil rig explosion, the Chernobyl nuclear plant disaster, Bhopal, the drug Thalidomide, the Dalkon shield contraceptive, the dangerously inflammable Ford Pinto, the P&O ferry sinking, and the Hatfield rail crash.[31] These potential exhibits in a Black Museum of corporate crime are but the most notorious instances of a much larger number of routine threats to life and limb.[32] The Health and Safety Executive (HSE) officially records about 600–650 fatalities a year arising from occupational injury. But it has been shown using the HSE's official categories and data that the official statistics are a considerable underestimate, and that there are closer to 1,500 occupational fatalities a year – double the homicide rate.[33] Studies of the investigation and adjudication of these deaths by police, coroners and courts demonstrate that there is a clear tendency to presume or find no criminal responsibility on the part of the employer,[34] despite a legal basis for prosecution. Such deaths are frequently as gruesome, and inflict as much suffering on victims and families, as the blood-drenched cases featured in *CSI* or *Wire in the Blood*, but they are not the subject of television drama and popular nightmares.

A distinction between the violence that is straightforwardly understood as crime, and work-related fatalities is that the former inflicts immediate, face-to-face injury. Occupational deaths usually involve complex chains of causality that make the attribution of moral responsibility more ambiguous. The serious injuries leading to death may not be seen immediately or at all by those who commit the culpable actions (say, deliberate violation of safety requirements) that predictably produce the fatal result. Similarly, the difference between a terrorist suicide-bomber and a war hero may be a plane and an altitude of 3,000 feet. But seen or unseen, their victims are blown to bits all the same.

The most vivid deconstruction of the morally tenuous, if not arbitrary, differences between the harms constructed as crime and those that are hidden by the complex chains of causality in modern social relationships, facilitating denial of responsibility, is J. B. Priestley's play *An Inspector Calls*, which should be regarded as a criminological classic. Priestley uses the narrative structure and conventions of the Agatha Christie cosy whodunit to show the moral similarity of the intentional harms perpetrated by the powerful and privileged and what is more commonly regarded as crime. A police inspector calls on a respectable bourgeois family, who are celebrating their daughter's engagement to a man from a more established wealthy background. The inspector is investigating the lonely, anguished death (from swallowing an acid disinfectant) of a poor young woman. He painstakingly establishes that each person present contributed something to the tragedy by a legal, but thoughtlessly cruel, action that they saw as justified and normal (sacking her for orchestrating industrial action; arranging for her dismissal from a job in a shop because of apparent rudeness; seducing, impregnating and abandoning her; refusing her charitable support when she was pregnant and destitute). Only the daughter and son of the family come to recognize their responsibility for the girl's homicide. The paterfamilias smugly denies it: 'I can't accept any responsibility. If we were all responsible for what happened to everybody we'd had anything to do with, it would be very awkward, wouldn't it?'[35] The inspector's parting shot has the appropriate riposte:

> One Eva Smith has gone – but there are millions and millions . . . still left with us, with their lives, their hopes and fears, their suffering, and chance of happiness, all intertwined with our lives, with what we think and say and do. We don't live alone. We are members of one body. We are responsible for each other. And I tell you that the time will soon come when, if men will not learn that lesson, then they will be taught it in fire and blood and anguish. Good night.'[36]

The criminal law, reflecting the outcomes of power struggles and moral panics and political exigencies over many centuries, scarcely maps even in a rough-and-ready way the boundaries of human infliction of serious pain and harm on others, and the moral responsibility for this.

(3) Social/cultural constructions

Durkheim's famous attempt to provide a sociological definition of crime suggested that 'Crime shocks sentiments which, for a given social system are found in all healthy consciences . . . an act is criminal when it offends strong and defined states of the collective conscience.'[37] This is as positivist, tautologous and relativist a definition as the standard criminal law textbook's, albeit emphasizing social/cultural rather than legal or normative construction. As Durkheim himself recognized, conceptions of the criminal vary considerably between and within societies, and over time. Crime is whatever happens to be reacted to as seriously wrong in a particular culture, with no objective standpoint for analysis or critique. 'Liberalism for the liberals, cannibalism for the cannibals.'[38]

What is actually treated as criminal in particular cultures differs not only from law, but also from professed moral beliefs. Respectable middle-class people who see themselves as staunchly law-abiding, and stoutly condemn crime, commonly engage in practices that constitute theft, such as padding insurance claims or paying cash for services and thus conniving at tax evasion.[39] They defend themselves from a self-perception as 'really' criminal by 'techniques of neutralization'[40] of moral guilt similar to those used by the street criminals they distance themselves from. For example, they might 'condemn the condemners', arguing that the insurance companies are ripping them off as clients, by extortionate premiums or unfair conditions such as extravagant household security requirements.

What is typically sanctioned as deviant in social practice will vary from the formal definitions of law or of professed morality, and different groups will treat different conduct as truly criminal. An occupational hazard for a criminologist at parties is to deal with irate demands to explain why the police and courts harass the speeding or drinking motorist instead of 'real' criminals. Is drink-driving socially deviant? It is in most circles nowadays, was not in England until at most some three decades ago, but was even then in Scandinavia for example. Will driving under the influence of mobile phones go the same way? Who is 'really' criminal – the 'honest, victimized' householder Tony Martin, or the young burglar he was convicted of killing?[41]

'It is a salient characteristic of "crime" in public perception that it is committed by "others".'[42] Dominant characterizations of 'crime' see it as conduct associated with 'inferior' classes, as the etymology of the terminology for offenders indicates. The Oxford English Dictionary states that 'villain' derives from the medieval French for peasant, and 'rogue' from the Latin for beggar. By contrast 'property' and 'propriety' share a common root, indicating a connection between privileged economic class and conceptions of 'good' behaviour. Inequalities in the administration of criminal justice, a perennial source of liberal concern, are rooted deep in cultural perceptions and hierarchical social structures that represent crime as the conduct of disadvantaged and dangerous outsiders. As the 'well-bred young man-about-town' Gerald Croft remarks in *An Inspector Calls*, 'After all, y'know, we're respectable citizens and not criminals.' To which the Inspector replies, 'Sometimes there isn't as much difference as you think. Often, if it was left to me, I wouldn't know where to draw the line.'[43]

(4) Criminal justice constructions

Who is formally processed by the criminal justice system as criminal, and for what offences, constitutes another construction of crime and criminality. Recorded crimes and criminals are a very small and almost certainly unrepresentative sample of all lawbreaking activities (let alone of culpably harmful behaviour). Only 2 per cent of crimes measured by the British Crime Survey end up with a convicted offender, and another 1 per cent result in a caution.

The proportion of known crimes leading to someone being sentenced to custody is 0.3 per cent. And they are in prison mainly for a variety of street crimes, not suite crimes – car theft, and burglary, not insider trading or pensions mis-selling. The imbalance starts with what is reported (or more often, not reported) by victims, and gets more marked as cases go through the criminal justice process. The overwhelming majority of those in prison are men from economically underprivileged groups, with a huge disproportion of black and other ethnic minority people.[44] Black people in particular are disproportionately represented at each step of the criminal justice process, but especially at the entry points (stop and search, arrest) and at the final stage (imprisonment). Black people are just 3 per cent of the population but 14 per cent of those stopped and searched by the police, and 15 per cent of the prison population.[45]

The pattern of offences for which people are processed and convicted is almost the obverse of the amount of space they get in typical criminal law books and journals. Most are charged with driving offences or thefts, and only a minority with the serious violent and sexual offences and homicide that occupy the attention of criminal law texts. The pattern of those who are processed as suspects or offenders is highly skewed towards the poor and powerless. Given the huge rate of 'attrition' – crimes that are not recorded let alone cleared up – those who end up with criminal convictions are the losers of the criminal justice lottery. Only the deprived are at serious risk of being treated as depraved.

(5) Mass media and policy constructions

The constructions of crime offered by the mass media – which are those that inform most policy debates – again have a very different pattern, a biased sample of a biased sample. Mass media representations follow a 'law of opposites' in the words of the American criminologist Ray Surette:[46] they are the obverse of what official statistics on recorded crime and criminals portray.

Mass media stories, news and fiction, overwhelmingly focus on the most serious violent and sexual offences, above all murder, even though these are thankfully rare in reality.[47] The 'law of opposites' has governed the pattern of newspaper crime stories over the last half century, but increasing in extent.[48] Homicide is by far the most common crime reported in news stories, with violent crimes the next most frequent (together they constitute about 70 per cent). Non-violent property crimes, the overwhelming majority of recorded offences, featured in around a fifth of newspaper crime stories up to the mid-1960s, and since then have almost disappeared (the few that are now reported usually have a celebrity element, like the theft of a pop star's luggage). The same pattern holds for fiction stories. Property crimes, always underrepresented compared to official statistics, have virtually disappeared as the principal crime animating fictional narratives.[49]

Victims and offenders portrayed in media accounts are disproportionately older and higher in the social scale than their counterparts in official statistics (though they share the common feature of being overwhelmingly male). The overwhelming majority of offenders processed by the criminal justice system are young men (under twenty-five), economically deprived, and disproportionately from ethnic minorities. The opposite is true of those featured in news stories (apart from their gender): most are men who are well above twenty, middle or upper class, and white (though an increasing proportion are ethnic minority).[50]

The criminal justice system's most visible face in the mass media is the police. They are mainly presented as successful, law-abiding and morally virtuous (negative portrayals have certainly increased over the last fifty years but they remain a small minority). In news and fiction stories the police almost invariably succeed in catching offenders, although in reality only a tiny proportion of crimes are cleared up. A further feature of media stories, especially fiction but also tabloid news, is that clearing up crime frequently requires violations of due process of law. Vigilante cops have ceased agonizing about means/ends dilemmas, as did Clint Eastwood's 'Dirty Harry' and his ilk back in the 1970s. In *24*, *The Shield* and many other contemporary screen examples they take abuse of force, even torture, as routine tools of the trade. Although stories featuring criminal justice corruption have increased, they remain a small minority.[51]

This mass media picture of crime, portraying tough, no-holds-barred 'law and order' as the source of security in the face of an increasingly serious and prevalent menace of violent predators, underpins most public and policy debate nowadays. Politicians are highly sensitive to the sensational but rare crimes that are the focus of most media attention, and policy-making is often an emergency panic response to them.[52] Increasingly the main focus is on the suffering of massively injured, vulnerable and ideal-typically innocent victims, as reflected in the new tendency to name laws after them. This generates a zero-sum frame-work in which harsh punishment of offenders is seen as the only way of adequately responding to the suffering of victims, a key element of the new crime control complex discussed in Chapter Five.

(6) Trespass: an overlapping core construction?

I have distinguished between five different constructions of crime in contemporary discourse, all offering very different images:

- *the legal*, representing the contingent outcome of centuries of legislation and case-law, united by the formal characteristics of criminal process, not the substantive nature of the multifarious behaviours subject to prosecution;
- *moral views* about what *should* be punished, varying between different cultures;
- *socially/culturally sanctioned* behaviour, stigmatized in everyday practice;
- *the criminal justice system* labelled pattern of offences and offenders;
- *mass media/public policy* representations, following a 'law of opposites' focusing on the rarest cases of homicide, violence and sex crimes.

It is difficult to see any common core. Some ideal-typical cases may in Durkheimian fashion unite all 'healthy consciences', say the murder by children of the toddler Jamie Bulger, or the Soham murders of two young girls. These highly unusual crimes are clearly regarded as criminal on all dimensions. But there will be alternative views on the gravity and even the 'really' criminal nature of most other cases, even if there is no doubt about their legal status.

Policy and popular debate about crime and control frequently involve people talking past each other. Legal constructions of crime are routinely attacked as oppressive, or as not punishing the truly criminal. 'Respectable' people, who regard themselves as law-abiding and moral, nonetheless engage in conduct that is criminal but attracts little or no social opprobrium or sanction, while claiming that 'real' criminals are treated too lightly. As *An Inspector Calls* illustrates, casual cruelties are the stuff of everyday life, often inflicting harm as severe as the most heinous crimes, with moral responsibility routinely denied by 'techniques of neutralization' dispelling potential guilt. The criminal justice system in practice processes the crimes of the disadvantaged, not all or even a representative sample of criminal behaviour – let alone seriously socially harmful actions carried out by the powerful. The mass media focus ever more feverishly on relatively rare, spectacularly violent offences, that then become the stuff of policy debate and new initiatives.[53]

However, I believe there is an overlapping core concept underlying this variation, which is not restricted to the highly exceptional Durkheimian cases that attract universal condemnation, but extends even to relatively minor volume crimes. This is the idea of physical 'trespass': literally 'breaking in' to the person or property of another. In his pioneering analysis of the changing law of theft since the Middle Ages, Jerome Hall seventy years ago showed that until the late fifteenth century 'trespass' was indeed an essential requirement of the offence. The 'Carrier's Case' in 1473 was pivotal in the slow process of freeing the concept of theft from restriction to physical seizures.[54] It laid the foundations for the modern, abstract concept whereby 'a person is guilty of theft if he dishonestly appropriates property belonging to another with the intention of permanently depriving the other of it' (Theft Act 1968, S.1(1)). As forms of property and modes of acquisition have become increasingly dematerialized, the legal ambit of theft has left the medieval notion of physical trespass far behind. But trespass, physical violation, lurks lingeringly behind popular notions of 'real' crime today.

This is a crucial element making 'white collar' and corporate crime, typically involving the misuse of property that is in the legitimate possession of the perpetrator (as in the Carrier's Case over 600 years ago), more 'ambiguous', even though it is easier to carry out, harder to detect, and usually involves far greater material loss for the victims.[55] In the same way, violent crime in domestic contexts has traditionally been seen as a 'private' or personal matter, less likely to be reported, harder to detect and prosecute.[56] Danger is seen as coming from a male stranger not a spouse: when women take elaborate security precautions to safeguard their homes they are often locking themselves in with the most likely source of violence against themselves.

The majority of crimes that are reported and recorded (as chapter 3 shows) are thefts and other property offences involving a clear element of physical trespass: thefts of and from cars, burglaries, vandalism, pickpocketing and snatches. Violent crimes by definition involve an element of trespass against the person. They are also disproportionately reported and recorded if they take place between strangers, or those who are not sufficiently closely related to each other for there to be legitimate and normal physical contact. But such offences are only a small proportion of all potential cases of lawbreaking, let alone culpable infliction of harm. They are also much more likely to be engaged in by those who do not legitimately possess much property, or the privacy that this brings with it.[57]

This is the primary reason for the concentration of criminal justice on the poor and powerless, prior to any issues of discrimination, direct or institutional. The socialist novelist Anatole France once ironically celebrated 'The majestic equality of the law, which forbids the rich as well as the poor to sleep under bridges, to beg in the streets, and to steal bread' (*Le Lys rouge*, 1894). The crimes that involve the element of obvious physical trespass on the property or persons of others are rarely resorted to except by the poor – but if they are, of course, they may be treated with 'majestic' impartiality (although the evidence suggests otherwise). Conversely, criminal opportunities favour the already privileged. 'The best way to rob a bank may indeed be to own one – or work in one – but, we assume, most of those in this position do not take advantage of it'[58] – but we are unlikely ever to know whether this assumption is correct.

The notion of trespass as a key element in conceptions of crime helps make sense of the concentration of the criminal justice system on crimes of the powerless. It also underpins the media and political focus on the most serious dramatic cases of violence and occasional spectacular robberies, which are paradigm instances of physical assault and 'break in' to the person or property of others. Popular conceptions of 'real' crime as carried out by 'them' not 'us', and involving clear physical intrusion or assault, also are related to the notion of trespass.

The law has over the last 500 years clearly and explicitly moved away from anchoring notions of crime in physical attack. Nor is a restriction of the idea of 'real' crime to physical invasion of space or body conceptually or ethically defensible. Neither the harmful consequences of actions nor the subjective moral responsibilities for conduct can or should be coherently or consistently restricted to physically direct trespass, even though harm and responsibility are clearest in such cases. This was one point made by *An Inspector Calls*, and as the zemiologists and other critical voices have long argued, the much broader ambit of criminal law is itself too narrow, excluding many serious forms of culpable harm. A further ethical objection to underpinning crime by the notion of trespass is that it has a built-in bias towards focusing only on the offences of the poor. Nonetheless it is the core idea in popular and media culture, and criminal justice practice, although not articulated explicitly. So all studies (the vast bulk of criminology) of officially designated crime and criminals, and of media and political discourse, are in effect primarily studies of trespass. As realists of the right and the left remind us too,[59] these conventionally defined crimes do inflict much cost and suffering, in particular on the poor and powerless, who are much more likely to be victimized by (as well as to perpetrate) them.

The concentration of popular culture and criminal justice practice on the most clear-cut types of trespass, committed disproportionately by the poor and excluded, is not just a result of its epistemological simplicity compared say to complex frauds, or even the physical violence involved in everyday work and other 'accidents', and the horrors of 'state crimes'. As generations of critical criminologists have argued, crime serves important ideological and control functions for societies characterized by inequalities of power and advantage.[60] It focuses the frustrations, pain, anger, insecurity and rage that are engendered by both the illegitimate – though largely undiscovered – crimes of the powerful, as well as many legitimate harms due to the everyday exercise of economic and political power, on to a scapegoat class of offenders, whose trespasses, evil as they may be, pale into insignificance relative to the other human sources of misery. The risks of physical or material harm from ordinary crime are dwarfed by those posed by either corporate or state crime, or the routine activities of a turbo-charged neocapitalist society. A burglary can be a frightening and often traumatic experience in addition to any material loss and inconvenience. But it is rarely life-trashing for whole families or communities in the way, say, that downsizing businesses to increase profitability and shareholder value is for many employees. Yet the former is a crime, the latter the basis for wealth, celebrity, and a peerage.

The diversion of fear and anger on to ordinary criminals by the media and politicians, facilitated by the more obvious element of clear physical trespass, helps secure the structures that themselves generate insecurity. Many critical voices have argued for the abandonment of criminology because of this, tied as it is to the concepts of crime embedded not so much in the law itself as in the functioning of the criminal justice system. Nonetheless the focus of the rest of this book will be on analysing the trends and patterns in crime conceived in this ultimately indefensible way. It must be borne in mind, however, that the pains inflicted by officially defined crime, and by criminal justice, are relatively minor compared to the even more severe and extensive harms done by the criminal and legitimate activities of the powerful. A plea in mitigation is that my analysis will show that the most damaging trends in crime and control can best be explained by the same neoliberal political economy that is also the source of those broader harms not dealt with by criminal justice.

3

A Mephistophelean Calculus: Measuring Crime Trends

> When Labour came to power in 1997 we inherited a grim legacy. Crime had doubled [since the 1970s]. . . . Overall crime is down by 30 per cent on 1997 . . . violent crime down by 26 per cent.
>
> Labour Party, 'Tackling crime', March 2005

> When I was Home Secretary crime fell by 18 per cent . . . Under Mr Blair . . . Overall crime is up by 16 per cent. Violent crime is up by over 80 per cent.
>
> Conservative manifesto, 'Action on crime', February 2005

> Around two-thirds (63%) of people thought crime in the country as a whole had increased . . . with nearly a third believing it had risen 'a lot'.
>
> British Crime Survey 2005–6

During the 2005 general election the hitherto somewhat arcane question of crime statistics became a thoroughly politicized Punch and Judy show. The parties assaulted each other with competing numbers, rubbishing those of their opponents. Labour's figures made Tony Blair the greatest crime-fighter since Batman; according to the Conservatives that accolade was Michael Howard's. The British Crime Survey shows that the majority of the public don't believe there is any success to squabble over.

Does this simply reaffirm the old cynical saw that statistics are worse than damned lies? Or can a way be found through the thicket of alternative measures to reach a judicious assessment of crime trends and patterns?

What are the Crime Statistics?

Official crime statistics are part and parcel of the administrative processes of the state, and evidently tied to a legal conception of crime. Until a quarter of a century ago all political and media debate about the 'crime rate' referred to a statistical series based on police records, published by the Home Office since 1856.[1] From 1983 an additional set of statistics has been regularly produced by the Home Office, the British Crime Survey (BCS), based on interviews with samples of the population.[2] It appeared as a separate volume from the police recorded figures until 2001. Since then the annual volume *Crime in England and Wales* provides data on the overall extent of crime from both sources, on victim reporting and police recording, the pattern of crime by offence and by region, recent trends, and the detection or 'clear up' rate.[3]

Problems of Interpreting Police Recorded Crime Statistics

Criminologists and statisticians have long been aware that the official crime statistics suffer from many pitfalls which make their interpretation hazardous.[4] Nonetheless, popular newspapers continue to present the police recorded statistics as if they were straightforward and unequivocal measures of crime.[5] What the tabloids unabashedly call the 'crime rate' the Home Office more cautiously labels

'Crimes recorded by the police'. If this was taken literally, there would be no problems: by definition the number of crimes recorded by the police is the number of crimes recorded by the police! It is a long time since any official sources referred to this as the 'crime rate',[6] and appropriate health warnings abound in current Home Office publications. But the basic issue remains: how accurately do the figures recorded by the police reflect rates and patterns of crime?

The 'dark figure'

As has long been recognized, the police recorded statistics are problematic because of the so-called 'dark figure' of unrecorded crime. In a well-worn metaphor, the recorded rate represents only the tip of the iceberg of criminal activity (and *a fortiori* culpable harm). At issue is what we can learn about the totality from the part that is visible. There is much evidence that the police statistics are 'supplyside' driven, reflecting the changing exigencies of Home Office policy-makers and police bureaucracies as much as the activities of offenders and victims.[7] If we could be confident that the recorded rate was representative of the rest it would at least be a reliable guide to trends and patterns. But the fundamental problem is that the recorded statistics are not only incomplete. They are biased. Some crimes and some criminals are much more likely to enter the records than others, with clear patterns of class, age, ethnic, gender, and area differences.

For an event to be recorded as crime it must get over two hurdles: (1) it must literally become known to the police; (2) it must be recorded as such by the police, using particular technical procedures. The 'dark figure' of unrecorded crime arises because many crimes do not overcome these hurdles. They are not known to the police, and/or are not recorded even if the police are aware of them. Let us examine how these hurdles may be negotiated.

Hurdle 1: Getting 'known by the police' There are two ways crimes may become known to the police: reporting by an individual victim; or discovery through proactive policing. How a crime comes to police attention depends on whether or not it has an aware victim.

If the victim of a crime is aware of their victimization, they may decide to report the crime to the police – although, for a variety of reasons, many do not. A substantial body of evidence about patterns of reporting by victims has now been assembled by victim surveys. For most crimes and victims the decision whether to report turns on a more or less explicit cost/benefit assessment. In the most recent BCS 73 per cent of victims who did not report a crime said that this was because the offence was too trivial and/or involved no loss, and/or that there was no point as the police wouldn't or couldn't do anything about it.[8] Another 6 per cent spoke of the inconvenience of reporting. These pragmatic reasons were more commonly offered in the case of property crimes. For violent crimes, however, another factor was important. Forty per cent saw what happened as 'private' or dealt with it themselves, as opposed to 45 per cent who saw it as not worth reporting. Another 7 per cent mentioned fear of reprisal as a factor in not reporting violence. Dislike or bad experience of the police was cited by very few (2 per cent overall) for any type of crime. Trends in overall reporting are thus likely to be highly sensitive to such pragmatic considerations as the value of property lost, the possibilities of making an insurance claim, and factors that affect the convenience of reporting (where the nearest police station is, whether crimes can be reported by phone, etc.).

Many crimes have victims who are unaware of what has happened to them. The victims may be children aware of their suffering but not that what was done to them was a crime. They may be adult victims of frauds that are so successful that the victim does not realize they have been deceived or even hard done by. Victims of theft may think they have lost the property involved.

Finally, many crimes do not have clear individual victims at all. In 'consensual' offences such as drug-taking, and 'vice' offences such as those relating to prostitution, pornography or gambling, the putative victim is a willing participant, even though others paternalistically regard them as harming themselves. The 'victim' of other offences may be the public at large, or substantial sections of it: examples include tax evasion, smuggling, pensions mis-selling, insider trading and other types of serious financial crime, motoring offences, public order offences and treason.

The common element of all these examples is that the police only come to know of them by chance or through proactive policing work, discovering the offence with the offender (for instance, through uniform patrol, surveillance of 'hot spots', undercover work, raids on pubs and clubs for drugs, analysis of financial transactions for fraud or other crimes, and searches of travellers at customs). Any estimation of trends and patterns for these offences can only be tentative.

Hurdle 2: Getting recorded by the police What surprises many people is that even if 'known' to them, the police do not necessarily record incidents as crimes. The first British Crime Survey estimated that in 1981 the police recorded only 62 per cent of all crimes reported to them, and 'less than half of those involving violence'.[9] Recent policy changes have increased the proportion recorded, but only to about 70 per cent.[10] Police officers still exercise discretion in the extent to which they record crimes reported to them, and in *how* they record them, although recording has become more tightly structured by Home Office counting rules and force policy. A recent Home Office research study monitored the outcome of calls to the police. Only 47 per cent of crime allegations were eventually recorded as crimes, although 71 per cent of those in which the caller was 'definite' a crime had occurred were recorded. In 21 per cent of cases where a crime was recorded it was classified differently from the initial allegation.[11]

The truly 'dark' figure is the extent of crimes without individual aware victims. This is both a conceptually and a pragmatically difficult area to estimate. The claim that crimes occur that have not been formally judged as such by an official recording process is contingent and probabilistic. It takes the form of an assertion that behaviour *would* have been recorded as a crime had it come to the attention of the relevant authorities. This relies on presuppositions that are more or less dubious, given what is known about police policies and practices concerning the recording of crimes that *do* become known to them, and the inevitable resource constraints on police capacity to uncover crimes not reported to them. The 'true' extent of crime is a metaphysical conundrum known, if at all, only by Mephistopheles. What is certain is that the number of crimes that could in principle be recorded is vastly greater not only than the police recorded figure but also than any alternative estimates, including the BCS.

Police exercise discretion not to record crimes for reasons varying from legitimate (for example if there is genuine doubt about the truthfulness or accuracy of a victim's report)[12] to completely corrupt (for example in return for a bribe). Until recently the Home Office counting rules left the decision to record a crime to the police themselves. The revised rules issued in 1998, further amended in 2006, specified that 'An incident will be recorded as a crime (notifiable offence) if, on the balance of probability: (A) the circumstances as reported amount to a crime defined by law; and (B) there is no credible evidence to the contrary.'[13] This still leaves open the issue of deciding *whether* a notifiable offence has become known. A recent Home Office study of police recording practices distinguished between two models that could underpin this decision in principle. On the *prima facie* model 'details of alleged crimes are taken at face value, and recorded without scrutiny'.[14] But on the *evidential* model 'the details of any incident will be challenged and validated, in the same manner that might be expected if the case were to be presented in court in order to charge a suspect'. Police forces and officers vary not only in their attachment to one or other model in principle, but in terms of practical procedures for recording crimes that have the (often unintended) effect of prioritizing a particular approach: for example, depending on what bureaucratic layers and processes intervene between initial allegations by members of the public and the final classification, and whether investigations are routinely concluded by phone, or whether visits to witnesses and to the scenes of incidents are required.

Recent major revisions of recording procedures, the new 1998 Counting Rules and the 2002 National Crime Recording Standard, aimed to prioritize the victim's perspective, and thus encouraged the *prima facie* model.[15] But legal and organizational pressures necessarily tend in the direction of the *evidential* model. The consequence of complete espousal of the *prima facie* approach would be the recording of many cases that lead nowhere. Certainly in the nineteenth century official pressure encouraged a strong evidential model for precisely that reason. Police forces were instructed to include in 'Number of crimes known' only 'such cases as, in their judgement, from the circumstances attending them, would, if discovered, be sent for trial'.[16] Thus the statistics for 'crimes committed' closely matched those for 'persons convicted'. The appearance of an efficient police force that cleared up most crimes was partly due to incidents only being recorded when there was from the outset sufficiently strong evidence for a trial to be an almost certain outcome. The desire to massage the figures in order to present an appearance of greater success (and enjoy an easier life) undoubtedly led to widespread practices of 'cuffing crimes' by not recording more difficult ones wherever possible. Perhaps 'crimes known to the police' might more aptly have been labelled 'crimes the police wish to make known'.[17] The increasing emphasis on performance measurement and results makes spinning the figures more tempting – and the impossibility of closing off all discretion always leaves some avenues for this. Certainly there have continued to be scandals about deliberate manipulation of statistics in recent years,[18] involving not only the police but the Home Office.[19]

Technical problems

In addition to the dark figure of crimes not reported to or recorded by the police, there are technical issues that affect the validity and reliability of crime statistics. Many questions are involved in moving from events to numbers recording them, and different decisions, whether made in good faith or bad, will produce very different counts of crime. The key questions concern the scope of offences eligible for the statistics, and the way that incidents are translated into numbers.

The Coverage of Recorded Statistics The police are required to record 'notifiable offences', a list that is mainly, but not entirely, identical with 'indictable' offences, that is, those that must or may be tried in a Crown Court. It thus includes most of what would generally be regarded as the more serious crimes, but excludes summary offences, those that are only triable by magistrates. No official records are kept of the number of the latter, only of offenders convicted or formally cautioned. This amounts to well over a million cases per annum. From time to time, most recently 1998 when common assault and assault on a constable were added, the Home Office changes the range of 'notifiable offences'. However strong the case for adjustments to take account of changing conceptions of seriousness, they necessarily introduce problems of comparison between statistics collected before and after the alteration.[20]

The Home Office tally of 'crimes known to the police' excludes offences that are recorded by other public forces such as British Transport Police, Ministry of Defence Police, the Royal Military Police and the UK Atomic Energy Constabulary Police. Other enforcement agencies, for example HM Revenue and Customs or the Health and Safety Inspectorate, investigate and sometimes prosecute offences. They primarily work through administrative procedures, and do not quantify the number of offences they deal with. Their cases will enter the Home Office criminal statistics only in the rare event that the police are involved and define an occurrence as a criminal violation.

How many and which offences to count? Another important set of technical issues arises in the translation of incidents into numbers. There are two main problems here. How many crimes should be counted in particular situations, and which offences should they be classified under? If an offender attacks a series of targets in a short time (say she or he breaks every milk bottle on the doorsteps of a number of neighbouring houses, or several windows), is that one offence or as many as the number of objects damaged? In many situations there is also ambiguity about what offence has occurred. For example, the scene of an alleged attempted burglary may contain no physical evidence at all, or only of criminal damage (a broken window, or scratch marks around a lock). Should the recording be guided by the possibly lurid perceptions of the anxious householder, or only by what the physical signs suggest? There is much scope in such cases for defining crime up or down according to what is most convenient for the police. At a much more serious level, how many crimes were committed in the terrorist attacks of 11 September 2001, or 7 July 2005?

There is no absolutely right or wrong answer to any of these questions, but consistency in handling them is necessary if the statistics are to be capable of any comparison across time and space. The National Crime Recording Standard (NCRS) was introduced in all police forces in April 2002 to try to achieve consistency in the way crimes are quantified, seeking a more victim-oriented approach. However desirable in themselves, such reforms always introduce problems of comparison before and after the change, and the published statistics have carried appropriate health warnings, as well as attempts to quantify the impact of the new procedures.[21]

Dimensions of the 'dark' figure

To get some sense of the extent to which recorded crime figures are incomplete it is salutary, if somewhat shocking, to consider figure 3.1 on what the Home Office calls the 'attrition rate', the disappearance of cases at different stages of the criminal justice process. The chart starts with a base that is described as 'offences committed'. This is

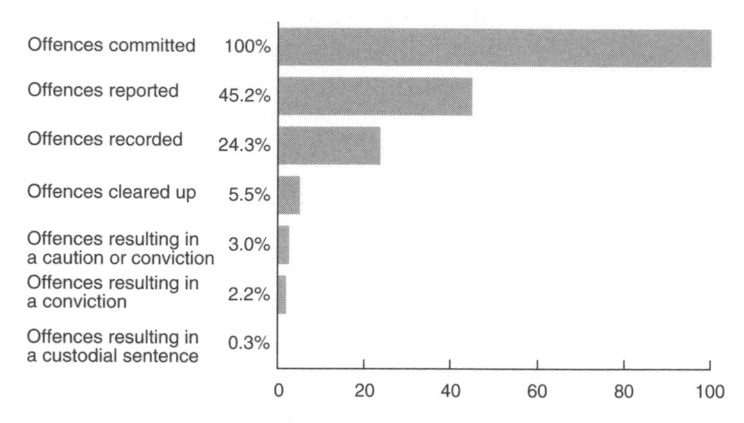

Figure 3.1 Attrition within the criminal justice system (percentage of offences committed)
Source: G. Barclay and C. Tavares, *Digest 4: Information on the Criminal Justice System in England and Wales* (London: Home Office, 1999), p. 29.

taken from the BCS total of crimes reported by its sample. This is at best an estimate only of crimes with individual aware victims. Completely absent from this base of 'offences committed' is the truly dark figure of crimes without individual aware victims. This *dark* dark figure encompasses offences that could involve very serious harm to persons or property, but which are not uncovered by the police or other enforcement agencies. They include vice offences, most major frauds, financial crimes, smuggling, tax evasion and breaches of safety standards that could lead to death or serious injury.

Given that it excludes all offences not measurable by the BCS, the chart understates the real dimensions of non-recorded crime. Even with that important qualification, it shows that fewer than half of offences counted by the BCS are reported by victims (45.2 per cent). Fewer than a quarter of BCS-calculated victimizations are recorded by the police. Only 5.5 per cent are 'cleared up' by them (that is, cases where the police have some reason to believe they know the identity of the perpetrator). Only 3 per cent of the BCS known offences end up with a formal identification of guilt (a caution or a conviction), and only 2.2 per cent in a conviction. Finally, 0.3 per cent result in a custodial sentence. Thus the officially recorded figures for levels of crime, and for identified offenders, relate to only a very small proportion of all crimes known about, and *a fortiori*, crimes committed.

The figure for recorded crimes is not just incomplete, but biased. Some crimes and some criminals are much more likely to appear than others. This has been demonstrated by a plethora of studies showing the influence of class, gender, ethnicity, age and other dimensions of social inequality on victims and suspects at all stages of the criminal justice process. This is shown by table 3.1.

It shows that people in the prison population are highly unrepresentative of the overall population. They are overwhelmingly male. Ethnic minorities are considerably overrepresented. The prison population is drawn predominantly from the most marginal economic groups in the population: 74 per cent were either unemployed, or employed at the lowest occupational levels, prior to incarceration. They have poor educational backgrounds and histories of family disruption. Jeffrey Reiman has summed it up most pithily in the title of his classic text of critical criminology, *The Rich Get Richer, and the Poor Get Prison*.

The extent of unrecorded offences means that apparent trends and patterns may be quite misleading. A rise in recorded crime, for example, may occur because of increased reporting by victims, and/or more recording by the police of offences reported to them, and/or more

Table 3.1 Prison and general population compared

	Prison population (%)	General population (%)
Under 25	40	16
Male	96	49
Ethnic minority	16	5
Semi/unskilled occupation	41	18
Unemployed	33	8.7
No permanent home	13	0.3
Left school before 16	40	11
Frequent truancy	30	3
Lived with both parents till 16	62	83
Taken into care before 16	26	2

Sources: R. Walmsley, L. Howard and S. White, *The National Prison Survey 1991* (London: HMSO, 1992); *Social Trends 1993* (HMSO).

successful proactive policing. The disproportionate representation of the economically marginal and of ethnic minorities in the suspect population may be because they commit more crime, or because the crimes they do commit are more likely to be recorded and cleared up – or an interaction between these possibilities. In short, changes in recorded crime levels or patterns may be due to changes in the balance of the dark figure of unrecorded offences relative to the rest. Until relatively recently these problems could be stated but no light could be shed on their possible dimensions. However, in the last four decades a variety of research instruments have cast some light on the 'dark figure' of unrecorded crimes.

Alternatives to the Police Statistics

Growing awareness of the limitations and biases of the police recorded crime statistics, together with the prominence of law and order as a political issue, have prompted the development of a variety of alternative measures since the 1960s. Victimization surveys (like the British Crime Survey) are by far the most significant, largely because they have been supported on a large-scale and regular basis. They offer an alternative measure of trends over time, as well as insights into reporting and recording processes which enable better understanding of the police statistics themselves. Other measures such as self-report studies can be used to assess the relationship between the characteristics of offending they reveal and the pattern shown in criminal justice statistics. However, they are not constructed so as to assess overall trends through time. An interesting measure developed recently is the use of data from hospital accident and emergency departments to assess trends and patterns of injuries sustained as a result of violence. This offers a useful alternative source of data capable of mapping trends in interpersonal violence, but not other offences.[22]

The advent of the BCS in particular has led many commentators, especially in the 'quality' media, to think of it as something like a 'true' measure of crime. It is commonly referred to as 'authoritative' or 'reliable',[23] by contrast with the police statistics. But *all* measures of crime have limitations inevitably associated with their particular techniques of construction. It is only with a reflexive awareness of these limitations that interpretations can be made with any degree of safety. The proliferation of alternative measures is nonetheless a boon to the understanding of crime trends and patterns. When the different measures point in the same direction (as they did in the 1980s and early 1990s) we can be much more confident that this corresponds to what is happening to offending and victimization. Even when they diverge (as for much of the 1990s and early 2000s) it is possible to understand some of the reasons for this, and to make appropriate allowances in interpreting each series of statistics.

Crime surveys

Victim surveys began during the 1960s in the US with three exploratory studies for the 1967 Presidential Commission on Law Enforcement. In 1972 a programme of annual national surveys (now the National Crime Victimization Survey (NCVS)) was instituted by the US Department of Justice.[24] In Britain limited surveys of victimization began in the 1970s. The General Household Survey (GHS) included a question about domestic burglary from 1972 to 1982. A pioneering survey in London was instrumental in the development of the methodology of later studies.[25]

Despite its regular appellation as 'authoritative', the British Crime Survey, even if conducted with faultless methodological rigour, has many limitations. These are succinctly identified at the very outset of the report of the first BCS.[26] First there are the thorny conceptual issues about how to define crime – and whose definition should prevail in a conflict. At best, a victimization survey will necessarily be limited to what can be gleaned from a putative victim's perspective. What the interviewed 'victim' may see as an assault may be regarded by the supposed aggressor as self-defence, or a playful push – and it is entirely possible that the latter's perspective would prevail if the matter came to the attention of the criminal justice system.

Secondly, victim surveys by definition can only measure crimes with aware individual victims. Entirely beyond their ambit are whole swathes of offences: crimes against business and other institutions; public order offences; successful frauds against unknowing victims; smuggling and tax evasion; offences with willing participants such as drug-taking or trafficking, and most 'vice' offences. Murder, generally seen as the most serious crime of all, cannot be included in a victim survey (for obvious reasons). These are not small exceptions. Each year the police record well over a quarter of a million thefts from shops, just under half a million burglaries other than from dwellings, and well over 100,000 drug offences.[27] None of these are within the scope of the BCS – but all are just a fraction of what is likely to be a huge dark figure of unrecorded crime in these and all other offence categories.[28]

Thirdly, as with all other surveys, there are sampling issues. The BCS began with interviews of a random sample of 11,000 households in England and Wales and 5,000 in Scotland. It has expanded considerably, to just under 48,000 interviews in England and Wales for the most recent sweep. The first limitation, however, is that certain groups are not included in the population sampled. The BCS is a survey of adults, so does not measure the victimization of children under sixteen.[29] As a household survey it does not cover crimes against the homeless.[30] The initial sampling frame used was the electoral register, but this became increasingly problematic as non-registration mounted during the 1980s, mainly because of the Poll Tax, leading to a switch to the currently used Postcode Address File.[31] The response rate has been about 75 per cent, very respectably high by most survey standards – but still allowing the possibility that the non-respondents may have different experiences from respondents. Finally, again as in all surveys, the accuracy of results is only as good as the honesty and memory of respondents, despite all the care taken with questions and interviews. All these issues are most acute with the gravest interpersonal offences, especially violent and sex crimes, where willingness to confide in a strange visitor from the Home Office is likely to be problematic, although improvements in methodology such as the use of computer-assisted self-completion techniques for such questions (to ensure respondent confidentiality) have been introduced over time.[32]

The regular publication of the BCS since 1983 allows comparison of different trend data, as well as analysis of the reasons why victims do not report offences, estimates of police non-recording, and other information relevant to interpreting the police statistics. As indicated earlier, the BCS is a valuable additional source of data but not a definitive calculation of crime rates. Triangulating with police statistics does allow greater confidence in judging trends, but not certainty. We must always bear in mind that changes in the police recorded figures may be due to alterations in victim reporting or police recording practices. Trends in the BCS may result from changing sample coverage or other methodological problems. There can never be certainty about any of this, but triangulation of different data sources allows more informed attempts at interpretation. In the next section we will try to describe recent trends and patterns in crime, interpreting the statistics with due caution in the light of the many problems.

What Happened? Unravelling Crime Patterns and Trends

As we have seen, the official police recorded crime statistics have severe limitations as an index of trends or patterns in crime. The advent of the BCS twenty-five years ago has shed much light on reporting and recording practices, allowing the statistics to be interpreted more confidently. Above all, because there are now two alternative measures of trends and patterns for offences covered by the survey, there can be greater confidence when they point in the same direction, as they did for most of the history of the BCS. However, in recent years the trends indicated by the police statistics and the BCS have begun to diverge, producing a politicization of the debate about their interpretation and the relative merits of different measuring instruments.

Patterns of crime

An important point to bear in mind is that recorded crime consists overwhelmingly of property crime, above all the so-called 'volume' crimes of burglary, other theft and handling, and thefts of and from cars. Nearly three-quarters (73 per cent) of crimes recorded by the police in 2005–6 were property crimes.[33] Violent crimes accounted for 22 per cent, and drugs and other offences 4 per cent. This is very similar to the picture given by the BCS, which estimated that 77 per cent were property crimes, and 23 per cent violent offences (as indicated earlier, the BCS does not include drug and other offences without specific individual victims). The pattern of an overwhelming preponderance of property offences has been true throughout the history of crime statistics, although there has been some

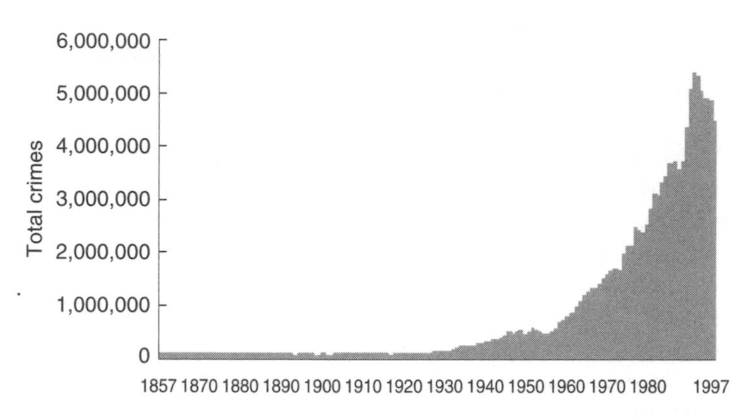

Figure 3.2 Crimes recorded by the police, 1857–1997
Source: G. Barclay and C. Tavares, *Digest 4: Information on the Criminal Justice System in England and Wales* (London: Home Office, 1999), p. 2.

growth of violent relative to property offences in the last thirty years, and particularly in the last decade (largely because of shifts in the recording rules). In 1976, for example, the proportion of recorded property offences was 94 per cent, and violent and sexual crimes were just 5 per cent.[34] This had changed only slightly by 1997: 91 per cent of recorded crimes were property offences, and 8 per cent were violent.[35] Thus trends in overall crime primarily track fluctuations in the level of property offences.

Trends in crime

Putting together the different sorts of data available, what can be said about the trends in the last half century? The most apparent trend is the spectacular rise in recorded crime since the late 1950s. Figure 3.2 sets this in a longer term historical context. It underlines the dramatic extent of the rise in recorded crime since the mid-1950s. Between the 1850s and the 1920s recorded crime remained on a plateau.[36] During the 1930s there was a period of substantial and sustained increase, continuing through the early years of the Second World War. In the decade following the war there were several short cycles of rising and falling rates, but no clear trend. But from 1955 recorded crime began a massive and sustained long-term growth.

In the early 1950s the police recorded fewer than half a million offences per annum. By the mid-1960s this had increased to around 1 million, and by the mid-1970s 2 million. The 1980s showed even more staggering rises, with recorded crime peaking in 1992 at over 5.5 million – a tenfold increase in less than four decades. By 1997 recorded crime had fallen back to 4.5 million. The counting rule changes introduced in 1998 and 2002 make comparison of the subsequent figures especially fraught, but on the new rules (which undoubtedly exaggerate the increase) just under 6 million offences were recorded by the police for 2003–4 – the highest on record – but this had fallen back to just over 5.6 million in 2005–6.[37]

The big question is to what extent the huge increase in recorded crime is a product of variations in reporting and recording, and how much of it is a genuine increase in offending. For all the reasons discussed earlier, it is impossible to be certain about either the level or trends in crime. Nonetheless, with the advent of regular alternative measures, and much more knowledge of reporting and recording processes, it is possible to interpret the trends with some confidence. Three subperiods can be distinguished, corresponding not only to the relationship between the recorded crime figures and alternative statistical series, notably the BCS, but also to major changes in political economy, culture and society. The three distinct periods are from the late 1950s to 1980; the 1980s and early

1990s; the 1990s and the early years of the twenty-first century.

Period 1, late 1950s–1980: rapid recorded crime rise

Until the 1970s there were no alternative measures of crime apart from the police statistics. Criminologists were wont to give cautionary warnings about whether crime really was increasing as the figures indicated, but it was impossible to know how much of any change was due to new patterns of reporting and/or recording crime.

However, during the 1970s the General Household Survey began to ask respondents about their experience of burglary. For the first time this allowed some insight into the extent to which reporting or recording changes contributed to rising crime rates. Burglary was not only a common offence, accounting for something like a fifth of recorded crime, but was of crucial importance for public anxieties about crime and the emerging politics of law and order. The GHS showed that during the 1970s the substantial rise in recorded burglaries was mainly accounted for by an increase in victims' propensity to report burglary to the police, *not* an increase in victimization. Between 1972 and 1983 recorded burglaries doubled, but victimization increased by only 20 per cent according to the surveys.[38] There was a considerable increase in the proportion of victims reporting burglaries to the police, and the reason is plain from the GHS. In 1972 the property stolen was insured in only 19 per cent of burglary incidents, but by 1980 this had increased to 42 per cent.[39] Thus the first set of victimization statistics, from the GHS in the 1970s, reinforced criminological scepticism about how much of the huge increase in recorded crime statistics was really due to increased offending.

It is impossible to be sure about whether the rise in the recorded rates for other offences was due to increased reporting on the same scale as burglary, and indeed how much of the increase in recorded burglary before the 1970s was a reporting phenomenon. But it is plausible that at least a substantial part of the rise in recorded crime was due to more being reported by victims. It was not only that a higher proportion of goods enjoyed insurance cover, but also that this reflected the spread of ownership of expensive consumer durables that were more likely to be reported if stolen. Thus a substantial part of the increase in crime rates from the late 1950s to the late 1970s was probably due to greater reporting rather than to increased offending. Nonetheless the public and political panic that (apparently) rising crime fuelled was a major factor in the 1970s politicization of law and order, and the Conservative election victory of 1979 with all the epochal changes it precipitated.

Period 2, 1980s–1992: crime explosion

However, as the BCS came to be repeated in several sweeps during the 1980s and early 1990s the discrepancy in the trends recorded by the surveys and by the police figures began to lessen. Although there was still some increase in reporting and recording, most of the huge rise in recorded crime in the 1980s and early 1990s corresponded to an increase in victimization. Between 1981 and 1993, the number of crimes recorded by the police increased 111 per cent, while BCS offences rose by 77 per cent. The proportion of offences reported to the police by victims increased from 31 per cent in 1981 to 41 per cent in 1993 according to the BCS.[40] In the most common types of property crime, such as car thefts and burglary with loss,

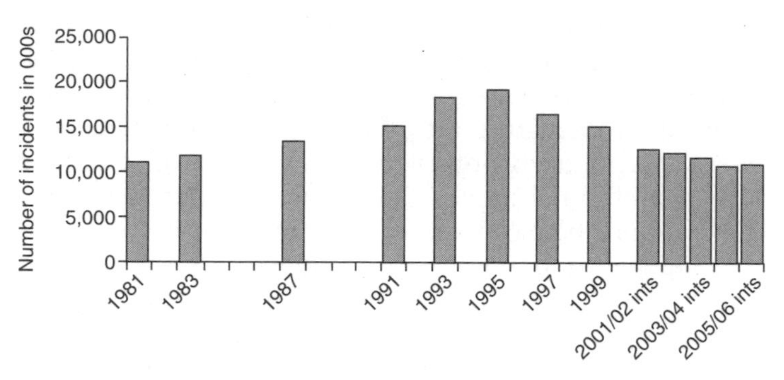

ints = interviews.

Figure 3.3 Trends in all BCS crime, 1981 to 2005–6
Source: A. Walker, C. Kershaw and S. Nicholas, *Crime in England and Wales 2005/06* (London: Home Office, 2006), p. 19.

reporting and recording rates had reached almost 100 per cent. When there is almost complete recording of victimization by the police the trends in the BCS and police figures will of course be almost identical. This is shown by figures 3.3 and 3.4 which chart the trends in BCS crime and police recorded crime since 1981.

Figure 3.4 shows that between 1981 and 1993 recorded crime roughly doubled. The reality of most of this increase is confirmed by the correspondingly huge increase in overall crime recorded by the BCS, which also went up by nearly 80 per cent, as shown by figure 3.3. The BCS also shows that there was an increase in the reporting of crime by victims, which accounts for the discrepancy in the trends. Nonetheless the overwhelming bulk of the vast increase in recorded crime during the 1980s and early 1990s seems to have been a genuine increase in offending and victimization. The 1980s were a decade of explosive crime increase.

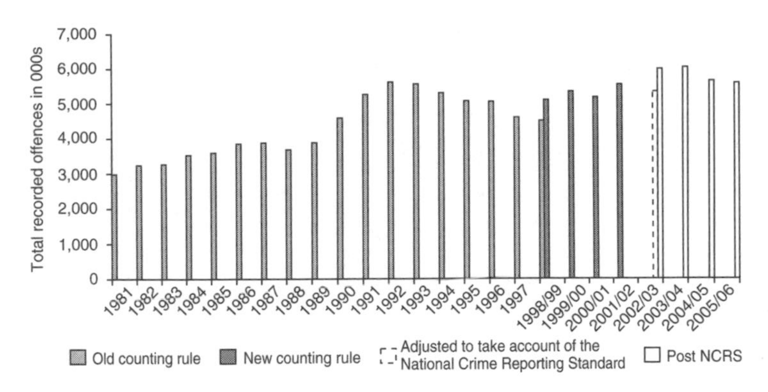

Figure 3.4 Trends in recorded crime, 1981 to 2005–6
Source: A. Walker, C. Kershaw and S. Nicholas, *Crime in England and Wales 2005/06* (London: Home Office, 2006), p. 19.

Period 3, 1992 onwards: ambiguously falling crime, rising fear

In the first decade of its existence the BCS seemed largely to confirm the patterns and trends shown by the police recorded crime statistics. While charting a somewhat slower rise in crime than the police statistics (because there was some increase in reporting by victims), for the most part the trends were similar. As the main volume crimes had reached rates of reporting that were nearly 100 per cent by the late 1980s, it could be anticipated that this parallelism would continue. From the early 1990s, however, the two sets of statistics begin to diverge, in complicated ways.

Between 1992 and 1995 the police statistics began to decline from their record height of nearly 6 million recorded crimes. But the BCS continued to register increasing victimization in these years. The 'missing crimes'

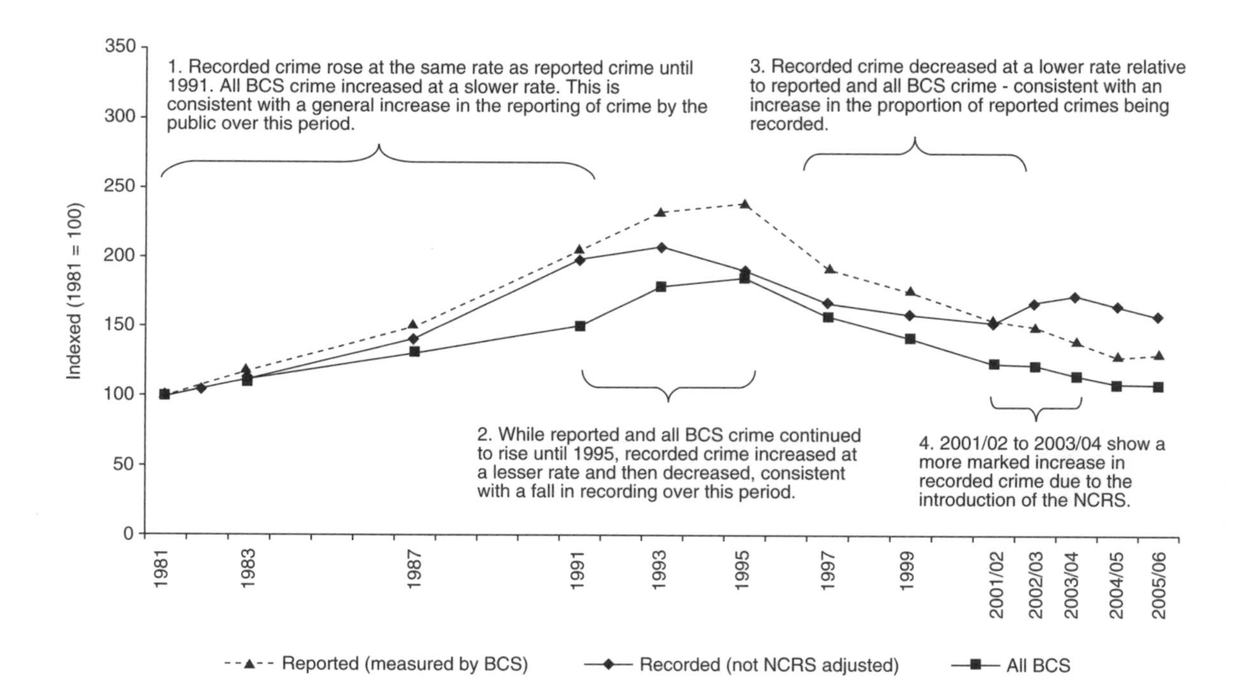

Figure 3.5 Indexed trends in the reporting of crime and all BCS crime, 1981 to 2005–6 (1981 = 100)

Source: A. Walker, C. Kershaw and S. Nicholas, *Crime in England and Wales 2005/06* (London: Home Office, 2006), p. 56.

in the police statistics were due to a reversal of the trend towards saturation reporting of the most common property offences.[41] Paradoxically, the very high levels of crime set in train processes leading victims to report less, and the police to record fewer of the crimes reported to them. Victims in higher risk categories faced more onerous conditions for insurance, reducing the incentive to report crimes (as making claims could trigger increased premiums, or other burdens such as expensive and stringent domestic security arrangements). The 'deductibles' (the proportion of claims victims themselves had to pay) were increasing for most insurance policies, creating further disincentives to reporting.

At the same time, the police were coming under a tighter performance measurement regime that began to bite hard in the early 1990s.[42] There were stronger pressures to record fewer crimes if at all possible, especially for key target offences. It was not only that overall crime levels, and rates for crucial categories like burglary, were in themselves performance indicators. Minimizing the recording of hard-to-investigate offences like burglary also helped boost detection rates, another key measure. The significance of declining recording by the police for explaining the fall in recorded crime from 1992 to 1995, at a time of increasing victimization according to the BCS, is shown in figure 3.5, which charts the shifting balance between recorded, reported and BCS crime since 1981. As can be seen, recording by the police fell from 1991 to 1995, while reporting by victims measured by the BCS continued to rise.

After 1997 the divergence between the police and BCS statistics continues, but in the reverse direction. The BCS figures, however, show continuing declines in total victimization from 1995 to 2005–6. The trend is substantial and sustained, with the risks of victimization by crime measured by the BCS now below the level of the first survey in 1981. This is the basis of the claims by Labour to have brought crime down substantially. By contrast, the police figures record increases from 1997 to 2004–5, if no allowance is made for the two major shifts in counting rules and procedures in 1998 and 2002 that were discussed earlier. However, if the impact of the new counting rules and the National Crime Recording Standard is estimated, there is only a very small increase in recorded crime from 1997 to 2004, and decline since then. The rise in recorded crime after 1997, at a time of sharp decline in BCS-measured victimization, is thus largely accounted for by the two changes in counting rules over this period.

Violent crime

Trends in overall crime largely track property crime. Violent crime, which is of the greatest public and political concern, has increased over the last quarter-century, according to police recorded and BCS measures. But the divergence between the BCS and the police figures for violence is especially marked in recent years, partly because it is in relation to violence that the changes in counting and recording rules have had their greatest impact on the police statistics.[43] This is shown by figures 3.6 and 3.7.

The BCS statistics on violence chart a similar trend since 1981 to that of overall crime. Violence is measured as rising up to 1997, with an especially rapid increase in the early 1990s. Thereafter it has fallen back to the levels of the late 1980s, but with a flattening of the decrease since 2001 (and an increase in robbery since 2004–5). The police figures shown in figure 3.7, however, show a sharp rise since 1998, attributable mainly to the counting rule changes (which added some more minor violent offences, notably common assault, to the 'notifiable' category), and

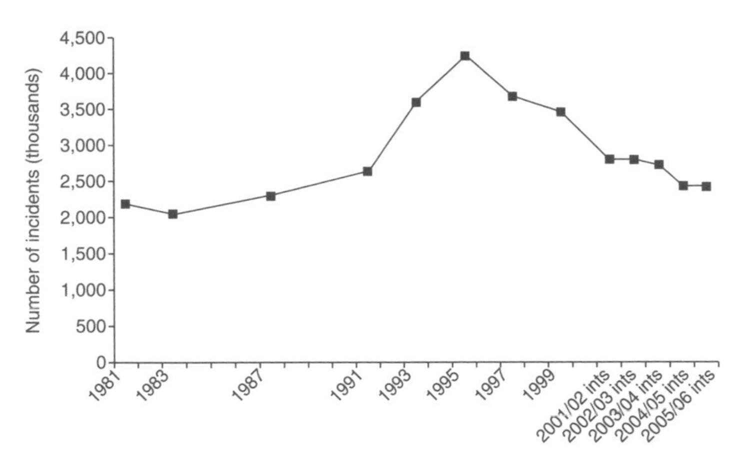

ints = interviews.

Figure 3.6 All BCS violent crime, 1981 to 2005–6
Source: A. Walker, C. Kershaw and S. Nicholas, *Crime in England and Wales 2005/06* (London: Home Office, 2006), p. 65.

the National Crime Recording Standard introduced in 2002 which, by adopting a 'victim oriented' approach, made the recording of violent offences more likely.

High anxiety

As the quotes at the outset of the chapter indicated, while the Conservatives see crime as falling until 1997 and increasing since (on the basis of the police statistics), and Labour see the reverse, celebrating a fall since they took office (as shown by the BCS), the public seem only to agree with the bad news, seeing crime as rising pretty well throughout. This is shown in figure 3.8.

As figure 3.8 shows, the majority of the public questioned by the BCS see crime as increasing for the country

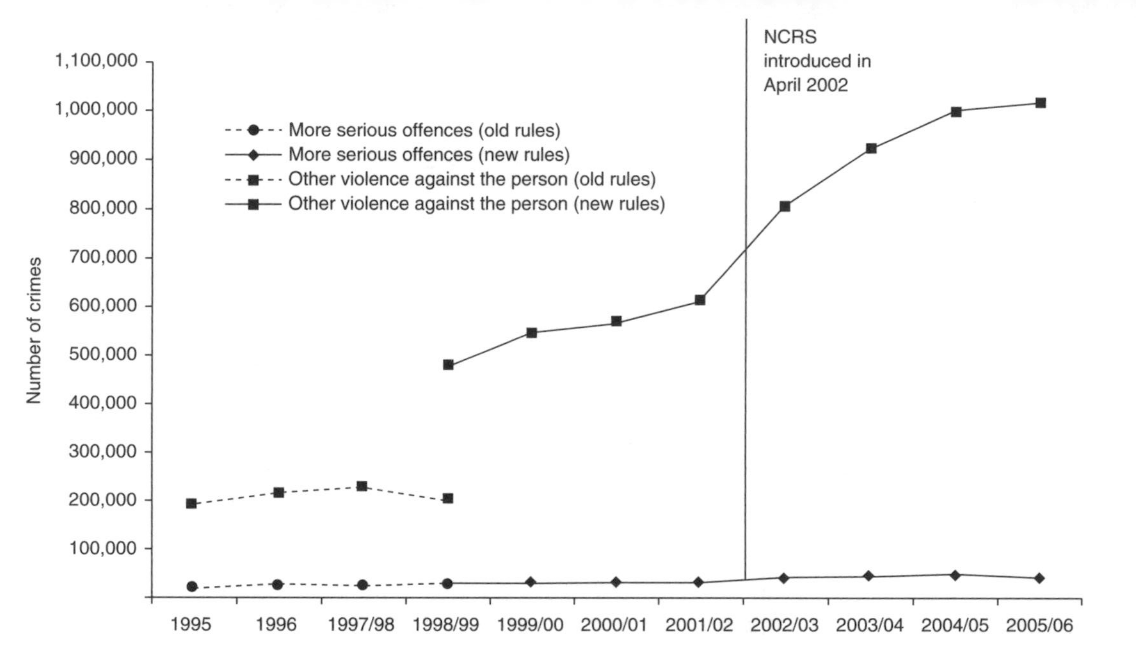

There is a discontinuity in the police recorded trend for violence in 1998 when new offence categories were added to police recorded violence, notably common assault, and new crime counting rules were introduced. The numbers of recorded violent crimes before and after this change should not be compared directly. The introduction of the National Crime Recording Standard (NCRS) in April 2002 also had an impact in following years on levels of police recording.

Figure 3.7 More serious violence offences and other offences against the person recorded by police, 1995 to 2005–6

Source: A. Walker, C. Kershaw and S. Nicholas, *Crime in England and Wales 2005/06* (London: Home Office, 2006), p. 67.

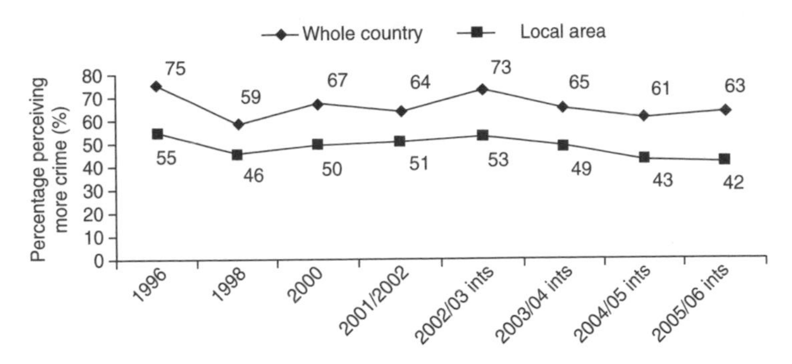

ints = interviews.

Figure 3.8 Perceptions of changing crime levels, 1996 to 2005–6
Source: A. Walker, C. Kershaw and S. Nicholas, *Crime in England and Wales 2005/06* (London: Home Office, 2006), p. 35.

as a whole in every year since 1996, although the proportion saying this varies from 75 to 59 per cent. There is a more optimistic picture for local crime, with a slightly declining proportion (less than half the sample in most years) seeing crime as rising in their areas. Nonetheless what is clearly underlined is a lack of correspondence between crime statistics and public perception.[44]

Conclusion: The Politicization of Crime Statistics

It is hardly any surprise that the relative significance and merits of the two sets of crime statistics has become highly politicized, with the Conservatives attempting to undermine the validity of the BCS during the 2005 general election campaign, aided by publications from sympathetic think-tanks.[45] The official crime statistics show crime rising almost continuously from the late 1950s, until they begin to fall sharply during Michael Howard's period as Home Secretary, but then rise again to new record levels under New Labour. The GHS and BCS victimization statistics, by contrast, suggest that until the Thatcher government much of the rise in recorded crime was due to increased reporting. As shown earlier, the spectacular rise in the 1980s and early 1990s was a genuine increase in offending, confirmed by both measures.

The apparent decline in recorded crime under Michael Howard, however, was largely a product of changes in recording – BCS crime continued to rise until after 1995 – while the growth of recorded crime under New Labour was mainly due to recording changes attributable to the revised counting rules. Victimization as measured by the BCS has declined to its lowest level since 1981, in the early days of the Thatcher government.

So whether Michael Howard or Tony Blair succeeded in being tougher on crime and its causes turns on which figures are more valid and reliable. The BCS cannot and does not claim to be a perfect barometer of crime – this is not possible, as it frankly admits. Most criminologists would argue, however, that as a measure of *trends* it is more reliable than the police statistics, which are notoriously subject to the vicissitudes of victims' reporting and police recording behaviour, and to changes in counting procedures such as the major reforms of 1998–2002. But then most criminologists are not fans of either Mrs Thatcher or Michael Howard (but probably not of Tony Blair either)!

Nonetheless it seems that the broad pattern of change over the last half century is clear. The overwhelming, most dramatic change is the huge increase in recorded crime. Probably a significant (but ultimately unascertainable) proportion of this was due to reporting and recording changes up to about 1980, so the statistics exaggerate the increase in crime. After 1981, with the advent of the BCS, it is possible to be more certain, especially about the 1980s when the two statistical series went in the same direction. Although a small fraction (about a fifth) of the recorded doubling of crime was attributable to more reporting by victims, there can be no doubt about the crime explosion that took place. After 1992 the two series diverge, and interpretation becomes vexed and controversial. Nonetheless, it seems most likely that there has been a diminution of overall crime, especially property crime, as the BCS indicates.

Violent crime is more controversial, as the BCS is particularly problematic here, and the contrast with the police figures most marked. But the most likely conclusion is that there has been a decline of overall violence too (but not some more serious stranger violence, notably robbery), as the BCS indicates, and that the police figures since 1998 are bedeviled by the effects of the major changes in counting procedures. Irrespective of what the figures indicate, however, the public perceives crime as rising. The next chapter will focus on the explanation of these trends.

4

Permissiveness versus Political Economy: Explaining Crime Trends

> We shall attack the social deprivation which allows crime to flourish. Our policies on fighting deprivation and social injustice, on arresting the decay of our inner cities, on youth employment and helping the family, will all contribute to a happier and more law-abiding society.
>
> Labour Party election manifesto, 1979

> Government must do all it can to see that the individual is not in perpetual fear of losing life, limb and property. Of course we cannot stamp out crime. But we . . . can reform the law to increase deterrence against violence and vandalism.
>
> Margaret Thatcher, Conservative election message, 16 April 1979

In the 1970s and 1980s law and order deeply polarized political parties. Put at its starkest, Labour and the left embraced a species of Clintonian criminology – 'it's the economy, stupid'. Crime was seen primarily as a consequence of economic deprivation, injustice and other social problems. Tory policy was to toughen deterrence. As in so much else, New Labour sought to triangulate between these poles, signalled succinctly in Blair's celebrated soundbite, 'tough on crime, tough on the causes of crime'. The

1997 Labour election manifesto made it plain that this mantra was calculated to synthesize two traditional extremes: 'On *crime*, we believe in personal responsibility and in punishing crime, but also tackling its underlying causes – so, tough on crime, tough on the causes of crime, different from the Labour approach of the past and the Tory policy of today.'

Blame it on the Sixties

The predominant account offered nowadays by the media and by politicians of the rise in crime since the 1950s was originally proposed by the 1970s right-wing backlash. It blames crime on postwar liberal social policies, culminating in 1960s 'permissiveness', which undermined social control that hitherto had held in check the personal and moral defects of offenders.[1]

The theme of permissiveness as the basic cause of rising crime has been emphasized many times by Tony Blair, most explicitly in a speech launching the Home Office's five-year Strategic Plan for law and order in 2004. Blair claimed it 'marks the end of the 1960s liberal, social consensus on law and order'. He explicitly blamed the '1960s revolution' for encouraging 'freedom without responsibility', when 'a society of different lifestyles spawned a group of young people who were brought up without parental discipline, without proper role models and without any sense of responsibility to or for others'.[2]

Blair's speech embodied the quintessential conservative analysis of rising crime. The Enlightenment values of personal liberty, autonomy and self-realization were dangerously democratized by 1960s 'permissiveness'. As this spread to the masses it brought the destruction of family, responsibility and self control – the bulwarks of civilization. This narrative overlooks the ways in which the 'permissive' legislation of the 1960s embodied a restructuring rather than relaxation of control.[3] It cannot explain why tolerant and liberal cultures like those of the Netherlands and the Scandinavian countries have not been racked by crime, violence and law and order politics – though these are emerging with the impact of neoliberalism and the weakening of social democracy since the 1980s.[4] Above all, it fails to realize that 'parental discipline . . . proper role models and . . . any sense of responsibility to and for others' have been undermined by the social devastation wreaked by neoliberal economic policies rather than by liberal ethics. Untrammelled free market economies undermine the family, education and other sources of informal social control. 'The experience of life year in, year out at the bottom of a harsh, depriving, and excluding social system wears away at the psychological and communal conditions that sustain healthy human development'.[5] As Blair's speech itself recognized, the greater liberalism associated with cultural changes since the 1960s are fundamentally desirable as an expansion of human self-realization. The problem is the deadly cocktail that ensued when 'permissiveness' was stirred with the greed, possessiveness and ruthless competition of the 'winner/loser' culture[6] ushered in by Thatcherite neoliberal economics. 'Make love, not war' became 'make love *and* war'. . . . and 'loadsamoney' too.

There have indeed been huge cultural changes since the 1950s in all Western societies: greater individualism, autonomy, concern with self-realization, more scepticism about authority, and less deference.[7] But while this 'desubordination'[8] may have reduced internalized controls restraining deviance, it cannot by itself explain rising crime. Many other factors need to be examined, including shifts in motivation, opportunity, formal controls, and the labelling of offences. Above all, the dimensions emphasized in the 'Labour approach of the past' (as New Labour's 1997 manifesto put it), such as the evils identified by the 1979 manifesto quote at the head of this chapter – deprivation, social injustice, urban decay, unemployment – all remain relevant to the explanation of crime and its control. Political economy and social justice are still crucial,[9] even though they have been sidelined in political discourse over the last two decades by an overemphasis on culture rather than social structure, on condemnation at the expense of comprehension, and above all by a resurgence of confidence in the power of policing and punishment to suppress crime.

Political Economy and Permissiveness

The account offered below will stress the overriding significance of political economy for the analysis of crime trends, focusing on the displacement since the 1970s of the postwar social democratic welfarist Keynesian consensus by neoliberalism. However, this is certainly not intended to substitute a one-club economic analysis for the cultural and control explanations that have become dominant. The term 'political economy' rather than 'economics' is used precisely to signify that economic factors must always be understood to interact in a complex and dynamic dialectic with political, cultural and social dimensions. The conceptual separation of the 'economic' from the 'political', 'social', 'cultural' and 'moral' was itself a reflection of the nineteenth-century liberal Holy Grail – revived by contemporary neoliberalism – of self-regulating markets, insulated from political and other 'interference'. As the great (but sadly neglected) political economist Karl Polanyi demonstrated most clearly sixty years ago, this was an impossible utopian aspiration: the economic is necessarily 'embedded' in other social relations that ultimately resist realization of the 'free' self-regulating market.[10]

Political debate about crime – and indeed much academic criminology – is riven by false antitheses and quarrels between rival theories that shed heat not light. The issue is not whether economic or social rather than moral or cultural or control factors explain crime: unemployment versus the decline of the family, inequality versus immorality. As Elliott Currie has expressed it most effectively, this either/or approach

> begins to get in the way of understanding both the multiplicity and the interconnectedness of the forces that operate to increase the risks of violent crime in specific, real world social circumstances. When we examine patterns of youth violence in, say, South Chicago or South London, we don't see evidence of 'strain' and *not* disorganization, for example, and *not* a weakening of 'parental' controls. We are likely to see great structural inequalities *and* community fragmentation and weakened ability of parents to monitor and supervise their children – and a great many other things, all going on at once, all entwined with each other, and all affecting the crime rate – with the combination having an impact that is much greater than the sum of its parts'.[11]

Five Necessary Conditions of Crime

To understand why crime rates have increased over the last fifty years we need to consider all the necessary ingredients both of offending, and of perceptions of crime. There are at least five necessary conditions for a crime to occur: labelling, motivation, means, opportunity, and the absence of controls (internal and external).

Criminological theories have frequently been proffered in imperialistic fashion, as *the* explanation of crime, denying the validity of all others.[12] There have also been attempts to synthesize these perspectives into what is then proffered as an integrated general theory. The view taken here is eclectic rather than synthetic. Explanations in terms of individual characteristics of offenders (psychological or biological) are complementary to, rather than contradictory of social analyses. Psychological and biological models can help explain the varying proneness of individuals in a population to behave in ways that come to be seen as criminal. People can be conceptualized as dominoes of different height in terms of their likelihood to engage in deviance in particular circumstances. But social factors are needed to explain rates of crime in a population: how many dominoes fall at a particular time. On the other hand, sociological accounts cannot explain by themselves why particular individuals, in what appear to be similar circumstances, behave in more or less deviant ways, a puzzle that may be illuminated by psychological or genetic models.

In a similar way, control and situational theories have been formulated since the 1970s in ways that deny the significance of motivation. For most of its history (roughly from the 1870s to the 1960s) criminology primarily focused on the question of motivation, with rival perspectives pursuing the Holy Grail of an explanation of why criminal behaviour occurs. The contributions of control and situation to the understanding of crime were largely overlooked, and their current dominance is making up for this. But concentrating on motivation, control, or situational context at the expense of the other dimensions is like seeking to explain the motion of a car in terms of either the accelerator, the brake, or road conditions alone. Although one or other may be the predominant factor in explaining changes at a particular moment, they are all continuously mutually interacting in the background.

Changes in rates and patterns of crime may occur because of changes in any or all of the five conditions of criminality at different times. To understand a particular historical trend we need to construct a narrative showing how wider changes in political economy and culture plausibly impacted on these elements of crime. This combines knowledge of broader historical change with what criminological research has suggested about the aetiology of offending. Before suggesting such a narrative, let us examine the five necessary conditions of crime.

Labelling

'Labelling' is primarily important for understanding perceptions of, and reactions to crime. Shifts in crime rates and patterns may frequently be due to labelling changes. For behaviour to be treated as 'criminal' it is necessary first for there to be an authoritative construction of the general category of crime it falls under. The behaviour must then be interpreted as such by victims, witnesses and official criminal justice agents. Shifts in criminal law, and in patterns of reporting and recording incidents, are major influences on apparent patterns and trends in crime.

Labelling may also act as a cause of criminal behaviour. Changes in how people treat labelled offenders (stigmatization, ostracism, denial of jobs) may contribute to further offending. Alterations in a person's self-identity as a result of such labelling can accentuate this. The so-called 'labelling' perspective that flourished in the 1960s emphasized the paradox that deviance can be explained as a consequence of attempts at social control, and claimed that this 'secondary' deviance was qualitatively and quantitatively more significant than primary offending. Whether the crime-producing consequences of official reactions to deviance outweigh their crime control effects cannot be settled once and for all; it is an open empirical question in particular circumstances. But apparent shifts in crime may well be accounted for by labelling.

Motivation

Detective fiction, as well as newspaper and 'true crime' stories, tend to portray the motives driving crime as complex, puzzling, often bizarre, requiring the sensitivity of a Dostoevsky or a Freud – or at least an Agatha Christie or a Cracker – to unravel. This is because they focus on extremely unusual, very serious, pathologically violent and sexual cases. Most offences are committed for quite conventional and readily comprehensible reasons, prompted by motives that are widely shared – money, fashionable goods, sexual pleasure, excitement, thrills, intoxication by alcohol, adrenalin or other drugs.[13] Many theorists have pointed out that criminals are often driven precisely by their immersion in the values and desires of a conventional culture that nevertheless denies them legitimate means of attainment or excludes them.[14] Offenders do not inhabit alien moral universes; the accounts they tend to give to justify or excuse their illegal behaviour do not exhibit a clash of civilizations but are extensions of dominant forms of ethical argument.[15] The fact that most crime is motivated by mundane, widely shared aspirations and pursuits does not, however, mean that understanding motives is not important to unravelling crime trends. The extent, nature and distribution of such motivations vary over time and between different places in ways that help explain offending patterns. To take a very straightforward example, neoclassical economic theory predicts that changes in economic conditions, say a rise in unemployment, will alter the perceived rewards relative to costs of illegal activity, and hence their prevalence and frequency – for all the emphatic denials of such a connection by the Thatcher government. Other things are frequently not equal, so the econometric evidence supporting this relationship is not unequivocal but is nonetheless strong.[16]

Social, cultural and economic changes affect the pressures and attractions of behaviour labelled as criminal, increasing or decreasing the numbers of people motivated to commit them. The most plausible account of how macro-social structures can affect variations in motivations to commit crime between cultures and over time is Robert Merton's theory of anomie, one of the most influential, but also frequently misrepresented and misunderstood, sociological theories of deviance.[17] This is often portrayed simplistically as 'strain' theory: explaining lower class crime as a direct product of lack of opportunities. It is then criticized for neglecting offending by the affluent and powerful, especially organizational and corporate crime; and conversely for deterministic overprediction that the deprived will become depraved. In fact, Merton's emphasis is very much on the *interdependence* of cultural interpretation and structure. Structural limitation of legitimate opportunities generates pressures for deviance not in itself but in the context of cultures that encourage widespread aspirations for all through a mythological fable of the possibility of rising from rags to riches – epitomized by the 'American Dream'. Even more fundamentally, Merton argues that cultures that emphasize material success, especially if this is defined primarily in monetary terms, generate strains towards deviance and crime at *all* levels of society, not least – indeed perhaps above all – among elites. There is no terminal point for monetary aspirations, and success breeds desire rather than satisfaction. Winning becomes all that matters, and notions of proper and legitimate means get pushed aside: nice guys or gals finish last; losers are zeroes. Cutting corners and coming first is all that matters, at all levels of society and all times. Deviance becomes the new normal.

Means of crime

As lovers of detective mysteries know, in addition to motive criminals need means and opportunity. Changes in political economy, culture, technology and social patterns can expand or contract the *means* of committing crimes. New types of crime become possible, old ones are blocked off, and new ways of committing old offences are created. The development of cheques, then credit cards, and more recently the internet, have provided successive waves of new technical methods for the old activity of relieving people of their money. 'The Internet is a particularly effective medium for criminal recruitment and the dissemination of criminal techniques,' found one pioneering study.[18] Cyberspace enables many new types of offence and novel ways of committing old offences, such as terrorism, piracy, fraud, identity theft, stalking, sexual offences against children, hacking security codes and racist harassment.[19] The increased speed and extent of travel and communications signified by globalization facilitates a variety of crimes: for example trafficking in people, drugs, arms, money laundering and terrorism.[20]

The commission of crime requires a variety of personal and technical resources. A recent analysis has identified at least seven resources needed for crime. These include (1) ability to handle emotional states (overcome fear, guilt, inhibitions); (2) personality traits (intelligence, courage, ability to manage appearance and demeanour); (3) appropriate knowledge (of victims' routines, organizational procedures, technical characteristics of tools and targets);

(4) skills (IT skills, driving, charm, dealing with safes, locks and other protective devices); (5) physical capacities (strength, speed, size); (6) tools or other facilitators (weapons, skeleton keys, crowbars, disguises); (7) social contacts, networks, associates (accomplices, specialists in appropriate criminal techniques, illegal markets).[21]

Opportunities for crime

Social and economic changes can increase or reduce the availability of criminal opportunities. In particular the proliferation of desirable and readily stealable consumer goods has frequently been linked to increasing theft of these items. In the last twenty-five years rational choice and routine activities perspectives have developed in criminology, focusing on the way that specific situations and patterns of everyday life create targets and opportunities for crime.[22] Opportunity is itself seen as a cause of crime: 'opportunity makes the thief', as two leading proponents claim.[23] These approaches are highly practical in aim and achievement, and there is much evidence of successful situational crime prevention interventions that have reduced specific types of offence by blocking or reducing opportunities to commit them. A particularly striking example is the reduction of suicide associated with changes in the British gas supply. This was analysed in a classic paper showing that the elimination of carbon monoxide after the introduction of natural North Sea gas in 1968 was rapidly followed by the virtual disappearance of suicide using domestic gas.[24]

Criminal opportunities can be expanded by a proliferation of targets (for example, the spread of ownership of cars, televisions, video and DVD players, home PCs, laptops, and most recently, mobile phones and iPods, each

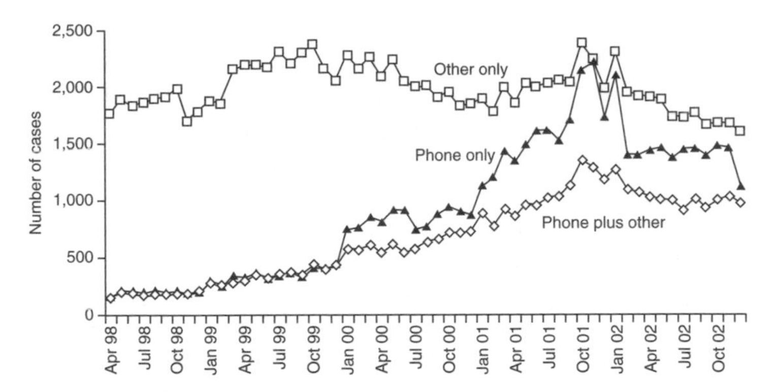

Figure 4.1 Monthly number of street offences involving theft of a phone, 1998–2002

Source: K. Curran et al., *Street Crime in London* (London: Government Office for London, 2005), p. 16.

in turn becoming the hottest items for theft), or shifts in 'routine activities' that make particular crimes easier to carry out. Figure 4.1 illustrates how the theft of mobile phones in the last decade responded to the spread of ownership of these ideal targets for robbery. It shows the very sharp rise in robberies of phones, especially from early 2000 to early 2002 (while thefts of other goods remained roughly static). This reflects the rapid rise in ownership of mobile phones in these years. 'The rate of increase in mobile phone ownership was particularly rapid from 1999 until 2001. In 1999 less than a third of the population aged 15 or over owned a mobile. By the end of 2001 this had risen to 75 per cent. Amongst 15–17 year olds the figure was already 70 per cent by mid 2000.'[25] The ebb and flow of opportunities for crime is thus a factor shaping trends and patterns of offending.

Controls

A crime will not occur unless the behaviour involved is labelled as such. Nor will this behaviour happen unless a potential offender acquires the necessary motivation and means, and suitable opportunities present themselves. But one further ingredient is necessary: an absence of controls. The potential burglar, say, may be eager to find a property to burgle, perhaps to feed her children or a habit. Equipped with jemmy and know-how, she comes across a relatively secluded house, milk bottles curdling on the doorstep indicating absent owners, and she spies the flashing LCDs of tempting electronic equipment through the ground-floor window. But her progress up the garden path may be arrested by the plod of a patrolling constable's feet, or the sound of a siren. Even in the likely event that the strong arm of the law is deployed elsewhere, one final intervention may hold her back. On the shelf she spots a Bible, and hears the still, small voice of her Sunday School teacher, 'Thou shalt not steal', and she goes home for tea and reflection.

Formal controls Changes in the efficacy of formal controls ('codes, courts and constables' in Malinowski's 1926 formulation) will alter the attractions or possibility of crime. The 1990s drop in crime in the US (indeed in most of the Western world) has been widely attributed to harder or smarter or simply more policing. 'Crime is down: blame the police,' boasted Chief Bratton of the New York Police Department.[26] Others give the credit to more and tougher punishment, claiming vindication for Michael Howard's 'prison works' slogan. Both interpretations explicitly or implicitly place much of the blame for the crime rise of the earlier postwar decades on a weakening of the severity, probability or effectiveness of formal sanctions.

Informal controls As the earlier quotes from Tony Blair and others attributing increasing crime to 1960s 'permissiveness' show, informal social controls are also important in interpretations of crime trends. Cultural trends such as liberalization affect the operations of internalized restraints, 'conscience' (the 'inner policeman'),[27] in the way that proponents of the 'permissiveness' thesis argue. The thesis that informal social controls – family, school, socialization, community and 'cultural capital' – are the fundamental basis of social order (for good or for bad) has a long pedigree in anthropology, sociology and criminology.[28]

The leading exponent of contemporary control theory, Travis Hirschi, started from the argument that as deviance is common, and committed for widespread and mundane motives, the real puzzle requiring explanation was conformity. His analysis suggested that 'social bonds' restrained most people from deviance. These bonds had four dimensions: *attachments* (strong social and psychological ties to conventional communities, making people sensitive to others' feelings and opinions); *commitment* (investments of time, effort, resources in family, education, work, career, property); *involvement* (in conventional social and leisure networks, not 'bowling alone' or with deviant others); and *beliefs* (in law, religion, conventional morality).[29] These bonds were socially and individually variable, changed over time, and had complex sources that required research and analysis (and bolstering by appropriate public policies). In a later version, Hirschi and Gottfredson pinpointed individual lack of self-control as the key factor explaining crime: criminal acts, they argued, are 'likely to be engaged in by individuals unusually sensitive to immediate pleasure and insensitive to long-term consequences

. . . The evidence suggests to us that variation in self-control is established early in life',[30] an analysis which is the root of conservative claims about 'permissiveness' and its discontents.

What's It All About? Explaining Postwar Crime Trends

Explaining the trends in crime depicted in chapter 3 requires us to consider how changes in political economy, social structure and culture have impacted on the five elements of offending.

Late 1950s–1980: rapid recorded crime rise

The huge and sustained rise in recorded crime that began in the late 1950s was mainly a product of the new mass consumer society that developed in those years. The era is frequently seen as full of optimism, supposedly summarized by Prime Minister Harold Macmillan's famous claim that 'most of our people have never had it so good' (in a 1957 speech to a Conservative Party rally in Bedford). It is significant that 'Macmillan's famous phrase is often misquoted as "You've never had it so good"'.[31] What Macmillan actually said implicitly recognized that not everyone shared in the new prosperity of the majority. Macmillan went on explicitly to worry whether it was 'too good to last?', and many were concerned about what negative social consequences mass affluence and consumerism might have.

The new consumer culture impacted both on the recording and on the occurrence of crime. The General Household Survey figures for burglary during the 1970s show that a substantial part of the rise in crimes recorded by the police was due to more reporting and recording by victims of property crimes, an understandable process in a society in which high value consumer goods were proliferating and an increasing proportion were insured against theft. It is plausible that much of the overall increase in the recorded crime rate, both in the 1970s and in the decade and a half before that, was also a recording phenomenon rather than a real increase in victimization, although it is impossible to be certain in the absence of any alternative sources of data to the police figures.

However, the culture and social structure of mass consumerism were also generating higher offending levels. Most obviously this resulted from the spread of tempting targets for crime: cars, radios and other equipment in cars, television sets, video recorders, etc. These all increased the opportunities for relatively easy, lucrative thefts, as did their successors in later decades like PCs, laptops, mobile phones and iPods.

Unemployment and inequality were of course at a historic low point and diminishing, and general living standards rising. This led many commentators and policy-makers to expect crime to fall, as indeed it did during much of the first decade after the Second World War [32]. Jock Young has spoken of an 'aetiological crisis' for social democratic criminology in this period:[33] rising crime in what Galbraith in 1958 dubbed the 'affluent society' dashed hopes that as deprivation diminished so would crime.[34]

While the idea that crime resulted straightforwardly from economic inequality and poverty may have been commonly held, social democratic criminology generally saw the relationship as much more complex. Culture and morality were crucial factors mediating the impact of economic factors on crime. Many social democratic theorists had indeed foreseen that the effects of mass affluence and consumerism would be likely to drive crime up, not down, because of the egoistic ethos and culture engendered by a materialistic society. This was the central theme of the criminological theory developed early in the twentieth century by Willem Bonger, the only example before the 1960s of a Marxist analysis of crime.[35]

The quintessential social democratic analysis of crime was Merton's theory of anomie.[36] As discussed earlier, this saw materialism as the key factor downplaying the importance of using only legitimate means to acquire goods, and stimulating deviance at all levels of society. Inequality in the structure of legitimate opportunities was a source of 'strain' in a culture that stressed the desirability and possibility of material success for everybody. Mertonian anomie became more not less acute in the era where the masses were told they had never had it so good, and it fanned motivations to steal. Social democratic criminologists in the early 1960s explicitly anticipated this. David Downes concluded his seminal study of delinquency in two inner London boroughs at the turn of the 1960s by anticipating the likelihood of

> an increase in delinquent activity, feasibly of a nihilistic, contracultural type, the more so since an increasingly affluent society has endorsed rising expectations and aspirations among male working-class adolescents who – unlike older members of the community – have had no experience of real adversities in the labour market.[37]

In the early 1960s, 'Even at this high point of modernity . . . with full employment, growing welfare provision and busy assembly lines, clear warnings were struck about the worsening social problems that would result from unchecked inequalities and the growth of consumerism.'[38] A Labour study group, whose report informed the Wilson government's thinking on criminal justice, argued that the 'get rich quick ethos' of mass consumer society led to a

> weakening of moral fibre . . . The values that prevail among those who dominate society may be expected to spread to all its levels. If men and women are brought up from childhood to regard personal advancement and ruthless self interest as the main considerations, material success will certainly not train them in social responsibility, and worldly failure may lead to social inadequacy and a resentful sense of inferiority.[39]

The more materialistic culture of mass affluence emphasized monetary success rather than the means of achieving it. It is perhaps no coincidence that the rise in crime began in the same year (1955) that ITV, the first commercial television channel, began to broadcast. It is not only that advertising invaded the home in a much more brash way. The television schedules were quickly saturated with game shows explicitly promoting the 'get rich quick ethos': *Double Your Money*, *The £64,000 Question*,[40] *Take Your Pick*, *The Price is Right*, and many others.[41] The stimulation of consumption by television advertising explicitly undermined norms of deferred gratification: 'Live now, pay later',[42] 'Take the waiting out of wanting'. This eroded inhibitions about illicit access to 'must have' goods, and not just the legitimate use of Access cards.[43] The pervasive stress on the desirability of glittering prizes for all increased the sense of relative deprivation among those sectors lacking in legitimate opportunities. The new consumer, wanting it all now with payment on the 'never never',[44] is in fact the character type of the delinquent – lacking self-control and the capacity to defer gratification – as evoked by right-wing criminology. In the words of a key text, criminals 'tend to be impulsive, insensitive . . . risk-taking, short-sighted',[45] a perfect description of the ideal-type consumer. All this was predicted by social democratic criminologists at the dawn of the era of mass affluence, and consumerism continues to fuel crime at a turbo-charged pace.[46]

The hold of informal and formal controls also weakened in this period. The beginnings of an independent youth culture in the mid-1950s,[47] and broader aspects of desubordination, reduced internalized restraints against offending. This is of course the key explanation proffered by conservative criminology: but it was consumerism, economic rather than moral liberalism, that wreaked havoc with traditional informal social controls.

Declining deference also began to make policing harder: police authority was more often questioned, and complaints against them more readily believed.[48] Detection rates began to fall, weakening the deterrent effects of criminal justice. This was not a primary cause of increasing crime, however, but a consequence of it. Falling clear-up rates were not so much a reflection of more incompetent policing, but of crime rising faster than police capacity to deal with it. As recorded crime began its precipitate rise (whether or not this was due to more offending), pressures on the police increased, leading to lower detection rates, and hence a decline in the deterrence and incapacitation effects of criminal justice, which may have further aggravated the crime rise.

In sum, after the late 1950s a variety of interlinked consequences of mass consumerism fed rising crime rates. These increased the labelling of crime (as more victims reported the theft of insured property), *and* expanded opportunities and temptations to offend. A more materialistic and egoistic culture not only fanned the relative deprivation that motivated crime, but weakened informal and internalized moral controls. Rising recorded crime put more pressure on the police and pushed detection rates down, thus eroding the probability of punishment and amplifying the initial growth of offending.

1980s–1992: crime explosion

In the 1980s and early 1990s crime rates reached historical record heights. The new British Crime Survey confirmed that this was primarily a real rise in victimization by crime, not just its reporting and recording. The processes that had driven crime up during the 1960s and 1970s all continued. But the critical accelerant behind the crime explosion of the 1980s came courtesy of Mrs Thatcher. The key change was the brutal displacement of the consensus, Keynesian, welfare state policies of the postwar decades by her eagerly espoused neoliberal monetarist policies. This produced the massive social dislocations of deindustrialization and resurgent mass unemployment – indeed long-term never-employment for increasing numbers of young men, especially among ethnic minorities and in inner city areas. Inequality sharpened into a yawning chasm between the top and bottom of the economic hierarchy, and poverty began to rise after a long historical process of increasing social incorporation and inclusion. Industrial and political conflict was sparked on a scale not experienced for half a century or more, with more violent disorders.

These trends are illustrated by figure 4.2, from the Institute for Fiscal Studies, charting registered unemployment, between 1961 and 1991. Figure 4.2 shows the huge surge in unemployment during the early Thatcher years, 1979–86. After a few years in which it fell back, unemployment rose sharply once more during the recession of the late 1980s and early 1990s. Income inequality also rose throughout the Thatcher era from 1979 to 1891 (figure 4.5 below).

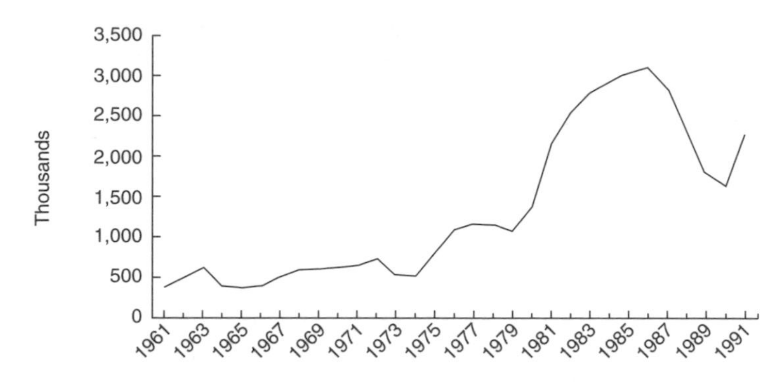

Figure 4.2 Trends in unemployment, 1961–1991 (claimants, excluding school leavers)
Source: A. Goodman and S. Webb, *For Richer, For Poorer: The Changing Distribution of Income in the United Kingdom 1961–1991* (London: Institute for Fiscal Studies, 1994), p. 9.

Rampant social injustice and exclusion eroded informal social controls of all kinds in the 1980s as whole communities lost the material basis of settled existence, with incomparably greater ramifications for stable, or indeed any, family life and 'morality' than the 'permissiveness' against which the right railed. Moral laissez-faire followed the economic. A culture of egoism, the 'me society', was stimulated under the guise of the ethic of individual responsibility. 'Greed is good' became the infamous watchword of a new Gilded Age. The unbridled turbo-capitalism of the Thatcher years had devastating consequences for order that far outweighed the strong state measures introduced to control it in a Canute-like effort to stem the social tsunami.

During the 1980s the Thatcher government consistently and firmly denied that there was any link between unemployment or poverty and crime. Does the evidence from econometric research support their denials?

Economic factors and crime: the econometric evidence In 1987 the late Steven Box published a seminal analysis of the relationships between recession, crime and punishment.[49] His comprehensive literature search found fifty studies that had tested for relationships between unemployment and crime levels.[50] Simply taking all these studies at face value, there were thirty-two which found that higher unemployment was associated with more crime, while eighteen found the opposite. This was the result that would be predicted by anomie theory, radical criminology, and indeed by neoclassical economics as well. Unemployment increases the pressures and incentives motivating crime, in particular the property crimes that constitute the bulk of the officially recorded figures. But the score-line was far from overwhelming! Those espousing theoretical perspectives making the opposite prediction, that recession reduces crime by decreasing the available targets of crime and increasing the number of unemployed 'guardians' staying at home (situational crime prevention and routine activities theories), could take some comfort from the fact that nearly half the studies went their way.

Box also highlighted the methodological weaknesses of many of the studies. In particular several used measures of crime such as arrest or conviction rates that are even more problematic than the officially recorded crime rates with all their limitations. There were also important conceptual and methodological issues concerning which variables should be controlled for in order to try to isolate the relationship between unemployment and crime, and about what measures of unemployment were used. Box further underlined the rather small relationship between unemployment and crime uncovered in most of the studies, in either direction, meaning that while they on balance provided some support for the hypothesis of a link, it was a weak one.[51]

Box also reviewed econometric studies probing links between income inequality and crime levels. Theoretically it would be expected that these variables were closely associated, because inequality would be likely to produce a sense of relative deprivation, motivating property crime in particular. Of the seventeen studies reviewed by Box (all but one were cross-sectional), twelve reported a positive relationship between inequality and crime and five did not.[52] The five exceptions were all studies of homicide. There was unanimous support for the view that greater inequality was associated with more property crime.

There are crucial limitations of all econometric studies from a criminological perspective that must be borne in mind in assessing their results. One is that the variables measured by econometricians have at best a rough-and-ready correspondence to the concepts in the criminological theories being tested. Unemployment or inequality rates, for example, may be related to anomie, but they are not direct measures of it. The social and psychological meaning of economic variables such as employment or income will vary according to different social, cultural and individual circumstances and interpretations. At best econometrics can establish correlations between economic indicators and official crime measures (with all the pitfalls of these statistical indices), not causal relationships. Interpreting such associations as causal explanations requires assumptions about the direction of causality. More fundamentally, the relationships have to be 'adequate at the level of meaning', as Weber put it.[53] There have to be plausible narratives linking the variables as sequences of comprehensible human action.

It is important to note that the studies reviewed by Box were all carried out before the mid-1980s. The social character, meaning and impact of such variables as unemployment and inequality changed fundamentally in the years immediately before Box's book.[54] The data for the studies he reviewed were gathered mainly during the post-Second World War decades of virtual full employment, when unemployment was mainly transitional and voluntary. Theoretically there would be little reason to expect such unemployment to be associated with crime.

After 1973, however, the recession and the advent of monetarism resulted in long-term, sometimes permanent exclusion from legitimate livelihoods of growing numbers of young men. In its social impact and meaning, especially in an increasingly consumerist culture, this was quite different from what unemployment represented in earlier decades. It signified a fatal combination of enhanced anomie and an erosion of the controls represented by legitimate work, and indeed marriage and family responsibilities.[55] The changed meaning of unemployment after the mid-1970s would be expected to produce a closer association between unemployment and crime levels than in earlier decades. This is confirmed by reviews of econometric research carried out more recently than Box's 1987 book.[56]

Although most studies conducted since the 1980s *do* find positive relationships between higher unemployment and higher crime rates (especially property crime), the strength of the association remains fairly modest. In part this may be because measures of total unemployment continue to include both voluntary and involuntary unemployment. Robin Marris has tried to estimate the significance of this, by assuming that unemployment rates below 4 per cent mainly involve transitional, voluntary unemployment and only levels above 4 per cent signify involuntary unemployment. He demonstrates that there were very strong associations during the 1980s and early 1990s between burglary and *involuntary* unemployment (estimated by including only levels over 4 per cent).[57]

Furthermore, unemployment statistics have become an *increasingly* problematic measure of levels of prosperity or economic hardship. Partly this is because official statistics on unemployment were considerably revised during the 1980s, in the context of the increasingly controversial increases in unemployment due to the Thatcher government's neoliberal economic policies.

It has also been argued that unemployment fluctuations lag behind changes in economic conditions. In a recession, for example, earnings will begin to fall before employment statistics do, because of wage cuts, reduced overtime and greater resort to part-time work. These cuts in conditions will generate stronger incentives for property offending *before* unemployment begins to rise, dampening the apparent effect of subsequent rises in the unemployment statistics.[58]

Wider transformations in the structure of the labour market, associated with the change from Keynesian economic management to neoliberalism, have also made unemployment statistics a less crucial index of economic exclusion and relative deprivation. Chris Hale has demonstrated the criminogenic significance of the emergence of a 'dual labour market' since the 1970s.[59] There is an increasing contrast between a *primary* or core sector of skilled workers, enjoying relative security, and buoyant earnings, benefits and employment rights, and a *secondary*, peripheral sector – mainly in service industries – lacking these advantages. Employment in the peripheral sector is low skilled, unstable, insecure, poorly paid and without employment rights and benefits. These 'McJobs' are much less likely to reduce crime in the way that work in the primary sector traditionally did.

Deindustrialization in the wake of neoliberalism during the 1980s enormously increased the peripheral relative to the primary sectors. This was associated with increasing crime rates, especially in economic downturns when earnings in the secondary sector are squeezed even more than they are in other parts of the economy.[60] Declining wages for unskilled workers have been shown to be associated with increasing property crime.[61] Conversely, the introduction of the minimum wage in 1999 was followed by greater decreases in crime in areas with disproportionately high numbers of workers previously earning less than the minimum, who thus gained most from the new policy.[62] While the changing structure of the labour market explains much of the growth and fluctuations in crime, it also means that the division between unemployment and marginal employment in the secondary sector becomes less clear-cut and significant.

Another factor complicating the crime–unemployment relationship is the contradiction between the motivational and opportunity effects of economic prosperity or hardship.[63] Simon Field's work for the Home Office has shown that both are important, but in different ways.[64] Analysing data between the Second World War and the late 1990s, Field found that the short-term cyclical effects of economic change must be distinguished from the long-term consequences of economic growth. In the short run there is an inverse relationship between economic fluctuations[65] and property crime,[66] and hence recorded crime overall. In the long term, however, crime has increased as affluence has grown. This discrepancy was accounted for by the contradictory short-run and long-run effects of prosperity. In the short term economic upturns reduce *motivations* for property crime. But the long-run result of affluence is the expansion of criminal opportunities due to the proliferation of goods to steal and routine activity effects, such as fewer homes guarded during working hours or leisure time.[67]

It was noted earlier that Box's 1987 review already showed overwhelmingly strong evidence that greater inequality was related to more property crime, but not homicide. Since then there has continued to be a sharp increase in economic inequality, with the partial exception of the last few years in Britain as New Labour's measures targeted at the alleviation of child poverty have begun to take effect.[68] More recent studies, in Britain and the US, have continued to confirm the strong association between inequality and crime.[69]

A significant change, however, is that homicide is no longer an exception. Studies in several countries now show strong associations between greater inequality and more homicide.[70] The difference from the earlier period is probably due to increases in the proportion of homicides involving poor young men as victims and perpetrators. In the 1980s, many areas suffered economic and cultural devastation as they lost the industries that were the basis of their whole way of life. The result was literally murder.

> Behind the man with the knife is the man who sold him the knife, the man who did not give him a job, the man who decided that his school did not need funding, the man who closed down the branch plant where he could have worked, the man who decided to reduce benefit levels so that a black economy grew, all the way back to the woman who only noticed 'those inner cities' some six years after the summer of 1981, and the people who voted to keep her in office . . . Those who perpetrated the social violence that was done to the lives of young men starting some 20 years ago are the prime suspects for most of the murders in Britain.[71]

The clear conclusion indicated by recent reviews of the econometric evidence is that there is a plethora of material confirming that crime of all kinds is linked to inequality, relative deprivation, and unemployment, especially if it represents long-term social exclusion.[72] The downplaying of economic factors in criminal justice policy discourse since the 1970s was due to shifts in dominant political and intellectual perspectives, not evidence that there are no significant economic correlates – arguably 'root causes' – of crime. Examination of the seminal work of Ehrlich, for example, shows this. In his 1970s papers pioneering the revival of interest in the economics of crime, Ehrlich's data clearly showed strong associations between poverty, inequality, unemployment and crime levels.[73] The emphasis on the significance of deterrence variables (probability and severity of sanctions) by Ehrlich himself and his primary audience of neoliberals was because policing and punishment were seen as desirable and available policy levers, while the economic factors either could not or should not be reversed by government action.

Political economy and crime: comparative perspectives
The econometric evidence reviewed above focuses on the relationships between economic factors and crime within particular social orders. As Ian Taylor has pointed out, the econometric literature is primarily concerned with

> the causal relations between 'economic crisis', 'the business cycle', or other *departures from normal economic conditions or circumstances* and the outgrowth of crime. There is often very little curiosity . . . about the ways in which the routine functioning of economies organised around the capital–labour relation or around individual self-interest may in itself be a factor in crime.[74]

We have seen that econometric studies *do* demonstrate by and large that economic factors – inequality, unemployment, poor pay and insecure conditions – are significantly related to crime fluctuations, especially in contemporary political economies. In these sections comparative and historical evidence will be reviewed, showing that the overall character of different political economies is related to variations in their patterns of crime and violence (the next chapter will show this applies also to their styles of criminal justice).

There has been little systematic comparative study of the relationship between crime and political economy. An obvious issue is that the problems of comparison between recorded crime rates in different jurisdictions are vastly greater than the acknowledged difficulties in comparing penal severity.[75] The well-known hazards of interpreting national crime statistics are amplified into another dimension altogether by the huge variations in legal definitions, police practices, and cultural conceptions of crime, order and morality affecting public perceptions and reporting. For these reasons the regular Home Office publication of comparative official crime statistics only reports league tables showing rates of change for each society, not absolute or even per capita levels of recorded crime,[76] for all offences except homicide where it believes the problems of comparison to be fundamentally fewer.

Since 1989 a group of criminologists in different countries has mounted several sweeps of the International Crime Victims Survey (ICVS) seeking to overcome some of these issues. They have attracted particular media attention in the UK because they show England and Wales as highest (with Australia) of the seventeen countries surveyed in overall incidence of reported victimization, as well as in the top three for every specific offence category.[77] The US, often assumed to be the world's crime capital, comes eleventh.

The survey is scrupulously rigorous in its methodology, and open about its possible limitations (such as the use of telephone interviewing). It is clearly an ambitious undertaking, representing a state-of-the-art attempt to provide data on comparative crime patterns and trends. For all that, the results obtained seem bizarre from the point of view of analysis in terms of political economy or indeed any other theoretical framework, and defy any attempt at interpretation or explanation. The authors themselves do not offer any account of the pattern of differences, beyond noting its consistency across the sweeps, although they offer some plausible suggestions about the possible sources of decline in overall victimization shown by their data.[78]

The ordering of the countries by the ICVS bears no relationship to their types of political economy, or to their relative punitiveness. It is thus equally mysterious to liberals, political economists and deterrence theorists. When crimes are weighted by their seriousness, as judged by the public in the surveys,[79] the pattern does approximate more closely to their types of political economy. The top three countries are neoliberal ones (England and Wales and Australia as in the unweighted tables, but with the US jumping to third place), and the bottom three are social democratic Denmark and Finland, and corporatist Japan. But it remains puzzling to note that the archetypal social democracy, Sweden, is in fourth place, not far off the neoliberals, with the Netherlands next.

It is difficult to avoid endorsing Jock Young's acerbic dismissal of the surveys as 'maverick results',[80] owing more to cross-cultural vicissitudes in perceptions of order, and indeed official interviewers, than to crime patterns. As Young suggests, the league tables of different societies run so counter to expectation that it is plausible that higher ranked societies may paradoxically be ones where the relative *absence* of serious violence makes respondents more sensitive to low-level incivility, and thus more likely to report incidents to interviewers, boosting the survey rate!

Table 4.1 Political economy and homicide (average per year 1999–2001)

	Homicide rate (no. per 100,000 population)
Neoliberal countries	
US	5.56
South Africa	55.86
New Zealand	2.5
England and Wales	1.59
Australia	1.87
Conservative corporatist	
Italy	1.5
Germany	1.15
Netherlands	1.51
France	1.73
Social democracies	
Sweden	1.1
Finland	2.86
Denmark	1.02
Norway	0.95
Oriental corporatist	
Japan	1.05

Sources: M. Cavadino and J. Dignan, *Penal Systems: A Comparative Approach* (London: Sage, 2005); G. Barclay and C. Tavares, *International Comparisons of Criminal Justice Statistics 2001* (London: Home Office, 2003).

There are fewer problems of international comparison of homicide statistics, because there is less diversity in legal definitions and recording practices. The international pattern of homicide rates does correspond systematically to variations in political economy.[81] Table 4.1 shows the variation in homicide rates between types of political economy in industrialized countries.[82] Neoliberal countries have the highest rates. The overall conclusion is clear: rates of lethal violence are highest in neoliberal political economies, and lowest in social democracies (with a glaring anomaly in Finland).

Some recent studies have offered cogent analyses of why serious violent crime rates could be expected to be much higher in neoliberal than social democratic political economies.[83] The earlier review of econometric studies showed considerable evidence that inequality, relative deprivation, and involuntary, exclusionary unemployment are linked to more property crime and serious violence. Neoliberalism is associated with much greater inequality, long-term unemployment, and social exclusion. In addition to economic inequality and deprivation, Currie has spelt out several other mediating links between political economy and greater pressures towards violent crime. These include 'the withdrawal of public services and supports, especially for women and children; the erosion of informal and communal networks of mutual support, supervision, and care; the spread of a materialistic, neglectful, and "hard" culture; the unregulated marketing of the technology of violence; and . . . the weakening of social and political alternatives'.[84] This link between neoliberal political economies and higher propensities towards serious crime is further supported by historical evidence about long-term trends in crime and disorder in many societies.

Political economy and crime: historical dimensions The post-Enlightenment incorporation of the mass of the population in industrialized capitalist liberal democracies into a common status of citizenship was associated with a secular decline in violence and disorder. Manuel Eisner has recently synthesized and updated the results of numerous historical studies exploring long-term trends in homicide in Europe. The long-term trajectory from the medieval period can be summarized roughly as a J-curve.[85] Homicide rates fall sharply up to the late eighteenth century. There was then a period of increase up to the middle of the nineteenth century, but to a much smaller extent than the earlier fall, taking the level back only to that of a century earlier. After the middle of the nineteenth century the decline resumed, until the last quarter of the twentieth century, when there is a return to the levels of the mid-Victorian period.

Focusing on the trend since the early nineteenth century in greater detail suggests a U-shape pattern in homicide and other serious crime over this period. Gurr shows that for the US, Britain, Australia and some European countries crime rates increased between the late eighteenth and mid-nineteenth centuries, declined in the later nineteenth century, and were fairly stable until the later twentieth century, when there was a return to rising crime.[86] Gatrell's detailed analysis of the trends in theft and violence in England during the nineteenth and early twentieth centuries supported this picture of decline in the later nineteenth century, followed by rough stability for the first quarter of the twentieth.[87] There have also been a number of historical studies showing a similar U-shaped pattern for the extent of violence in political and industrial disorders: secular decline from the mid-nineteenth century to the last quarter of the twentieth century, with an increase thereafter.[88]

Attempts to explain these long-term trends involve a complex mix of interdependent considerations. Eisner and Gurr themselves primarily invoke Elias's analysis of a broader 'civilizing process'.[89] This depicts a secular cultural, social and psychic tendency of greater sensitization towards control and display of bodily processes generally, including violence, during modernization. While the emphasis in Elias's analysis is on cultural and psychic sensibilities, these are interlocked with developments in state formation, as well as disciplinary and stabilization processes associated with the emergence of markets and factories.[90] The state came to monopolize the means of violence, as part of a process of pacification of social and economic life, with the police emerging as the institutional locus for this.[91] The changes in cultural sensibilities analysed in Elias's account of the civilizing process were bound up with broad shifts in the political economy. A sharpening of social conflicts, crime and disorder in the early stages of industrial capitalism during the late eighteenth and early nineteenth centuries was succeeded by a long-term process of inclusion of the majority of the population in legal, political and (to a lesser extent) economic and social citizenship. This was the precondition for the mix of mass seduction and discipline represented by 'penal welfarism' during the first three-quarters of the twentieth century.[92]

The emergence of a globalized neoliberal political economy since the 1970s has been associated with social and cultural changes that were likely to aggravate crime, and to displace all frameworks for crime control policy apart from 'law and order'. The spread of consumerist culture, especially when coupled with increasing social inequality and exclusion, involved a heightening of Mertonian 'anomie'. At the same time the egoistic culture of a 'market society', its zero-sum, 'winner–loser', survival of the fittest ethos, eroded conceptions of ethical means of success being preferable, or of concern for others limiting ruthlessness, and ushered in a new barbarism.

The insecurities and pressures engendered by neoliberalism and consumerism affected all levels of society, as indicated by Karstedt and Farrall's study of 'The moral maze of the middle class'. This charts the growth of fraud and unethical business practices in the UK and Germany, and the techniques of neutralization facilitating it. Although it is impossible to quantify this, corporate, white-collar and state crime were similarly stimulated by the anomic pressures and moral ambiguities of neoliberalism.[93]

Informal social controls, the inculcation of a 'stake in conformity', through family, education and work, become forlorn dreams. The eclipse of social democratic hopes shuts off prospects of alleviating deprivation (absolute or relative) by legitimate collective industrial or political action, leaving the 'responsibilized' individual to sink or swim in a world of risk.[94] Sometimes, as neoclassical economics would predict, offending is the 'rational choice' in adverse labour market conditions. The reversal of the 'solidarity project',[95] the long-term incorporation of the mass of the population into a common status of citizenship, which underpinned the 'civilizing process' of declining violence and crime, has formed the dark couple of rising crime and harsher control efforts that took root after the 1970s.

1992 onwards: ambiguously falling crime

Recorded crime peaked in 1992, and then began to fall. The drop in recorded crime during the period 1993–6 was a recording phenomenon rather than a real decline in offending, as argued in chapter 3. Michael Howard may not have succeeded in his aim to be tough on crime, but the 'businesslike' police performance targets that he sponsored were certainly tough on the causes of crime recording.

Since the mid-1990s the British Crime Survey has registered a substantial fall in victimization, returning to the levels of the early 1980s. Rising recorded crime rates for some years after 1997 were primarily due to new counting rules, and they have begun to come down recently.[96] In the 1990s, recorded crime rates began to decline, first in the US, but then in most Western countries.[97] The dramatic fall in New York City, formerly seen as a world crime capital, attracted particular media attention. This has caused a reverse 'aetiological crisis' to that associated with the 1950s crime rise.[98] No 'grand narrative' seems satisfactory. Neoliberalism, the left's prime suspect, retains its global economic hegemony. But conversely there has not been any reversal of 'permissiveness', the right's dominating bête noire. The favourite criminal justice accounts all have some plausibility, and will be reviewed in the next chapter, but also do not provide complete explanations. The zero tolerance policing explanation in particular, celebrated by many promoters of the supposed New York miracle, has been demolished definitively by close analyses.[99] Nor has the enormous expansion of punitiveness, above all the staggering and gross levels of imprisonment, contributed more than marginally.[100] This is seen most sharply by comparing the experience of two sets of adjacent countries: Scotland versus England and Wales; Canada versus the US. In each case, the former jurisdiction has pursued a much less punitive penal policy than the second over the last quarter-century, but has seen similar crime reductions and lower serious crime levels than its tougher neighbour. These cases establish that it is possible to have 'Less crime without more punishment'.[101]

Within the array of explanations, economic factors are certainly significant, if peculiarly unheralded by governments wishing to appear 'tough on crime'.[102] But they too cannot provide more than part of the explanation. Unemployment has certainly been at much lower levels than during the crime explosion of the 1980s, having fallen substantially and continuously since the early 1990s

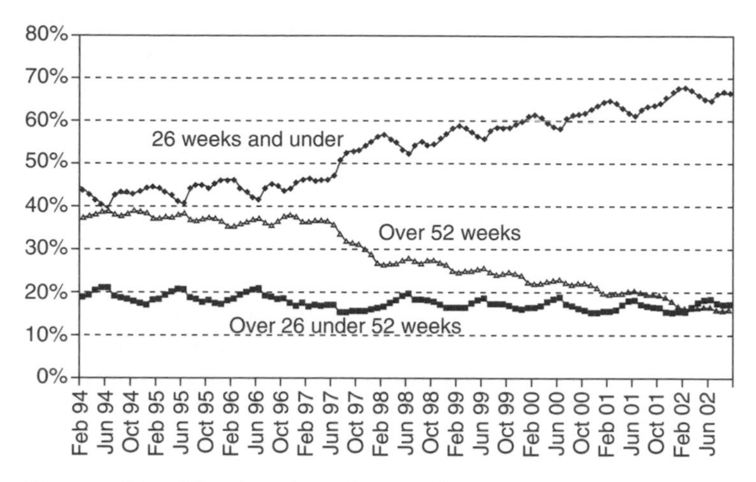

Figure 4.3 The duration of unemployment, 1994–2002 (percentage distribution, claimant count, monthly)
Source: C. Pissarides, 'Unemployment in Britain: a European success story', working paper, Centre for Economic Performance, London School of Economics, 2003, p. 25.

(although it remains nearly three times higher than in the early 1970s).[103] Of particular significance for social exclusion and crime, Figure 4.3 shows that longer-term unemployment (over fifty-two weeks) has fallen since 1997 (accounting for the overall fall, as shorter-term unemployment has not decreased). This has been achieved largely by the expansion of secondary labour market jobs.

Figure 4.4 shows that in recent years unemployment and property crime rates track each other quite closely. The decline in unemployment in the 1990s parallels the falls in theft and burglary (and hence overall crime too). The figure also shows that the huge rise in unemployment in the 1980s was associated with the crime explosion in

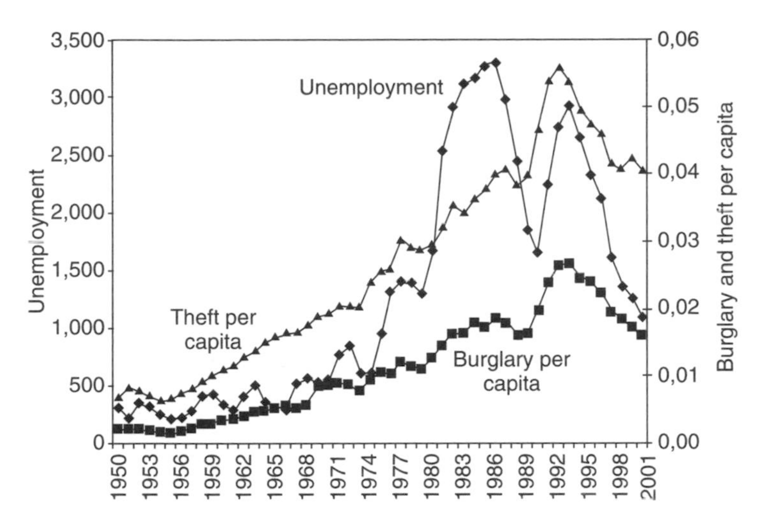

Figure 4.4 Trends in unemployment and property crime, 1950–2001

Source: D. Deadman and Z. MacDonald, 'Why has crime fallen? An economic perspective', *Economic Affairs*, 22 (Sept. 2002): 5–14, at 6.

those years, but that there does not appear to have been a close relationship before that (for reasons that were discussed earlier).

Overall there has not been any significant change in the extreme level of economic inequality and insecurity that New Labour inherited, despite welcome improvements in crucial aspects of poverty (especially child poverty). As summed up by the Institute for Fiscal Studies: 'Between 1996/97 and 2001/02, income inequality rose on a variety of measures, to reach its highest ever level (at least since comparable records began in 1961) as measured by the Gini coefficient.[104] Since then, income inequality has fallen, and it is now at a similar level to that in 1996/97:

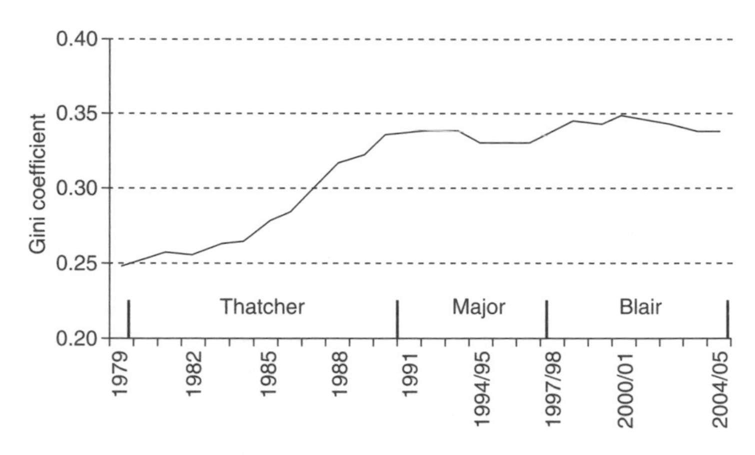

Figure 4.5 Income inequality, 1979 to 2004–5
Source: M. Brewer et al., *Poverty and Inequality in Britain: 2006* (London: Institute for Fiscal Studies, 2006), p. 24.

the net effect of eight years of Labour government has been to leave inequality effectively unchanged.'[105]

Figure 4.5 depicts the huge rise in inequality during the Thatcher years, which fuelled the crime explosion. It remained on a rough plateau under John Major, but then rose slightly in the early Blair years, falling back since 2001, but only to the level inherited in 1997. Inequality, a key driver of crime, has remained generally steady in recent years, but has not fallen significantly. The crime drop remains something of a mystery, defying any simple account.[106] But economic factors – falling unemployment, a brake on the acceleration of inequality and poverty – are an important part of the explanation.

The paradox of security

The blessings of property can be double-edged. As property increases, so does anxiety about retaining it. As the Gershwin brothers expressed in this song:

Folks with plenty of plenty,
They got a lock on the door;
Afraid somebody's gonna rob 'em
While they're out a-making more . . .
What for?

(Ira Gershwin, *Porgy and Bess*)

While emphasizing that crime overall has been declining, New Labour has struggled to benefit from this, above all because of the evidence from surveys and from media discussions that public fears have not declined. This has been labelled the 'reassurance gap' by policy-makers, and stimulated the so-called 'reassurance policing' agenda to try to plug it.[107] This is underpinned by the notion of 'signal crimes',[108] the idea that particular offences have special power to symbolize broader crime and disorder and thus to stimulate unwarranted anxiety, outweighing the general statistical decline in crime (not a million miles away from the old Marxist notion of false consciousness).

There may, however, be a rational kernel to the stubborn refusal of public anxiety to decline with the crime rate, beyond blaming the messengers of the sensationalist and bad news addicted media (though they are very significant). Within the decline in overall crime, the most worrying serious violent crimes (especially robbery) have tended to rise, especially according to the police recorded statistics.[109] Perhaps even more significant is what can be called the paradox of insecurity. An increasing obsession with security practices and paraphernalia, even if successful in reducing risk, can exacerbate the sense of insecurity by acting as reminders of danger. In so far as the decline in crime overall is due to more successful adoption of protective equipment and preventive routines by crime-conscious citizens, rather than any reduction in the root causes of offending, the burden falls on potential victims above all. While prevention tactics, burdensome as they may be, are preferable to victimization, they are a product and index of insecurity, and indeed may reinforce rather than reduce fear. What is required is reassurance not about crime but about the causes of crime. The root causes of crime have not diminished appreciably in the 1990s. Declining crime has been a product of fragile economic prosperity, unevenly shared and insecure, and of holding the lid down on potential criminality that has not abated.[110] This may well be a temporary upturn for the forces of order in an arms race between them and potential offenders. Febrile anxiety on the part of the public may not just be due to overexposure to the *Sun*, or a *Mail*strom of moral panic. The right-wing media nonetheless do contribute greatly to the growth of law and order politics and policies that will be analysed in the next chapter.

5

A New Leviathan? Law and Order Politics and Tough Crime Control

The early 1990s saw a hardening of public and political discourse about law and order and about crime control policies, initially in the US and UK, but eventually in most Western countries. The decline in crime during the 1990s, in the UK as well as the US and elsewhere, has been commonly attributed to these tougher crime control policies, notably rising imprisonment, and 'zero tolerance' policing and other 'hard cop' tactics. This chapter will analyse the rise of the politics and culture of 'law and order', and assess its impact on crime control.

Many books and articles have been written about this already. David Garland's 2001 book *The Culture of Control* in particular offers a tour de force analysis that has deservedly become exceptionally influential and stimulated a veritable library of debate and commentary. My account is deeply in its debt, but diverges from it in some ways. Garland constructed a Foucault-inspired 'history of the present', weaving together many strands of cultural, social, political and economic change. The developments in crime and control are a complex dialectic of many influences and interdependencies. Nonetheless, in my view the growing dominance of neoliberalism in the globalizing political economy of the late twentieth century is primus inter pares in understanding what has happened. At the same time, it is also important to recognize that there has not been an unbroken and unilinear march towards the 'culture of control' since the 1970s. There was a step change in the early 1990s, most marked in the US and Britain, but experienced more generally too. The change was not a reversal but rather a sharp accentuation of a trend towards harder crime control discourse and policies, embedding them much more deeply. This is not to deny the existence of countertrends and resistances to greater punitiveness,[1] but important as these are, the overall trajectory has been in the direction of harsher crime control policies, especially since the early 1990s. As many critics of Garland's thesis have pointed out, the 'culture of control' is not equally prominent in all societies, and many jurisdictions have succeeded in resisting it to varying degrees.[2] These variations are closely related to the extent to which different political economies have embraced neoliberalism. However those 'varieties of capitalism'[3] that have succeeded to date in retaining some form of welfarism and social democracy face increasing pressure from global markets and from the hegemony of consumerist culture. This threatens to push them in the direction not only of more neoliberal economic policies but of the more repressive law and order control policies that are their Janus face.

The Rise of Law and Order Politics

Until the late 1960s criminal justice policy had not been a partisan political issue, at least since the early nineteenth century. According to Downes and Morgan's definitive study it did not feature in any party's election manifesto between the Second World War and 1970.[4] Nor was crime an important issue to the public until the 1970s, at least as registered by opinion polls, although it has been a favourite theme in all branches of popular entertainment for centuries. Some specific aspects of criminal justice policy *were* politically controversial, notably capital punishment, and competing penal policy lobbies campaigned vigorously over it.[5] Particularly spectacular or salacious crimes have always been regular topics of popular fascination, part of a perennial tendency for respectable opinion of the middle-aged to bewail the supposedly declining moral standards of young people.[6] But the overall state of crime was not a widespread cause of concern, nor was criminal justice policy subject to political controversy and conflict.

'Law and order' first became politicized in the US in the 1960s.[7] Barry Goldwater had blazed the law and order trail in his abortive but prophetic Presidential bid in 1964. In the hands of the political right, the demand for law and order condensed a number of specific meanings: above all that law could and should produce order, but failed to do so because of weak enforcement. In this view, the unequivocal purpose of law was crime control, but it was shackled by excessive due process restraints that frustrated effective enforcement.[8] The law and its front-line troops, the cops, should be unleashed to restore order. Law and order was a successful campaigning slogan for Richard Nixon in his 1968 election victory, becoming a codeword for race, culture and generational backlash. As we now know, Nixon, Spiro Agnew and the rest of the elite Republican cadre of 1968 knew what they were talking about in relation to crime, mostly ending up on the wrong side of the bars a few years later.

The politicization of law and order was heralded in Britain in the 1970 general election, when the Conservative manifesto said that 'the Labour Government cannot entirely shrug off responsibility' for rising 'crime and violence'.[9] The manifesto also linked crime with industrial disputes as instances of 'the age of demonstration and disruption'. The Labour manifesto replied by attacking the Conservative attempt 'to exploit for Party political ends the issue of crime and law enforcement'. With the hindsight of the last thirty-five years, these seem remarkably genteel opening shots in the coming political war about law and order!

Politicization of law and order accelerated under Margaret Thatcher's leadership of the Conservative Party. During the late 1970s, in the build-up to her election victory in 1979, Mrs Thatcher blamed the Labour government directly for rising crime and disorder, pledging a 'ring of steel' to protect people against lawlessness.[10] She promised to boost the resources and powers of the police to prevent and clear up crime, and to toughen penal policy, reversing the softness on crime that she attributed to Labour. The Tory's law and order campaign was greatly helped by the emergence of the police as a political lobby, backing up the Conservatives' agenda in a series of advertisements and speeches.[11] The issue was a major factor in Thatcher's 1979 election victory, according to polls monitoring the shifts in public opinion.[12] The police were directly rewarded for their open support when the Conservative government implemented in full a recommended pay rise as one of its first acts in office.

The party political gulf on law and order reached its widest point in the mid-1980s. The key conflicts were over the policing of the urban disorders and of the miners' strike of 1984–5 (both results of the economic and social dislocation engendered by the Thatcher government's monetarist policies), the Police and Criminal Evidence Act 1984, and the campaigns for democratic police accountability. On all these issues Labour took a civil libertarian stance, attacking the Conservative government for violating the principles of the rule of law. Labour also attacked Conservative law and order policies for being counterproductive in increasing social divisions, and aggravating rather than reforming the root causes of crime that lay in social inequality and relative deprivation. While this position may have had the support of the majority of criminologists (at any rate until the late 1970s), it was an electoral liability for Labour. In the 1984 and 1987 general elections the Tories attacked Labour for being 'soft' on crime because of its concerns about civil liberties, its 'permissiveness', links with trade unionism (associated with disorder) and failure to develop any short-term solutions to bolster public protection.

In the late 1980s signs appeared of a new cross-party consensus on law and order. The Conservatives (with Douglas Hurd as Home Secretary) began to offer a more nuanced approach, perhaps because of the apparent failure of toughness to stem rising crime. They began to emphasize crime prevention, proportionality in penal policy, and value for money (a major Thatcherite theme, of course). The new tack culminated in the 1991 Criminal Justice Act. For its part, Labour began to try to repair some of the 'soft on law and order' image that the Tories had successfully foisted on them, culminating in Blair's legendary 1993 soundbite, 'tough on crime, tough on the causes of crime'. This began to be widely touted during 1993 in media interviews and articles, in the wake of the anguish and national soul-searching about crime and moral decline triggered by the tragic murder of the Liverpool toddler Jamie Bulger by two young boys.[13] It is perhaps ironic that the formulation was probably 'borrowed' from its original author, Chancellor of the Exchequer Gordon Brown.[14] 'Tough on crime, tough on the causes of crime' touched all bases, finely balancing the new realist recognition that crime really was a problem with a more traditional social democratic criminological concern with 'causes'. But the main departure was rhetorical: the double whammy of toughness packed into one short, sharp sentence.

Since 1993 there has developed a new 'second order' consensus on the fundamentals of law and order policy[15] – toughness, toughness, toughness – with frenzied partisan conflict on specifics: anything you can do, I can do tougher. Law and order politics has become a dominant discourse of the age.

During the 1970s and 1980s law and order had been the exclusive slogan of the political right. David Downes vividly labelled the new turn as the 'theft of an issue'.[16] As the emerging school of New Left Realism argued, the primary victims of crime were the poorest and most vulnerable groups in society, those that the left had traditionally seen as its constituency.[17] Crime could best be explained by the social ethos and conditions of unbridled capitalism, as the left had traditionally argued, but the acute suffering of crime victims meant that urgent remedies to alleviate their plight and reduce victimization were needed as soon as possible, and could not wait until the deeper root causes of crime were tackled.[18] The missing link that New Left Realists urged was the identification and implementation by the left of short-term crime control policies that might offer some protection while long-term economic and social reforms addressed the basic causes.[19]

In the early 1990s, as Labour tried in earnest to recapture the ground lost on the issue of law and order, they began to attack the Tories not only with the old social democratic arguments about crime being produced by inequality, egoism and exclusion, but by pointing to failures of Conservative criminal justice policies. Given the record increases in crime in the 1980s, despite burgeoning expenditure on policing and punishment, this was an open goal – as even Tory cabinet ministers conceded.[20] Apart from the general increase in crime, the media propelled many individual cases (notably the murder of Jamie Bulger) into moral panics symbolizing a general breakdown in moral and social order that transcended their particular tragic circumstances. Specific instances of failure in criminal justice policy or practice were transformed into major scandals by the media.[21]

The wrong-footing of the Tories on law and order came to a head in 1993, with Tony Blair's emblematic pledge 'tough on crime, tough on the causes of crime'. Michael Howard fought back vigorously with his 'prison works' speech to the October 1993 Conservative Party conference, and policies inspired by it. Nonetheless the game had changed dramatically. Having ditched its electoral 'hostages to fortune' such as exclusive association with civil liberties, trade unionism, and an analysis of crime primarily in terms of social justice,[22] Labour was making the political running on what had hitherto been one of the Tories' most secure policy areas. As with the whole New Labour project, the ditching of old commitments was seen as a price worth paying for its electoral rewards.

The 1992–3 period was a decisive watershed for the politics of law and order, as for other policy areas. While, during the late 1970s and 1980s, neoliberal and neoconservative political parties, ideas and policies had become dominant in Britain, the US and most of the Western world, they were fiercely if unsuccessfully contested. On a world scale the New Right's ascendancy was marked by the fall of the Soviet Union in 1991. But what really confirmed the global hegemony of neoliberalism was the acceptance of the fundamentals of its economic and social policy framework by the erstwhile social democratic or New Deal parties of the West. The Clinton Democrats and New Labour, and their embrace of the 'third way'

– neoliberalism to a cool beat – marked a new, deep consensus, sounding the death-knell of the postwar settlement of a Keynesian mixed economy that the conservative parties had accepted when they returned to power in the early 1950s. Blatcherism was Butskellism in reverse.

The Crime Control Consensus

The new political terrain of neoliberal triumphalism was signified in 1993 by Labour's seizure of the law and order agenda. The post-1993 crime control consensus has five core elements.

(1) Crime is public enemy number 1 Crime and disorder – and since 2001, terrorism – are seen as *the* major threats to society and to individual citizens, by the public and politicians. Many opinion polls have demonstrated that crime (and more recently terrorism) have moved to the forefront of public concern. The polling organization MORI, for example, has conducted surveys on what people see as 'the three most important issues facing Britain today' for more than thirty years. In the early 1970s, just as law and order was emerging as a political issue, under 10 per cent rated it among the top three. It was easily eclipsed by a plethora of other economic and social issues, such as inflation, unemployment, the national health service and education. By 1977 the proportion putting crime in the top three issues had increased to 23 per cent, and during the pre-election months in 1979 it was as high as 41 per cent. In the 1980s and early 1990s it generally fluctuated between 10 and 20 per cent. But after 1993 the proportion putting crime in the top three issues was often above 30 per cent, and generally in the high twenties. Since 2001 crime has consistently been rated a leading concern,

rivalled only by 'terrorism' and 'race relations/immigration' – cognate issues in the tabloid world of law and order discourse.

(2) Individual not social responsibility for crime Crime is the fault of offenders, due to their free choice, individual or cultural pathology, or to intrinsic evil. It is *not* caused by social structural factors, according to the crime control consensus. This was expressed most bluntly in 1993 by the then Prime Minister John Major: 'Society needs to condemn a little more and understand a little less.'[23] Major had earlier told the 1992 Conservative Party conference:

> To excuse crime may seem understanding. But it's wrong. Sympathy doesn't curb crime. If society wants to protect itself it must condemn crime, not condone it. We must create a climate in which people know the difference between right and wrong and yours and mine. We must spell out the truth. Crime wrecks lives, spreads fear, corrupts society. It is the fault of the individual, and no one else.

Tony Blair has frequently echoed these sentiments, as in a recent article when he claimed that 'the left, by the 1980s . . . had come to be associated with the belief that the causes of crime are entirely structural . . . we had eliminated individual responsibility from the account'.[24]

(3) Foregrounding victims versus offenders The victim has become the iconic centre of discourse about crime, ideal-typically portrayed as totally innocent. Crime discourse and policy are predicated on a zero-sum game: concern for victims precludes understanding – let alone any sympathy for – offenders.[25] Michael Tonry quotes a sharp example of this zero-sum ethos, citing 'a senior US Justice

Department official . . . "People are either for victims or for criminals" '.[26] John Major's speech to the 1992 Conservative Party conference offers an example from this side of the Atlantic:

> We are cracking down hard on crime – particularly violence . . . There's another problem we are dealing with – the illegal occupation of land by so called 'new-age travellers' . . . They say that we don't understand them. Well, I'm sorry – but if rejecting materialism means destroying the property of others, then I don't understand. If doing your own things means exploiting the social security system and sponging off others, then I don't want to understand. If alternative values mean a selfish and lawless disregard for others, then I won't understand. Let others speak for these new age travellers. We will speak for their victims.

(4) Crime control works Since the early 1990s can-do optimism has reinvigorated law enforcement agencies around the world: criminal justice *can* control crime provided it is tough (*and* smart). Criminal justice professionals and conservative politicians celebrate this as a triumph of common sense over the 'nothing works' pessimism and over sensitivity to civil liberties that are said to have hampered crime control for much of the twentieth century. Policing and punishment, they claim, can control crime through effective deterrence, prevention and incapacitation, if given sufficient powers and resources. 'Prison works', as does 'zero tolerance' policing, and the 'responsibilization' of citizens to take self-protective measures against victimization.[27] Civil liberties and human rights are at best marginal issues, to be subordinated to crime control exigencies, and deeper social causes of crime are denied or played down.

Tony Blair's recent speeches have reflected this confidence that a properly empowered criminal justice system can control crime effectively.

> Looking back, of all the public services in 1997, the one that was most unfit for purpose was the criminal justice system . . . above all, there was a resigned tolerance of failure, a culture of fragmentation and an absence of any sense of forward purpose, across the whole criminal justice system. . . . In the first few years we took some important first steps. We stopped the fall in police numbers. . . . We halved the time to bring persistent juvenile offenders to justice. We introduced the first testing and treatment orders for drug offenders. We introduced and implemented a radical strategy on burglary and car crime which cut both dramatically. We toughened the law. As a result, on the statistics we are the first Government since the war to have crime lower than when we took office. But that's the statistics. It's not what people feel. Building on these foundations, we started to become a lot more radical in our thinking. We introduced the first legislation specifically geared to Anti-Social Behaviour. We asked the police what powers they wanted and gave them to them. The latest Criminal Justice Act is a huge step forward. We put a £1 billion investment into CJS [criminal justice system] technology. We have introduced mandatory drug testing at the point of charge in high crime areas. We have established the first DNA database. There will be a new framework for sentencing. Probation and prisons are to be run under one service. Community penalties are being radically restructured. And we have 12,500 more police than in 1997. There is a real feeling within the CJS that change is happening. But as fast as we act, as tough as it seems compared to the 1970s or 1980s, for the public it is not fast or tough enough. What we signal today is a step-change. . . . The purpose of the CJS reforms is to rebalance the system radically in favour of the victim, protecting the innocent but ensuring

> the guilty know the odds have changed . . . our first duty is to the law-abiding citizen. They are our boss. It's time to put them at the centre of the CJS. That is the new consensus on law and order for our times.[28]

(5) High-crime society normalized David Garland's book *The Culture of Control* shows how popular culture and routine activities have become increasingly focused on crime risks and the perception that we live in a 'high-crime society'.[29] Lucia Zedner has vividly described some of the ways in which crime concerns have penetrated everyday life, and the paradox that they enhance fear rather than security:

> The home owner who sets her alarm each time she leaves the house is constantly reminded of the possibility of burglary during her absence. Likewise the ubiquitous signs warning that property is mark-protected, that CCTV cameras are in operation, or guards patrolling are akin to anxiety makers advertising the risks of crime at every turn . . . Less obvious products are also increasingly marketed as security-enhancing, for example mobile phones are sold particularly to teenagers and women as safety devices enabling anxious parents to maintain constant surveillance over their offspring or their users to summon help. Likewise sports utility vehicles (SUVs) are made the subject of aggressive marketing campaigns that emphasise their bullish capacity to protect their passengers from unknown external threats . . . Paradoxically, the subjective security created by the armoured environment of the SUV only exacerbates the sense of personal vulnerability encountered on leaving the vehicle. Hence the proliferation in the United States of drive-in fast food joints that do not require one to risk even the few meters between car and restaurant . . . Personal segregation, whether in cars, suburban residential communities, doorman-protected apartment buildings, or exclusive leisure facilities is predicated upon risks 'out there'. . . . The more provision for security is

> made, the more people regard as normal or necessary, and the greater their anxiety when it is not available. And for those who cannot afford to buy into these 'bubbles of security' in the first place, the sense of standing outside protection, of inhabiting dangerous places only increases.[30]

The new hegemonic law and order consensus that prevailed is part of a broader shift in politics and culture, dubbed by Rose the 'death of the social'.[31] The rise of neoliberalism, individualism and the 'risk society'[32] have eclipsed the Keynesian, mixed economy, welfare state consensus that prevailed for the first three postwar decades. In the sphere of UK domestic politics this was confirmed above all by the ascendancy of New Labour in the 1990s and early twenty-first century, with its promise of a 'third way' 'beyond Left and Right'.[33]

The Toughening of Crime Control

The 'second order' consensus about tougher crime control that emerged in 1993 marked a crucial step change in the hardening of policy. In many ways the Thatcher governments of the 1980s mounted only a phoney war on crime, for all the fiery speeches by the leader that made Vlad the Impaler seem a bleeding heart liberal. Mrs Thatcher certainly talked the talk of toughness, but the rather more pragmatic home secretaries she appointed, above all William Whitelaw (1979–83) and Douglas Hurd (1984–9), walked a softly, softly, subtle walk in practice.

Phoney war on crime: the Thatcher era

Thatcher-era policing was not as tough as she made it sound in campaigning speeches. The one area where there was a clear new hardline approach was the militarization of public order policing, symbolized vividly through the rapid introduction of riot control uniforms and equipment, dramatically transforming the police image from Dixon of Dock Green to Darth Vader. The space for this was created largely by the urban riots of the early 1980s in Brixton, Toxteth, Broadwater Farm and elsewhere, and by a resurgence of union militancy, above all in the 1984–5 miners' strike. These were direct products of the devastation wreaked by the Thatcher government's enthusiastic espousal of neoliberal economics, and by its attack on the trade union movement. Nonetheless the new public order policing tactics were largely reactive to new levels and forms of violent disorder, rather than spearheads of a broader toughening of police and penal policy. The major extension of statutory police powers in the 1984 Police and Criminal Evidence Act (PACE) was immensely controversial, and vigorously campaigned against as the harbinger of the Orwellian police state signified by the year of its birth. The impact of PACE was and remains disputed, and it certainly did not introduce the perfectly balancing set of safeguards that the rhetoric of its proponents promised. But it transformed the position of suspects in police custody in primarily positive ways, considerably reducing the possibility of the gross abuses revealed later in the 1980s by the Court of Appeal decisions on several spectacular miscarriages of justice that had occurred in the 1970s.[34]

The penal policies of the Thatcher governments became markedly more sophisticated in the later 1980s. The impending crisis signified by rocketing crime levels facilitated the adoption by the liberal pragmatists at the helm of the Home Office of a set of more finely nuanced and evidence-based (to anticipate the Blairite slogan) approaches. Crime prevention, in the form of both physical/situational and community-based techniques, moved to the forefront of policy. The Criminal Justice Act 1991, which had followed many years of consultation and planning, deriving from a 1988 Green Paper and the 1990 White Paper *Crime, Justice and Protecting the Public*, was the high-water mark of the growing recognition that prison was 'an expensive way of making bad people worse' (as the White Paper put it pithily). The Act sought to limit the use of imprisonment, reserving it for offences that were 'so serious that only a custodial sentence could be justified'. Proportionality of punishment, whether custodial or not, was the paramount principle. This was embodied most explicitly in the unit fine system introduced by the Act, seeking (albeit rather unsatisfactorily in practice) to match payment to the offender's means.

Tough on crime, 1993 onwards

This more balanced and pragmatic approach was rapidly abandoned in October 1993 when Michael Howard made his notorious 'prison works' speech to the Tory Party conference. The volte-face was in part due to a series of scandals, mishaps and causes célèbres that were feasted on by the tabloids. However, the key change was the conversion of Labour to Blair's new toughness. From opposing the Conservatives' law and order approach from a civil libertarian direction suddenly Labour began attacking them from the opposite flank, deploring their failure to crack down on crime. The significant shift in policy following the emergence in 1993 of the 'second order' consensus on tough crime control is shown in figure 5.1 and table 5.1.

Figure 5.1 charts the long-term trends in the prison population of England and Wales since the early twentieth century. It shows that the prison population declined in

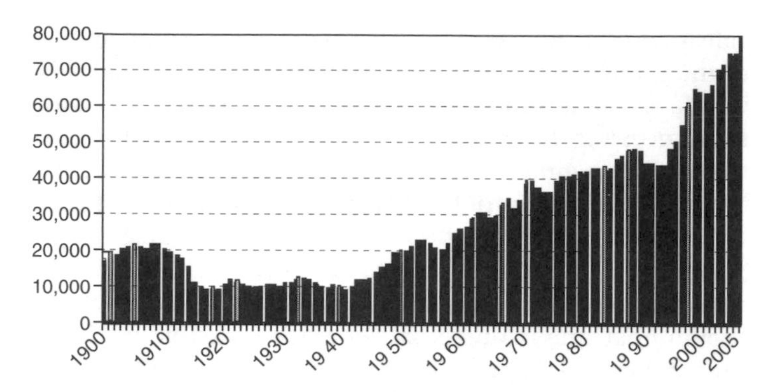

Figure 5.1 Prison population in England and Wales, 1900–2005

Source: T. Newburn, '"Tough on crime": penal policy in England and Wales', in M. Tonry and A. Doob (eds), *Crime and Justice 36* (Chicago: University of Chicago Press, 2007), fig. 7.

Table 5.1 Projected prison population in England and Wales, 2007–2013

	High	Medium	Low
2007	80,420	79,380	78,380
2008	84,670	82,730	80,730
2009	89,410	86,290	83,320
2010	94,020	89,810	85,700
2011	98,310	92,970	87,590
2012	102,280	95,630	88,980
2013	106,550	98,190	90,250

Source: N. de Silva, P. Cowell, T. Chow and P. Worthington, *Prison Population Projections 2006–2013, England and Wales*, Statistical Bulletin 11/06 July 2006 (London: Home Office).

the interwar years from its pre-First World War level of around 20,000. Since the end of the Second World War it has generally gone up, but with several periods of decline. During the early 1980s it was at a historic height of just over 40,000, but by the end of the decade it had risen sharply to nearly 50,000. There were then a few years of decline in the early 1990s, reflecting the approach of the 1991 Criminal Justice Act. But following the U-turn signalled by Michael Howard's 'prison works' speech in 1993 the numbers in prison began a sharp, relentless rise, reaching 77,000 by 2006.

This rise is projected to continue substantially on present policies, as table 5.1 indicates. It shows the current Home Office projections of the prison population on three alternative scenarios, 'high', 'medium' and 'low' (these are based on regular consultation exercises with samples of 'stakeholders' in the sentencing process). On the *low* scenario numbers in prison are projected to grow from the 2006 all-time record of just over 77,000 to more than 90,000 by 2013. On the high scenario they are expected to be over 106,500.

By themselves, increasing imprisonment rates do not establish that penal policy has indeed got more punitive. They may reflect more crime and convictions, or more serious ones. However, several recent analyses of the 1990s trends show conclusively that these factors do not account for the rising prison numbers, and that they are due to greater penal severity.[35] The number of offenders caught and convicted has remained roughly stable. There does not seem to be any significant increase overall in the seriousness of the offences or offenders being sentenced. But there *has* been a significant increase in the probability of those convicted receiving custodial sentences, *and* serving more time. Defining severity of punishment as a combination of the probability and the length of custodial

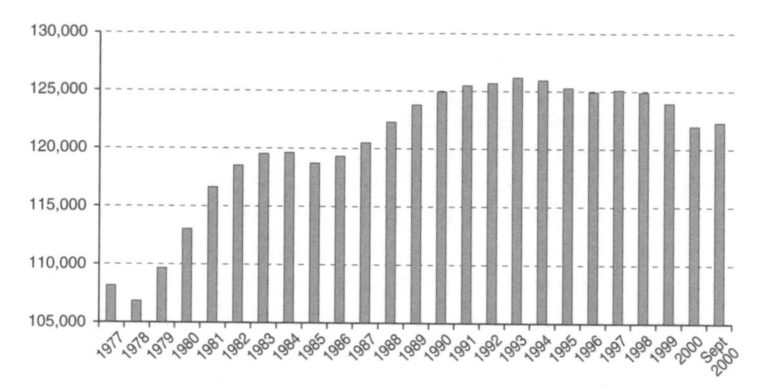

Figure 5.2 Police service strength in England and Wales, 1977–2000
Source: 'Police service strength England and Wales, 31 March 1977–30 September 2000', Research Paper 01/28, House of Commons Library, London, 16 Mar. 2001, p. 7.

sentences, an exhaustive recent analysis concluded that 'for serious property offences, the severity of punishment stayed constant or decreased between 1981 and the early 1990s and then increased dramatically. For serious violent offences, the severity of punishment increased steadily from 1981 to 1999.'[36]

Expenditure on police went up substantially during the 1980s. It then levelled off until 1997, since when it has gone up even faster. Police numbers show a roughly similar trajectory, reaching a peak of over 125,000 in the mid-1990s (as shown in figure 5.2). After a fall in the mid to late 1990s, the numbers begin to rise sharply after 2000, reaching an all-time record of over 143,000 by early 2006.

It is important to bear in mind also that these police officers are supported by a growing body of civilian staff, nearly a quarter of a million people in 2006. In addition there is an increasing body of community support officers (nearly 7,000 as of March 2006), as well as traffic wardens and special constables. These uniformed adjunct officers within police forces are just the tip of a huge iceberg: the 'pluralization' of policing, a proliferating array of organizations, some under the auspices of national or local government, but the majority private, that are providing policing and security services.[37] The numbers game is not all there is to the increase in policing resources. PACE in 1984 extended statutory police powers considerably, albeit with a set of safeguards for suspects intended to provide balance. As will be shown below, however, since 1993 there has been an accelerating expansion of police powers, usually without any accompanying safeguards.

The trends in imprisonment and in police numbers and resources refute the widespread political and popular belief that the criminal justice system has become 'softer' on crime, and needs toughening and strengthening. Tony Blair recently launched a major Home Office initiative predicated precisely on the proposition that criminal justice had been tilted against the protection of 'the law-abiding majority', and that it needed 'rebalancing' in their favour.[38] As this chapter documents, policing, punishment and prevention have grown extensively in resources, personnel, powers and scope over the last three decades. Nonetheless political initiatives and media-sparked panics relentlessly feed the myth that crime control has gone soft.

It is important to note that imprisonment and policing have grown particularly rapidly since the early 1990s, when crime rates began to fall, as compared with their more modest (but still substantial) expansion during the 1980s crime explosion. The early 1990s mark a watershed in punishment and policing both in the UK and the US: there has been spectacular growth at a time of falling crime. The key reason for this was the espousal by New

Labour, Clinton Democrats and other 'third way' devotees of the new 'tough on crime' mantra. This removed from the centre of the political arena the main forces that had sought to balance crime control with respect for due process and human rights.

New Labour, Old Punitiveness

New Labour's crime control policies embodied its characteristic 'modernization' project, seeking to 'triangulate' what it portrayed as the old-fashioned polarities of right and left. This was epitomized by the flagship 1998 Crime and Disorder Act, a quintessential 'third way' synthesis of the tough and the smart. It aimed at 'evidence-led', 'joined up' policy in the duties it placed on police, local authorities and other relevant agencies to develop a coordinated 'strategy for the reduction of crime and disorder in the area', culminating in the ambitious Crime Reduction Programme launched in 1999. But it also offered tabloid-appeasing toughness: minimum mandatory sentences, ASBOs, curfews.

The Janus-faced tough/smart policy combination is encapsulated above all in the restructuring of youth justice in the 1998 Act: systematic, evidence-based attempts to address and prevent offending by early prediction of risks and appropriate remedies, coordinated by interagency teams in the form of the local Youth Offending Teams, and centrally by the Youth Justice Board.[39] Alongside this, however, were a variety of new powers for the police and the courts to control youth crime and disorder, such as ASBOs, child curfew schemes, abolition of *doli incapax*,[40] and detention and training orders. The net result was an increase in the use of custodial penalties for young offenders.

Gradually 'tough on crime' has eclipsed 'tough on the causes of crime'. There has been a remorseless growth of police powers, for example. The legislative trend since 1993 has been extensions of police powers without corresponding safeguards, with the Human Rights Act of 1998 constituting the only balance. New powers to intercept communications, conduct covert operations, stop and search and arrest, and new public order offences were created in the early years of New Labour by the Police Act 1997, Crime and Disorder Act 1998, Regulation of Investigatory Powers Act 2000, Terrorism Act 2000, and the Criminal Justice and Public Order Act 2001. In 2002 the Home Office conducted a review of PACE. The review was premised on the view that the regime of safeguards created by PACE adequately protected suspects. The review's concern was to provide a 'useful tool supporting the police and providing them with the powers they need to combat crime'. It was deemed necessary to 'simplify police procedures; reduce administrative burdens on the police; save police resources; speed up the process of justice'. Accordingly the review floated a number of proposals to dilute the safeguards of PACE. The Criminal Justice Act 2003 authorized detention for thirty-six hours for all (not just 'serious') arrestable offences, and added criminal damage to the possible grounds for stop and search. The Serious Organised Crime and Police Act 2005 created a power of arrest for all offences, ending the category of non-arrestable offences. It enhanced powers of search and fingerprinting. It also allowed for the creation of civilian custody officers, overturning the PACE requirement that they should normally be police sergeants. The pressures on the police to achieve results have intensified in the new crime control climate, and they are increasingly armed with new powers unfettered by safeguards. This is likely to reduce the legal accountability of the police, despite the welcome enhancement of the complaints process represented by the Independent Police Complaints Commission that became operational in 2004.

New Labour has been repeatedly jolted into new 'tough' laws and initiatives by particular media-driven moral panics, and since 2001 – and *a fortiori* 2005 – the threat of terrorism. This was epitomized by Tony Blair's 'street crimes summit' at Downing Street in March 2002, and the accompanying initiative pledging to get robbery 'under control' by September. Michael Tonry has documented no fewer than thirty-three such get tough on crime initiatives announced between June 2001 and May 2003 alone,[41] with thirteen 'crime summits' between 1999 and 2003. It has been estimated that over 3,000 new criminal offences have been created by New Labour since 1997, one for every day the Blair government has been in power.[42]

New Labour itself sees toughening policing and punishment as a step forward, necessary 'modernization' for 'a criminal justice system and thinking shaped by the need in Victorian times to counter the gross unfairness of the past';[43] Blair's mantra is that 'twenty-first century crime requires twenty-first century solutions'. This means 'rebalancing the criminal justice system in favour of the law-abiding majority', as plans unveiled in July 2006 express it.[44] Nonetheless, as several commentators have pointed out, there are many aspects of penal regression in the punishment policies of the last thirty years in Britain as well as North America, Australasia and elsewhere.[45] The policing changes outlined earlier also have many echoes of premodern forms, in particular the resurgence of private and citizen involvement in providing policing and security services.[46] The proliferation of gated communities, enclosed and privately secured shopping and leisure complexes, and other forms of 'mass private property' have been referred to as a 'new feudalism'.[47] While Tony Blair is of course right that 'turning the clock back' is not possible, pointing out the regressive elements in current penal and policing trends is more than just a polemical branding of them as old-fashioned or uncivilized. Penal regression reflects the reversal of the 'solidarity project' of post-Enlightenment modernity, the attempt to incorporate all sections of society into the common rights of citizenship.[48]

The law and order paradigm, with its 'can-do' confidence about bringing crime under control by tougher penal and policing policy, might get some superficial vindication from the overall fall in crime in the last decade indicated by the British Crime Survey. However, the fall has mainly been in the less serious 'volume' crimes, while robbery and more serious violent crimes have increased. The role of criminal justice policy relative to wider socio-economic and cultural factors in explaining these crime trends is in any case complex and debatable, as will be explored in the assessment of the impact of law and order on pp. 154–62 below.

Explaining Toughness

There have been many attempts to explain the complex causes behind the rise of tough law and order politics. 'Eight different plausible stories' have been distinguished by Michael Tonry among recent attempts to answer the question 'Why did American crime control and punishment policies become so much harsher than in earlier American times or in other places now?'[49] These are that harsher punishment results from: (1) more crime; (2) public pressure; (3) exploitation of law and order by politicians as a popular issue; (4) the rise of single-issue politics; (5) the advent of 'risk society'; (6) 'postmodern' angst and insecurity; (7) special cultural characteristics of the US grounded in its particular historical forms of inequality; (8) cyclical changes in public and political attitudes and reactions to deviance. Underlying these narratives are three basic master accounts: (a) truth will out – penal policies are a reaction to crime trends (Tonry's first story); (b) democracy in action – cultural shifts, largely induced by the media and politicians, generate changes in sentiment and policy regarding crime, victims and offenders (roughly Tonry's stories 2–4); (c) root causes – deeper structural changes in political economy shaped the developments in penal culture and policy (Tonry's stories 5–8).

(a) Truth will out? Proportionate and pragmatic response to rising crime

The 'truth will out' account of the emergence of 'law and order' portrays it as simply a rational, realistic response to the increased incidence of victimization. We saw in chapter 3 that recorded crime has grown greatly since the 1950s, and in the 1980s and early 1990s there was a veritable explosion of crime. Even more crucially for understanding why crime became a political issue, crime did not just increase overall, but it came to victimize middle-class and elite groups who had been relatively sheltered from risk, and who (at least the liberal professionals among them) constituted the bulwark of support for penal liberalism.[50] As has often been quipped, a conservative is a liberal who has been mugged – and the likelihood of liberal professionals becoming crime victims has increased in recent decades, even though it remains much less than the risks faced by the poor.

There has also been a resurgence of optimism that criminal justice *can* reduce crime, displacing the 'nothing works' pessimism engendered by research on both policing and penal measures during the 1970s. The keystone of the police studies calling into question the impact of policing on crime was the Kansas City Preventive Patrol Experiment.[51] On the penal front the most influential paper was Robert Martinson's famous review of the research to ascertain 'what works' – which was usually simplistically summarized as 'nothing works'.[52] Martinson was in fact a liberal opponent of imprisonment who hoped that his critique of the effectiveness of the rehabilitative programmes (which were used to justify long sentences in order to enable treatment) would reduce the use of prison. He later wrote a paper criticizing the simplistically negative interpretation of his results, and pointing to many successful rehabilitative programmes, especially outside prison, but to no avail.[53] In despair at the take-up of his research by neoconservatives, who used it to justify tougher penal policies, he committed suicide in 1980.[54]

The crime drop of the 1990s has been used by the police, many politicians, and by conservative criminologists to refute the nothing works pessimism of the 1970s/1980s. They claim that tough criminal justice policies *can* contain crime without addressing social root causes – if these existed at all. We shall consider the evidence for such claims below.

(b) Democracy in action? Public discourse and punitiveness

Greater public and political support for tough law and order politics can at best be explained only to a very limited extent by a 'truth will out' narrative. Public support for 'law and order' in the US has been shown to be closely tied to prior media and political campaigns, but is *not* related to crime rates.[55] In Britain, the rise of 'law and order' to its current prominence in public opinion polls *followed* the politicization of law and order in the 1970s by Margaret Thatcher's Conservatives and by Police Federation lobbying.

Media narratives – news and fictional – have been framed in 'law and order' terms increasingly since the 1970s. As inequality and social divisions have been exacerbated in the last quarter of a century, politicians have found crime concerns to be a way of constructing consensus in limited areas through focusing attention on fear of criminal folk-devils.[56]

The media have always featured crime stories as a prominent aspect of news and entertainment. But in the last four decades there has been a hugely increasing media focus on crime. A historical study found that the proportion of crime stories in two major British newspapers (*The Times* and the *Mirror*) doubled after the late 1960s, from 10 per cent to 20 per cent.[57] Crime stories began to construct crime as a much more pervasive and threatening phenomenon than before. Stories about specific incidents were much more likely to represent a case as only part of a wider context of growing danger. Violent crimes, especially murder, have always been the main focus of news and fiction stories. But the concentration on stories of murder and sex crimes became much more marked. Stories about property crimes in which no violence occurred have almost disappeared from news and fiction, only appearing if they have a celebrity angle. Paradoxically this means that although the media vastly exaggerate the risks of violent crime, characters in crime fiction are now in much less danger of victimization by property crime than the audiences watching them.[58] There is also much more emphasis on the fear and suffering endured by victims, who have moved to the centre stage in crime news and fiction.

Three fundamental changes in the narrative structures of news and fiction stories about crime can be observed.

Accentuate the negative Bad news increasingly drives out good. A sharp illustration of the change can be found by comparing two almost identical reports on the annual crime statistics from the *Mirror*, one in 1961, some years before the politicization of law and order became evident, the second from 1977, when it was reaching its height.[59] Reporting a 10 per cent rise in overall recorded crime, and a 14 per cent increase in violence, the 1961 headline spotlighted the one bit of good news in the statistics: 'Fewer sex crimes'. The 1977 story, headlined 'Crime soars to new peak', says that 'grim Home Office figures show' a 10 per cent increase in violence, a 15 per cent rise in muggings, and growth in other types of offences against the person. Given much less prominence is the figure for overall recorded crime increase, at only 1 per cent, and the finding that sex offences fell. The later story not only singled out the bad news from a similar array of figures, it presented them in much hotter emotional language.

Victim culture Crime is represented increasingly as a zero-sum game of victim versus offender. One-dimensionally evil villains inflict frightening suffering on innocent and appealing victims, who increasingly often occupy the subject position of narratives, and with whom readers and viewers are invited to identify.

News reporting of crime stories has not always been founded on this zero-sum perspective. Before the politicization of law and order in the early 1970s there was also often a measure of concern for offenders, both to understand and if possible to rehabilitate them, but since then any compassion for offenders, even any effort to understand them, is represented as callous and unjust to victims. Two contrasting pairs of news stories can be taken as examples.[60] The first pair concern violence against a child, the second pair both involve a marital triangle.

On 27 February 1945 the *Daily Mirror* front page prominently featured a photo of a two-year-old girl, looking sad and in pain, headlined 'Another cruelty victim'. Even in a murky photocopy, even after more than half a century, the child's pitiful, anguished face cries out for comfort. The story is the main home news of the day. One paragraph details the poor girl's injuries: black eye, bruises – 'Red weal marks extended over her temple and across her cheeks.' Beyond this clinical detail there is no attempt to spell out the trauma and suffering of the victim, or the evil of the assault. Approximately two-thirds of the story is focused on the offender, a Birkenhead man of twenty-six who lived with the girl's mother, and was sentenced to six months with hard labour. The last part of the story concentrates on his account of his own actions. He claimed, it said, that 'the child's crying got on his nerves and that he "couldn't help himself"'. This was explained by the fact that 'he had been torpedoed three times and that his nerves were very bad'. What is noteworthy is the absence of demonization of the perpetrator, and the concern to understand how he could have carried out such an act from *his* point of view. Attempting to understand the offender is not seen as incompatible with the greatest concern for the victim, and condemnation of the act is taken for granted.

This can be contrasted with the way *The Times* reported a child murder case on 25 November 1989. This is of course a much more serious offence: murder rather than assault. Nonetheless the presentation of the story suggests a fundamental transformation in discourse about serious crime since 1945. The story is the lead story on the main home news page (until the late 1960s *The Times* hardly ever gave crime stories any prominence). A banner headline reads 'Martial arts fanatic gets life for killing daughter aged five', and a smaller headline above it tells us that the 'Girl died from a combination of pain, shock and exhaustion after vengeful beating'. A sub-headline says that 'Social workers held many case conferences but she slipped through the safety net'. Three pictures illustrate the story: a large one of the unfortunate victim, happy and smiling; her mother weeping; and her father, the killer, looking dishevelled and menacing. All are Afro-Caribbean.

The most immediately noticeable contrast with the 1945 story is the use of much more emotionally charged language to emphasize the victim's suffering and the perpetrator's evil – not only in his actions but his essence. The assault leading to the girl's death is elaborated in brutal detail, and the victim's pain and fear are stressed. He is portrayed as essentially violent, behind a facade of respectability and concern for his children. 'Outwardly he was a doting father, proud of his children and anxious that they should do well at school, but inwardly he was a moody fitness fanatic' and martial arts expert. His 'three children were placed on the at-risk register following incidents in which Sukina and her three-year-old sister were taken to hospital with broken limbs'. The only glimpse at the defendant's perspective offered, reporting his admission that 'he lost control and did not realise what he was doing', is undercut by its placement in the middle of a detailed, gruesome account of his actions. The sole comment showing any sympathy towards him comes from the mother: 'Whatever they do to David will never bring my daughter back to me. I have got no feelings whatever towards him. But I cannot condemn him as he was a good father in a loving way. He just had a bad temper that he would not control.' The victim's mother is contradicted at once by the Detective Superintendent who was in charge of the case: he tells us that the perpetrator had previous convictions. The killer is not the only character in the story attracting blame, however. Considerable attention is given to the failure of social services to protect the child adequately despite repeated warnings.

The presentation of these stories is radically different in a number of ways. The 1945 *Mirror* story describes a tragic situation of a child assaulted by a man who is portrayed as himself a victim rather than an essentially evil person. The injury suffered is presented in degree zero clinical language, and no emotional or evaluative adjectives are used to colour the report. The 1989 *Times* story by contrast is replete with adjectives stressing the victim's anguish and the perpetrator's pathologically violent character. It is noteworthy that by 1989 *The Times* was using more emotive styles of reporting than a tabloid had forty-five years earlier. The stories illustrate a profound change in discourse about crime. By 1989 it has become a zero-sum game in which only the victim is represented as a suffering human being. Her death is seen as caused by two villains. A demonised brute who attacked her, and a negligent authority that failed to protect her. Instead of a complex human tragedy we have a one-dimensional battle of good versus evil.

This is illustrated further by the following two cases of violence in the context of a marital triangle. On 13 December 1945 the *Daily Mirror* published a story on its front page under the headline 'Three years for "savage" cripple who branded rival'. The story continued on the back page, under another headline, 'Cripple and branded woman "in a fervour"'. Nearly all the front and back page stories concerned crime, but this was the most prominent. It concerned a crippled woman who had branded another woman that her husband had 'associated' with while his wife was in hospital. The story highlights the judge's comments while sentencing her to three years for the 'savage' offence. His emphasis is not so much on the brutality of her attack per se as that she took 'the law into her own hands' and used a punishment – branding – that 'our laws' now regarded as 'too revolting to the civilised mind to be inflicted for any offence whatsoever'. The bulk of the story concerns the anguished expressions of guilt by all three parties in this triangle. The husband pleads for mercy for his wife, while the victim is described as having accepted the branding as a deserved punishment after confessing to the 'association'. Both the victim and the husband seemed to accept primary responsibility for what had occurred. Altogether this is presented as a tragic human situation, with no innocent parties, in which all are victims of their own wrongful actions, and filled with remorse. The punishment is necessary to maintain the integrity of the law rather than to avenge harm done, to placate the victim's pain, or to incapacitate or deter an evil perpetrator.

On 6 July 1991 both the *Mirror* and *The Times* reported another case arising from a marital triangle. *The Times* covered it on the front page with a photo spread, and more fully on an inside home news page. The *Mirror* spread it over two full pages (2–3), with many photos. The case involved an armed man who held his ex-wife's lover hostage in a car for twenty-nine hours, surrounded by armed police. The kidnapper had been alarmed that his children were to be taken into care – apparently a mistake as they were to stay with his ex-wife. The pictures in both papers exhibit much of the iconography of thriller movies: the surrounded car, police marksmen in bullet-proof vests, the hostage emerging with blood pouring from his left arm where he'd been shot, the handcuffed offender with face blacked out being led away. No doubt the prominence given the story owed much to the availability of this dramatic visual material.

There is a sharp contrast with the 1945 story, the narrative being constructed with a clear hero/victim and villain/perpetrator. Although the incident is referred to as tragic, the sympathies expressed are entirely one-sided. The violence is emphasized: the victim was threatened with a noose, the perpetrator was armed with a crossbow and gun, and shot the victim in the arm as police converged on the car. The perpetrator is continuously described in one-dimensionally villainous terms as 'the gunman', and we are told that he had been involved in a 'tug of love drama' twenty years previously in Australia. His arsenal of weapons is described in detail. By contrast the victim is extolled in heroic terms: 'Hero is Mr Cool' reads a subheadline, and the police credit him with 'remarkable resilience and patience'. What could be read as a tragic personal conflict in which everyone was a victim (as the 1945 story had been constructed) is transformed into a straightforward fight of good versus bad.

These pairs of stories illustrate the key change in the discourse of crime news reporting since the Second World War. The narratives have become personalized and sensationalized, as a battle against one-dimensionally evil villains who inflict dramatic and frightening suffering on individual victims.

This pattern is also found increasingly in crime fiction.[61] Crime is represented as an increasingly serious threat. Murder has always been the most frequent focus of crime fiction, but is now portrayed as a widespread threat rather than a rare, one-off incident. The pain and fear of the victim becomes prominent. Until the 1950s the predominant form of crime fiction had been the 'cosy' Agatha Christie-style whodunit. A structural feature of these stories is that the victim has to be an 'exceptionally murderable' person,[62] so unpleasant that they are hated by many people in order to generate the maximum possible number of suspects as 'red herrings'. The culprit is usually portrayed as a sympathetic character so that there is considerable surprise at their unmasking. The consequence is that audience identification and sympathy in the classic mystery story is frequently with the perpetrator, *not* the victim. The drive to clear up the crime stems not from justice but respect for law; there is no serious questioning of the necessity for legal sanctioning of even a likeable offender.[63] This is quite different from the narrative structure prevailing since the late 1960s in which perpetrators are demonized and victims are portrayed as vulnerable, cruelly suffering innocents.

People questioned in surveys tend to place fiction lower down the list of sources of information about crime and criminal justice, compared to news stories or vicarious experience.[64] But it is clear from focus group discussions that fiction is a major source of the information shaping public perspectives.[65]

Empirical research has been ambiguous about the effects of media representations on the (highly vexed) issue of 'fear of crime'.[66] But the media have considerable significance for framing popular beliefs about the prevalence and problems of crime, and what is to be done about them,[67] shaping law and order discourse. However, this begs the question of what shapes media representations. They are not impartial messengers bringing objective messages from the gods, but reflect as much as influence social and cultural trends. The increasing individualism, sensation seeking and declining deference exhibited by media stories are interdependent with the same patterns in broader cultural change. They are wrapped up with the underlying development of neoliberalism, and the more competitive, egoistic ethos it entails. Most directly, all media organizations are increasingly subjected to the rigours of intense, ever more globalized competition for audiences.

In both news and fiction (and the two are increasingly similar in presentation and narrative structures)[68] crime is now portrayed as a much greater risk than before, not just because it is more common, but because it is represented in much more highly charged emotional terms as a serious threat to ordinary people. There is much greater individualism underlying media narratives. Crime is seen as problematic not because it violates the law or other universalistic moral reference points, but because it hurts individual victims with whom the audience is led to sympathize or empathize. Offenders are portrayed not as parts of social relations that victims and the public are also embedded in, but as pathologically evil individuals. Any attempt to understand them, let alone any concern for their point of view or rehabilitation, is seen as insensitive to the suffering of their victims. These features also testify to desubordination and the decline of deference. Crime is seen as wrong not because of acceptance of legality as a benchmark of how people should behave, but because it causes personal harm to individuals we identify with. The police and other authorities are themselves portrayed as increasingly immoral and illegal in their practices. Crime is represented as bad because it hurts sympathetic individuals, not as an offence against authoritative law or morality. No deference to legal or other authorities is shown or suggested. The moral evaluation of individuals is established in specific narratives, not derived from their status in the social or legal system.

Law and order solutions Although police officers and other criminal justice officials cannot be automatically trusted or respected, and there is greater recognition of the possibilities of corruption and abuse,[69] nonetheless they are the only game in town as far as any protection or justice for threatened innocents can be contemplated. Forceful policing and tough punishment are looked to both as social security blankets, deterring or incapacitating evil, and as seeking rough justice, offering the only sliver of solace available for the victimized, and a small measure of security and emotional closure for the audience. This increasingly justifies vigilante-style policing methods.[70] The vigilante *Dirty Harry* has ousted the overgrown Boy Scout *Dixon of Dock Green*; the play-it-by-the-book Los Angeles Police Department of *Dragnet* has become the corrupt and brutal *LAPD Confidential* and *The Shield*, only marginally – if at all – lesser evils than the hoodlums they wipe out.

(c) Root causes: new times, new crime control?

A complex, mutually reinforcing set of changes in culture, social structure and political economy since the late 1960s undoubtedly underlie the emergence of law and order politics and policies. Some of these were deep structural transformations, others were contingent policy choices, but once these had occurred they set in train processes that embedded them, making reversal hard if not impossible. The library of work seeking to analyse these changes contains a variety of accounts of their sources, significance and staying power. This is partly signified by the many labels purporting to characterize the era that is emerging. Is it postmodernity or late modernity (i.e. a fundamental break from the 'modern' – however that is analysed – or its unfolding)? Are the main changes cultural, or in political economy, or social relations? Is the key theme greater individualism; heightened concern with risk and insecurity; weakening of family and community organization and ties; declining deference; globalization, that is, the heightened speed of communications and movement, compressing space and time and eroding national and communal frontiers; shifting modes of governance; the revolution in information technology; the growth of social divisions and exclusion . . .? Are economic changes paramount? Neoliberalism; post-Fordism; disorganized or turbo-capitalism?

The argument of this book is that the concepts of 'anomie' and 'egoism' provide the key to integrating explanations of the trends in crime and control. Anomie has the fundamental meaning of a weakening of the hold of moral controls, but the notion of anomie does not indicate primarily a cultural process, as found in conservative accounts of growing 'permissiveness'. Rather it implies an interlinked analysis of the nature of the ends held out as valuable in a particular culture, beliefs about the way that access to these ought to be distributed in the population, and how life chances actually are distributed by the social and economic structure. Egoism is a particular version of individualism, competitive and possessive as opposed to reciprocal and mutually responsible individualism. Chapter 4 showed how the changes induced by neoliberalism and consumer culture vastly fanned all aspects of anomie and egoism, driving up offending and the recording of crime. The limited attenuation of this in the 1990s is a major factor in the crime drop. In the same way, neoliberalism and the social and cultural changes that went with it altered public discourse about crime and opened the way to law and order as the widely favoured solution.

Tougher attitudes and policies concerning crime and control are not directly related to trends in crime. The rise in crime predates the changes in punishment and policing, and fluctuations in popular opinion track media and political campaigning rather than crime statistics. The toughening of attitudes and policy reached its height in the 1990s when crime began to fall. Nonetheless the huge rise in crime over four decades is a crucial background to the shift in popular opinion. However, it is not sufficient to explain why tough law and order came to be seen as the solution.

There are at least two crucial changes that provide the necessary mediating links, both consequences of neoliberalism. The first is an intensification of egoistic individualism. This might (as neoliberals hope) engender more sense of responsibility for oneself, and perhaps one's family or others with whom one can closely identify, a prospect that underlies the 'responsibilization' practices of greater attention to private security. This is the core of what Garland has dubbed 'the criminologies of everyday life', but it can also result in lack of concern for a growing mass of those defined as the 'other', who are increasingly demonized, feared and regarded as suitable objects for harsh punishment.[71]

Perhaps even more fundamentally, neoliberalism weakens the levers available to governments to regulate the economic and social divisions, exclusion and injustice that are the root causes of crime. The fading of hopes of social amelioration, at any rate on a foreseeable time-scale, leaves people with no prospect of comfort against the turbulent sea of multiplying insecurities unsettling their lives except the mantras of criminal justice and exclusionary barriers against threatening 'others'. Since many of the sources of insecurity and risk are neither criminals nor these 'others', support for law and order is at best only partly directed at the appropriate issues, and is partly displacement of anxiety against the most visible targets. The intensity of anger directed at a select number of 'folk devil' criminals (however horrific their crimes) is a form of 'acting-out',[72] concentrating on a symbolic few the frustration and fury that has been inflamed by a much wider range of threats.

Comparative studies have established clearly that punitiveness is related to variations in the political economy of different societies. An inverse relationship between levels of welfare spending and the severity of punishment, over time and between different places, has been demonstrated by econometric analysis of different states in the US, and different countries.[73] A major recent book studied penal policies in twelve countries.[74] It demonstrates that punitive cultural attitudes and policies are highest in the most neoliberal societies studied (US, South Africa, England and Wales, Australia, New Zealand), and much lower in social democracies. Although the Scandinavian social democracies remain less characterized by law and order politics and by punitive policies, they are moving in that direction as globalization exposes them to more pressure to adopt neoliberalism.[75] This is only partly related to rising crime. It was shown in chapter 4 that social democracies are less prone to homicide, although they do have comparatively high rates of more minor violence and property crime – possibly because of greater civility paradoxically producing more reporting. In sum, contemporary comparisons suggest that neoliberalism tends to be more punitive than social democracy.

Tough on Crime? Assessing the Impact of Law and Order

To what extent, if any, can the 1990s crime drop, in Britain and the US, be attributed to the politics of law and order – tougher policing and the new punitiveness? The police have not been slow to claim credit, particularly in the US, and especially New York City with its highly publicized precipitous decline in crime. 'Crime is down: blame the police,' William Bratton, NYPD Commissioner between 1994 and 1996, unabashedly trumpeted.[76] Throughout the world the New York experience has stimulated a new 'can-do' confidence among the police, palpably relieved that after two decades when 'nothing works' seemed to be the clear conclusion of research, new policing tactics seemed at last to be vindicating their crime-busting credentials.[77]

Independent research suggests a much more complex and indeed enigmatic picture than the prophets of 'zero tolerance' and toughness present. Most commentators do not question that substantial declines in crime have occurred in the US and in Britain, but explaining this is far more problematic. Indeed it is precisely the widespread character of the crime drop that calls into question some of the most popular explanations, in particular 'zero tolerance' policing. As many analysts have argued, crime fell in most parts of the US despite the considerable variations in policing styles. While the celebrated New York City drop was especially marked, crime declined to a comparable extent even in cities that did not pursue the same (or indeed any) reform strategy.

The crime drop: blame the cops?

Close analysis of the New York experience itself suggests problems in attributing most of the falls in homicide and other serious crime to policing changes, because of the timing of these.[78] Certainly some of the huge decline in New York City is plausibly due to policing changes, but there is considerable doubt about how much is attributable to the celebrated 'zero tolerance' aspect of the changes. Even Bratton has played down the label of 'zero tolerance' for his reforms, and most analysts see the much more rigorous and speedy analysis of crime, and the stricter local managerial accountability for crime trends, summed up as 'Compstat', as the most important element in the NYPD's success.[79]

The most vigorous arguments for the significance of criminal justice policies for the crime drop come from a celebrated article by the economist Steven Levitt, the basis for a chapter in his best-selling book *Freakonomics.*[80] Levitt's analysis gained huge notoriety for its claim that a major factor in the crime drop was the impact of the legalization of abortion following the 1973 US Supreme Court decision in *Roe v. Wade*. Indirectly this argument is really one about how legalized abortion resulted in a fall in the size of the impoverished and excluded underclass, implicit testimony to the significance of economic and social exclusion – though hopefully more humane programmes can achieve this compared to what amounts to a form of eugenics, the ultimate in pre-emptive incapacitation!

Levitt also attributes the crime drop to criminal justice factors, notably the expansion of police and prisons. He specifically relates the crime fall to increasing numbers of police, not the new tactics that have attracted most of the attention,[81] whether hard cop like zero tolerance, soft cop (community policing), or smart cop (problem-solving, better management and analysis of information). Levitt points out that the 'universality of the drop in crime' militates against its explanation in terms of factors that varied considerably between places, such as police innovation. Levitt attributes 'between one-fifth and one-tenth of the overall decline in crime' (i.e. 5–6 per cent) to the approximately 14 per cent increase in police officers per capita in the US during the 1990s.[82] This is based on other studies (including one of his own) calculating that increasing police numbers by 1 per cent is associated with a reduction of roughly 30 per cent in the crime rate. There is no specification of the causal mechanisms bringing this about (presumably there is a taken-for-granted assumption that a larger police force deters crime and also catches more criminals). There is also a tacit presumption that the elasticity of crime to police (the per centage crime drop attributable to a 1 per cent increase in police numbers) is constant for all levels of police strength, and in all jurisdictions.[83] Both assumptions are highly questionable.

Nobody would claim that police have no effect on crime, that disbanding the police, or at the other extreme saturation policing, would make no difference. What is debatable is the impact on crime of the relatively marginal changes in police numbers that are economically or politically feasible (for example the 14 per cent change over a decade that is cited by Levitt). The experimental studies that were the basis for the 'nothing works' pessimism of the 1970s bore this out. As Home Office research argued, this is because of the very small chance that patrolling police officers will encounter crime at all, even in high crime metropolitan areas. A 'patrolling policeman in London could expect to pass within 100 yards of a burglary in progress roughly once every eight years – but not necessarily to catch the burglar or even realise that the crime was taking place'.[84] The problem lies not in police ineffectiveness, but in the huge number of potential targets of crime, vastly outstretching any conceivable level of police resources. As an Audit Commission report calculated, a typical patrolling constable has to cover an area with 18,000 inhabitants, 7,500 houses, 23 pubs, 9 schools, 140 miles of pavement, 85 acres of park or open space, and 77 miles of road.[85] Not a happy lot for the poor constable expected to provide meaningful cover for so many possible crime victims. The response to this from police forces over the last two decades has been the search for new tricks, innovative strategies that by analysing information and crime patterns can hopefully target scarce resources at hot spots and hot offenders so that meaningful prevention and detection become possible. These have contributed to the crime drop, through more effective protection and better investigative techniques, and because the fall in crime levels itself enables a higher proportion of offenders to be detected. Increasing police strength may well have facilitated the adoption of innovative methods. But for the reasons indicated by the Home Office and the Audit Commission, relatively marginal increases in numbers by themselves are unlikely to have had a significant effect.

Prison works?

Did prison work, as promised by Michael Howard and his American counterparts? What role has the huge American prison expansion, and the smaller but still historically and comparatively very large imprisonment rise in Britain, played in the crime drop? Recent comprehensive reviews in both countries[86] show that while the considerable growth of imprisonment certainly played a part, in conjunction with other social and criminal justice changes, this was achieved at enormous cost, economically, but even more in human terms. The scope for further reduction through further increases in imprisonment is now much less, and there are other less costly alternative policies that offer more potential.

According to the traditional utilitarian rationale, imprisonment (and most other forms of penalty) may work to reduce crime in four possible ways: rehabilitation – interventions enabling the offender to live a law-abiding life; special deterrence – frightening an offender away from future offending; general deterrence – persuading potential offenders not to commit crime because of the prospect of punishment; incapacitation – removing the practical possibility of offending.[87] Recent official reviews, notably the Halliday Report, expressed renewed optimism about the prospects of rehabilitation through the use in prison of new techniques such as cognitive behaviour therapy.[88] This was based on favourable results from exploratory programmes, but subsequent research has come up with more disappointing outcomes, in particular because the early initiatives worked with atypical small, self-selected groups.[89] In any case the prospects of these therapeutic techniques succeeding is greater with non-incarcerated offenders. Rehabilitation may work even in prison contexts, but the prospects for successful programmes have been greatly undermined by the remorseless expansion of the last decade.[90] In truth when Michael Howard spoke of prison working it was not rehabilitation he had in mind, but deterrence and incapacitation.

Although from time to time claims have been made about the special deterrence effects of new tough regimes, these have seldom if ever withstood empirical evaluation.[91] Many claims have been made that more severe punishment reduces crime through general deterrence. On a rational economic actor model it should follow that raising the cost of crime through increasing severe penalties would lead, other things being equal, to less offending. Nonetheless most recent assessments of the empirical research literature 'conclude that there is little or no consistent evidence that harsher sanctions reduce crime rates in western populations . . . sentence severity has no effect on the level of crime in society', in the words of a comprehensive North American review of the research.[92] The economic model has a number of flaws; for example, potential offenders may not know of sentencing trends, they are frequently not acting in a rationally calculating way but under the sway of drugs, alcohol, sexual or other excitement, or they may be in such a desperate state (perhaps because of hunger or addiction) that they are willing to take risks. Above all, however, the rational attractions of committing crimes even if penalties are severe may still be considerable, as only a very tiny minority (around 2–3 per cent) of offences that are known about (a minority of all that take place) result in an offender being sentenced.

The common finding of studies of active offenders is that the prospect of punishment is not prominent in their consciousness. Given the almost infinitesimal chance of being punished for any specific offence, this is far from irrational.[93] Empirical research confirms the old view of the eighteenth-century classical school in criminal law that the certainty of punishment is much more important in deterrence than its severity.[94]

The most plausible link between the massive rise in incarceration and the 1990s crime drop is in terms of incapacitation. Prisoners cannot victimize the general public while they are behind bars. A recent Home Office estimate suggested that 'the prison population would have to increase by around 15 per cent for a reduction of crime of 1 per cent'.[95] This is based on the self-reported offending of people entering prison in early 2000. The many American studies seeking to evaluate the impact of the rise in imprisonment on crime come to a variety of estimates depending on their particular methodologies, some much higher, some lower.[96] It is hard to deny that the massive increase in imprisonment had a significant part to play in the crime drop, but what is much less plausible is that it will continue to do so. Unless people leave prison less likely to commit crime than when they entered – and the evidence about rehabilitation and special deterrence does not make this plausible – then only by continuously jacking up the prison population can incapacitation produce a decline in crime (in a steady state, the same number of people are leaving prison as entering it, and the only difference is in the people committing the crimes not in how many crimes are being committed). Even if the prison population continues to rise, however, there are diminishing returns in terms of incapacitation. This is because the offenders caught first are more likely to be the serious and prolific ones. Thus even in purely economic cost-benefit terms there comes a point (already long past in the most plausible calculations) where prison does not pay from a hard-headed economic cost-benefit perspective, especially compared to putting the equivalent resources into alternative policies such as policing or economic regeneration. Jobs may do better than jail as a way of reducing crime.[97]

The most rigorous assessments of the 1990s crime drop in America find that socioeconomic and demographic changes (particularly the more buoyant labour market, the decline in the high-crime age groups in the population, and shifting drug markets) made a significant impact, albeit in conjunction with criminal justice policies.[98] Toughness was certainly not the key factor. Smart policing played a bigger part than hard policing. While the huge expansion of imprisonment played a part, cost-benefit analysis suggests that it reached a point of diminishing returns many years ago in economic terms (never mind considerations of humanity). In Britain too, the success of New Labour in maintaining relatively low levels of unemployment and reducing poverty (but not overall inequality) to a limited extent are key factors, as the last chapter demonstrated. More intelligence-based assessments of risk underlying patterns of policing, prevention and punishment have also played a part. Certainly the marked reductions in the highest volume property crimes such as car crime and burglary owe much to vastly improved prevention practices.

Minding the reassurance gap

While emphasizing that crime overall has been declining, New Labour (and indeed police leaders) have struggled to benefit from this, above all because of the evidence from surveys and from media discussions that public fears have not declined. This has been labelled the 'reassurance gap' by policy-makers, and stimulated the so-called 'reassurance policing' agenda to try to plug it. As suggested in chapter 4, there may be a rational kernel to the stubborn refusal of public anxiety to decline with the crime rate, beyond blaming the messengers of the sensationalist and bad news addicted media (though they are very significant). Within the decline in overall crime, the most worrying serious violent crimes have continued to rise. In so far as the decline in crime overall is due to more successful adoption of protective equipment and preventive routines by crime-conscious citizens, rather than any reduction in the root causes of offending, the burden falls on potential victims above all. While prevention tactics, burdensome as they may be, are preferable to victimization, they are a product of insecurity, and indeed may reinforce rather than reduce fear. What is required is not reassurance about crime but about the causes of crime. However, this cannot be provided so long as neoliberalism, the fundamental source of increasing criminality, and of the accentuation of insecurity and law and order solutions by media and political discourse, remains triumphant.

6

Conclusion: Law and Order – A 20:20 Vision

> If the past teaches us one thing, it is that there is always an alternative, the game is never over, and history never ends.
>
> Jeremy Gilbert, 'The second wave'

> Being trapped between the knowledge that radical change is necessary, and the sense that very little is possible, produces at least the appearance of confusion.
>
> Ruth Levitas, 'Shuffling back to equality'

Law and order has moved to the centre of public and political concern in recent times. The politics of law and order focus on a very narrow range of offences and offenders, as was shown in chapter 2. The ambit of criminal law itself leaves out many forms of serious, culpable harm, especially harm perpetrated by corporations or states. But the criminal justice system filters this down even further, processing almost exclusively crimes committed by the poor and the disadvantaged. Public policy debate, egged on by the media, is focused primarily on an even smaller range of spectacular violent offences (although this has been complicated recently by the rise of the anti-social behaviour agenda).

The last fifty years have witnessed a huge increase in crime rates, throughout the world, although by most measures crime has fallen back since the mid-1990s. Interpreting official crime statistics is notoriously fraught with problems. Nonetheless, the overall rise to a high-crime society in which vulnerability to victimization has become 'a normal social fact'[1] cannot be denied, as chapter 3 established. However a comparison of victimization surveys with the police recorded rate suggests that most of the increase in offending was concentrated in the 1980s and early 1990s, when a crime explosion took place. The earlier recorded rise was largely, though certainly not entirely, due to victims reporting a higher proportion of the crimes from which they suffered. This was stimulated by the advent of a mass consumer culture, which meant that more valuable goods were being stolen, household contents insurance became widespread, and the incentives to report crime increased. The rise in offending that occurred after the late 1950s was also mainly a result of the advent of mass consumerism, with its proliferation of tempting targets for crime and the anomie it generated, especially among the relatively deprived.

As chapter 4 showed, the crime explosion of the 1980s was a direct result of the social tsunami brought by neoliberalism, with spiralling long-term unemployment, poverty and inequality. Conversely, the decline in the later 1990s was due in part to a limited brake on these anomie-generating pressures, achieved by New Labour's economic and social policies ameliorating (but not getting tough on!) the causes of crime, and because of smarter, more effective criminal justice and crime prevention. Despite the fall in victimization, concern about crime remains acute, partly generated by media and political focus on atypical instances of spectacular violence, but partly because of widespread awareness that – although better security has suppressed crime – the causes of criminality remain largely intact.

The development of the crime control complex analysed in chapter 5 has brought about an increasingly authoritarian society. The adjustment of the routines of everyday life to crime prevention and security measures brings with it a huge accentuation of social divisions and exclusion, symbolized most clearly by the proliferation of gated communities and other types of 'mass private property'. Prison numbers have rocketed due to tougher sentencing, despite the fall in crime, and police powers have expanded considerably – without the balancing safeguards that accompanied increasing police powers in the 1980s. Contrary to government rhetoric, the criminal justice system has already been rebalanced – in favour of the forces of law and order. The insecurity and anxiety due to the war on terror has contributed greatly to public acceptance of this.

All this paints a depressingly dystopian picture of where we are heading, in particular for anyone concerned about civil liberties, social justice and democracy. Victimization by routine crime has fallen substantially in recent years, but serious violent crime has not. The crime drop is partly the result of rapidly and hugely increasing the prison population, especially in the US, but with England and Wales following in its wake. Leaving aside ethical considerations about this, however, even many conservative criminologists recognize that prison expansion has long ceased to be a cost-effective way of cutting crime, because of diminishing returns: the offenders being incapacitated by successive waves of expansion are the less prolific and serious ones. As Spelman's rigorous econometric study of the effects of the growth of imprisonment in Texas concluded recently, jobs not jail are a more promising direction for future crime reduction.[2] Unless prisons considerably improve their performance in terms of rehabilitating prisoners – which the extent and speed of the expansion of imprisonment makes almost impossible – their contribution to crime reduction through incapacitation will diminish. Nonetheless, on current official projections the prison population will grow over the next six years by at least 12 per cent, and possibly by more than 25 per cent, from its current all-time record level.

Smarter policing and crime prevention more generally has undoubtedly been a major factor in reducing victimization in recent years, as discussed in chapter 5. These improvements are likely to continue. However, negative social consequences are also likely to multiply. Many crime prevention strategies take the form of what Pat O'Malley and David Garland have called 'responsibilization'.[3] Victims and potential victims are induced by a variety of pressures and incentives to take responsibility for their own protection, learning about and analysing the risks they face, adjusting their routines accordingly and adopting suitable technical equipment and other measures from the burgeoning repertoire made available by the rapidly expanding security industry. This is one aspect of a broader shift of responsibility for security and welfare from government and corporations to private citizens, a core feature of neoliberalism's project of diminishing the scope of collective provision and bolstering profitability.[4]

In the crime context it amounts to a process of double victimization: victims and potential victims of crime are expected to restrict their own liberty and comfort by burdening themselves with a variety of techniques and routines that are at best inconvenient but at the extreme can amount to virtual house arrest. While they may work to reduce actual victimization, at least in the short run, these strategies serve as constant reminders of the threat of crime, and exacerbate rather than bolster a pervasive sense of insecurity.[5]

Crime control through smarter policing and prevention has another major negative social consequence, however effective it may be in the short run: it reinforces social divisions and exclusion. Identification of likely future offenders and offending is primarily based on analysis of past records: the 'usual suspects' are recycled, and self-fulfilling predictions lock people into their past patterns. A class of recurrently targeted 'persistent and prolific offenders' is consolidated and separated, bearing electronic marks of Cain on their persons and in official databases.

Preventive practices create or reproduce social boundaries and exclusion even more clearly. A quarter of a century ago, a pioneering analysis of the growth of private security anticipated the development of a new feudalism, as a result of the spread of what was labelled 'mass private property': spaces that were legally privately owned, but in practice social in that they contained large numbers of people.[6] The key examples were shopping malls, gated residential areas, and leisure complexes such as Disneyland-style theme parks. Although the extent to which such mass private property has spread is variable, and certainly less developed in Britain than in North or South America, there is a clear trend towards the growth of such spaces throughout the world.[7] Visible crime and disorder are much less in such places, but there is evidence of displacement to less protected areas,[8] so that the tacit policy is 'burgle my neighbour'.

Public criminal justice has very little purchase in mass private property: policing is by private security, electronic surveillance and a variety of architectural and design features (well illustrated in Shearing and Stenning's fascinating analysis of social control in Disney World).[9] Private security agents lack any special police powers such as arrest. But this is amply compensated by the powers derived from the private property rights of their employers. This gives them the ability to search, exclude, and impose conditions on entry, frequently exercised in highly discriminatory ways against anyone deemed suspicious or undesirable – largely those from poorer or disadvantaged groups.[10] This undoubtedly suppresses the occurrence of crime and disorder. The offences that do take place in mass private property (such as theft by employees or visitors) are frequently dealt with by informal means and not reported to or recorded by the police – or in victimization statistics such as the British Crime Survey. Part of the decline in recorded crime may well be attributed to the spread of mass private property leading to a decline in official recording. The immediate suppression of crime inside mass private property must be balanced against displacement effects, and the long-term accentuation of social exclusion and division, which is likely to exacerbate crime in the future.

The exclusionary approaches to crime control represented by mass imprisonment or the spread of mass private property are problematic ethically from any humane or liberal perspective. 'Tough on crime' policies are also deceptive in terms of pragmatic effectiveness. As Elliott Currie argued some years ago, they may suppress or hide crime, and thus lower the officially recorded rate. But they do not alter – indeed they are likely to increase – the *criminality* rate: 'the tendency of our society to produce criminals'.[11]

The evidence reviewed in chapters 3–5 above pointed to the advent of neoliberalism as the underlying factor in both the crime explosion and the shift to more authoritarian and exclusionary law and order crime control strategies. Rosa Luxemburg's stark choice, socialism or barbarism, remains apposite.[12] But actually existing socialism as practised in Eastern Europe *was* barbarism. Its collapse pulled down in its wake the more ethical democratic socialism in the West that *had* produced more peaceful and just societies, and the promise of further improvement. Whether there is any possibility of its revival in the face of the more individualistic ethos engendered by three decades of neoliberal hegemony, and the globalizing tendencies that have made more difficult if not impossible the agenda of social democracy in one country, is a crucial question, not least for crime and criminal justice.[13]

Certainly a major difficulty is that neoliberalism has relinquished the tools that had been available to social democratic states to try to remedy inequality and exclusion. For example, greater mobility of capital flows, partly because of technological and cultural changes associated with globalization, but crucially because of liberalization of controls over financial movements, has weakened the regulatory and taxation capacity of individual governments in relation to corporations. However, the extent to which this has systematically and irretrievably weakened governments' abilities to tax for redistributive and welfare purposes is debatable, and the position still varies considerably between different countries.[14]

There is considerable evidence that variations in the political economy of different states is associated with the character of their penal sytems, as well as their patterns of serious and violent crime, as shown in chapters 4 and 5. The more neoliberal states tend to be the most punitive, while more social democratic and welfare-oriented states also have less harsh penal regimes.[15] There is also extensive historical and comparative evidence of links between serious violent crime, inequality and social exclusion.[16]

Gramscian pessimism of the intellect suggests that the dystopian extrapolation of current trends is the most likely future. Law and order 2020 will confirm the worst fears held in the past about law and order 1984, but not realized then. An equally Gramscian optimism of the will, however, suggests that it might still possible to espouse TIA – there *is* an alternative – and forsake the Thatcherite TINA. The mild attack on the causes of crime by New Labour's largely *sotto voce*, stealthy redistribution, mitigating some of the worst aspects of poverty inherited in 1997, and at least halting the spectacular rise of inequality, combined with general economic prosperity and low unemployment, *did* contribute to a substantial overall reduction in crime during the late 1990s.

But serious violent crime remains a growing threat, and the containment of volume crime is fragile in the face of the continuing resilience of its basic causes, in particular the anomie of a consumerist society fuelling egoistic aspirations while bracketing off issues of the legitimacy of means. Economic collapse, with a return of mass unemployment and deprivation, remains an ever-present threat in market economies, and would almost certainly trigger a repeat of the 1980s explosion of crime and disorder – or worse – and more authoritarian control efforts. Even if overall inequality is no worse now than when Labour took office in 1997 (though it did get much greater in its first term), the grotesque gap, growing spectacularly by the day, between the wealth of the super-rich and the majority of society (let alone the poor) provides a model of aspiration that fuels rampant anomie.

A major factor in this burgeoning inequality between the very rich and the rest is the extent to which the wealthy succeed in minimizing (legally) their taxation, thus exacerbating the burdens of the majority. This provides a model of social irresponsibility that bolsters a culture in which winning by any means possible is what counts – with huge consequences for crime at all levels of society. The proliferation of devices for tax avoidance in effect 'defines deviancy down' for the wealthy.[17] At the same time the tabloid-fuelled law and order culture for 'them' exacerbates the hunt for welfare cheats and scroungers at the other end of the social scale.[18] This postmodern spin on 'one law for the rich, one for the poor' deepens the anomie that drives street crime. When Tony Blair in his 2006 speech calling for a 'respect' agenda cited Tawney's analysis of 'the breakdown of society on the basis of rights divorced from obligations', he completely inverted the point. Tawney's critique in *The Acquisitive Society* was directed against the rich, whom he regarded as enjoying rights without responsibilities. This analysis remains pertinent now. If the wealthy withdraw from their social obligations by exploiting legal loopholes to minimize their tax burdens, if the powerful are shown revelling in a culture of casual cruelty (in TV programmes like *The Apprentice* and *The Weakest Link*), why the shock horror when those without the same access to legitimate opportunities ape their 'superiors'? New Labour's pride in its relaxed stance on people getting filthy rich undermines its capacity to be tough on the causes of crime.

Certainly the regulative capacity of states to achieve social democratic ends has been undermined by globalization under the neoliberal auspices of the 'Washington consensus'. But this could be seen as a challenge not a fatal conclusion. The social democratic deficit of states could lead to a search to develop 'collaborative mechanisms of governance at supranational and global levels'.[19] Unless there is some mitigation of neoliberalism, and the inequality and egoism it carries with it, there is no real hope of reversing the deep pressures that have driven crime up, and assured the ascendancy of law and order politics.

It is often said that there is no constituency for such a change, that the public has been moulded by three decades of neoliberalism to see this as unquestionable common sense. In the penal sphere in particular popular opinion appears to be harshly punitive, precluding any other approach apart from law and order. New Labour (and the Clintonian Democrats) saw public feeling as constraining them to the tough neoliberal social, economic and criminal justice policies they pursued. But analysis of research suggests that public opinion is more complex and nuanced, and that leverage for changing it through political campaigning does exist – although of course the failure of the centre-left governments of the 1990s to do so has consolidated the hegemony of neoliberalism as common sense. Nonetheless, despite decades of propagandizing in the other direction, there is evidence of latent public support for elements of a more liberal or even social democratic analysis of crime, hidden behind the more overt punitiveness revealed on the face of surveys.

In one recent study, for example, 65 per cent of Americans saw tackling causes as the key to controlling crime, compared to only 32 per cent favouring greater toughness – a substantial increase since a 1994 survey when the respective proportions were 48 and 42 per cent.[20] The punitive first reactions of people to survey questions about crime and sentencing are largely framed by misinformation about penal practices coming from the popular mass media. When exposed to more accurate information provided by researchers, views of appropriate penal policy move away from the automatic lynch-mob punitiveness of the tabloid press. Similar latent support for more social democratic economic and social policies can also be discerned in studies of public opinion more generally,[21] despite the massive propagandizing for neoliberalism over many decades from business-oriented think-tanks, the mass media, and politicians.[22]

History has been stained by the bloody consequences of premature declarations of the arrival of Utopia. Marxism, and arguably the socialist tradition more generally, has been beguiled by what has been called the 'obstetric' fallacy,[23] the view that capitalist society was pregnant with the embryo of socialism, requiring just a little push to bring the good society. It was this confidence above all that seduced people into accepting that even violent means could be used to achieve the imminent birth of an earthly paradise. After the bitter experience of the devastating consequences of such dirty hands arguments, Lukes is surely right to raise the issue of whether the future ideals to which Marxists (and socialists) aspire are 'unapproachable through the violation in the present and in the future of the limits that basic or human rights impose'.[24] The trouble is, as he gloomily adds, 'Of course, it might also be unapproachable through respecting them.'

But it took more than three decades for the neoliberal ideas that Hayek began to campaign for in 1947 at Mont Pellerin in Switzerland[25] to move from being seen as eccentric, if not lunatic fringe – tilting against the inevitability of the Keynesian, mixed economy, welfare state consensus – to becoming the new common sense. The social democratic ideal is harder to get across than either revolutionary socialist or free-market utopianism, as the Polish philosopher Leszek Kolakowski put it in a stirring but pessimistic assessment:

> The trouble with the social democratic idea is that it does not . . . sell any of the exciting commodities which various totalitarian movements . . . offer dream-hungry youth . . . It has no prescription for the total salvation of mankind . . . It believes in no final easy victory over evil. It requires, in addition to commitment to a number of basic values, hard knowledge and rational calculation . . . It is an obstinate will to erode by inches the conditions which produce avoidable suffering, oppression, hunger, wars, racial and national hatred, insatiable greed and vindictive envy.[26]

But even the tiny moves in this direction by the centre-left governments of the 1990s have brought considerable benefits to the most vulnerable people in society, as reflected in falling crime rates. This hints tantalizingly at what might be achieved by a less covert critique of the egoism encouraged by their predecessors. But every little helps.[27] This book began with an epigraph from the Talmudic tract *Ethics of the Fathers*, and another saying from it sums up the conclusion. 'It is not your duty to complete the work, but you are not free to desist from it.'[28]

Notes

Full titles and publication details are in the references list on p. 210.

Chapter 1 Introduction

1 See Dumenil and Levy, *Capital Resurgent*, Harvey, *A Brief History of Neoliberalism*, and Glyn, *Capitalism Unleashed*, for full analyses of neoliberalism. 'Keynesianism' refers broadly to an approach to economic policy inspired by the work of John Maynard Keynes, the great British economist, which sought to rescue capitalism from the ravages of the Great Depression of the 1930s, and came to dominate the management of economies by Western governments in the decades after the Second World War. It aimed to contain economic fluctuations by a combination of fiscal and monetary policy. It implied a larger role for the state, and a mixed economy of public and private provision. During the Second World War, the British coalition government developed plans for a postwar expansion of the welfare state, consolidating the solidarity of classes necessitated by the war effort. After the war, the Labour government led by Clement Attlee implemented much of this, establishing a National Health Service, free universal secondary education, and an aspiration to provide security to all 'from cradle to grave'. Similar developments occurred

in thc US under President F. D. Roosevelt's 'New Deal' of the 1930s, and during and after the war. For an illuminating contrast between this social democratic and Keynesian consensus, and the neoliberalism and monetarism that displaced it in the 1970s, see Paul Krugman's essay on Milton Friedman, the anti-Keynesian economist who died recently, 'Who was Milton Friedman?'.

2 Kay, *The Truth about Markets.*

3 The classic exposition is Hayek, *The Road to Serfdom*; for critical assessments see Tomlinson, *Hayek and the Market*, and Gamble, *Hayek*.

4 Osborne and Gaebler, *Reinventing Government*, is a seminal exposition of this case. McLaughlin, Muncie and Hughes, 'The permanent revolution', analyses the impact of NPM on criminal justice policy; Leys, *Market-Driven Politics*, is a comprehensive critical analysis.

5 Hayward, *City Limits*, S. Hall and Winlow, 'Rehabilitating Leviathan' and 'Barbarians at the gates', Winlow and Hall, *Violent Night*, and Lawson, 'Turbo-consumerism', analyse consumer culture's impact.

6 Zedner, 'Opportunity makes the thief-taker'.

7 Harvey, *A Brief History of Neoliberalism*, p. 33.

8 Glyn, *Capitalism Unleashed.*

9 Dumenil and Levy, *Capital Resurgent*; Harvey, *A Brief History of Neoliberalism.*

10 Harvey, *A Brief History of Neoliberalism*, p. 80.

11 ESRC 'Society Today', *Wages and Distribution of Wealth in the UK* (2005), at www.esrc.ac.uk.

12 Esping-Andersen, 'Inequality of incomes and opportunities', p. 12.

13 Galbraith, *The Affluent Society.*

14 T. Jackson, *Chasing Progress.*

15 Pollock, *NHS plc.*

16 Bakan, *The Corporation*, pp. 56–9.

17 Gottfredson and Hirschi, *A General Theory of Crime*, pp. 89–91.

18 Sennett, *The Corrosion of Character*. 'A shortened framework of institutional time lies at the heart of this social

degradation; the cutting edge has capitalized on superficial human relations. This same shortened time framework has disoriented individuals in efforts to plan their life course strategically and dimmed the disciplinary power of the old work ethic based on delayed gratification' (Sennett, *The Culture of the New Capitalism*, p. 181).

19 Tawney, *The Acquisitive Society*, p. 33.

20 Wilkinson, *The Impact of Inequality*, is a comprehensive recent review of the voluminous empirical evidence. Chapter 4 below reviews the extensive evidence demonstrating links between crime and the economic and social concomitants of neoliberalism, such as inequality, social divisions and exclusion.

21 It might be said that the world has disastrously followed the lead of the wrong one of two Austrian refugees from Nazism who in 1944 both wrote seminal studies of capitalism, liberty and democracy.

22 Polanyi, *The Great Transformation*, p. 265.

23 Gamble, *The Free Economy and the Strong State*.

24 Jacobs and Skocpol, *Inequality and American Democracy*.

25 Palast, *The Best Democracy Money Can Buy*.

26 Adding insult to invective, Wilson declared that against 'root cause' explanations 'I am sometimes inclined, when in a testy mood, to rejoin: "Stupidity can only be dealt with by attacking its root causes"' (*Thinking about Crime*, p. xv).

27 The pioneering texts were Becker, 'Crime and punishment', and Ehrlich, 'Participation in illegal activities'.

28 The seminal books were Lea and Young, *What is to be Done about Law and Order?*; Kinsey, Lea and Young, *Losing the Fight against Crime*; Matthews and Young, *Confronting Crime*.

29 Wilson, *Thinking about Crime*, p. xiii. On this view, 'crime amidst plenty' became 'the paradox of the sixties' (ibid., ch. 1). Left realists, notably Jock Young, spoke in similar terms of the 'aetiological crisis' faced by social democratic criminology as crime rose in spite of mass affluence (Young, 'The failure of criminology'). This is considered further in chapter 4.

30 For a general analysis of social democratic criminology see Reiner, 'Beyond risk'. Even a supposed economic determinist like Willem Bonger, the first Marxist to write systematically about crime, saw economic factors as linked to crime through the egoistic culture and ethics that were shaped by capitalist political economy (Bonger, *Criminality and Economic Conditions*).

31 It must also be borne in mind that the supposedly discredited experiment in trying to reduce crime by welfarist programmes, Lyndon Johnson's 'Great Society' programme, had at most four years, from LBJ's 1964 election victory to Richard Nixon's 1968 triumph on a law and order platform, before it was written off as failed. Stan Cohen has incisively shown how liberal approaches were deemed disproved not as a result of real evidence of their failure, but because they were eclipsed by a sudden shift in dominant fashions of thought (Cohen, 'The revenge of the null hypothesis').

32 Martinson, 'What works?'; Kelling et al., *The Kansas City Preventive Patrol Experiment*. The Home Office, in particular, interpreted these evaluations as showing that rehabilitative penal interventions, and traditional police tactics, had at best a very limited capacity to reduce crime, and that the way forward was crime prevention activity to limit criminal opportunities (Brody, *The Effectiveness of Sentencing*; Clarke and Hough, *The Effectiveness of Policing*; Clarke and Mayhew, *Designing Out Crime*).

33 Garside, *Crime, Persistent Offenders, and the Justice Gap* and *Right for the Wrong Reasons*. Crime levels do seem sensitive to changes in the *certainty* of punishment (Farrington and Jolliffe, 'Crime and punishment'), so improving the clear-up rate can help reduce crime, but only marginally.

34 Bottoms, 'Empirical evidence'; Tonry and Farrington, *Crime and Punishment in Western Countries*.

35 Smith, 'Less crime without more punishment', and 'Crime and punishment in Scotland'; Welsh and Irving, 'Crime and punishment in Canada'; Tonry and Farrington, *Crime and Punishment in Western Countries*, pp. 1–2.

36 Garside, *Crime, Persistent Offenders, and the Justice Gap*, p. 17.
37 Prime et al., *Criminal Careers*.
38 Garside, *Crime, Persistent Offenders, and the Justice Gap*, pp. 14–18, deconstructs the government's case incisively.
39 L. Taylor, *In the Underworld*; Hobbs, *Bad Business*; Wright and Decker, *Burglars on the Job* and *Armed Robbers on the Job*.
40 Marcuse, *Eros and Civilization*; Freud, *Civilisation and its Discontents*.
41 Some of the arguments put by Émile Durkheim to this effect are looked at further at the beginning of chapter 2. An earlier formulation, at the dawn of quantitative social science, was the claim by Quetelet – a founding father of modern statistics – to be 'able to enumerate in advance how many individuals will stain their hands with the blood of their fellow creatures, how many will be forgers, how many poisoners' because 'The crimes which are annually committed seem to be a necessary result of our social organisation' (cited in Vold, Bernard and Snipes, *Theoretical Criminology*, pp. 31–2; see also Beirne, *Inventing Criminology*).
42 Durkheim, *The Division of Labour in Society* and *Suicide*; Merton, 'Social structure and anomie'. This is not to assume that their concepts are the same, or even that their own usages are unitary or unchanging. It has often been suggested that Merton's version of anomie differs significantly from Durkheim's. Horton's claim that Merton 'dehumanises' the 'radical and utopian' thrust of Durkheim is a particularly hard-hitting version of this (Horton, 'The dehumanisation of anomie and alienation', pp. 294–5). But it was based on a gross misreading of Merton, unsupported by any citations from Merton's work, that reduces it to an identification of anomie and inequality of opportunity (see Reiner, 'Crime, law and deviance', pp. 192–4).
43 Ben Zoma and Hillel (see chapter epigraph above) were among the many rabbis whose epigrams are collected in

the Talmudic volume *Pirkei Avot*, usually translated as *Ethics of the Fathers*. They date roughly from the third century BCE to about 600 years later. The son of a rabbi, and descended from a long line of rabbis, Durkheim would doubtless have been familiar with this source.

44 Messner and Rosenfeld, *Crime and the American Dream*.

45 Tunstall, *The Media are American*. In an important new work, Jeremy Tunstall now argues that American hegemony over media around the world has been challenged with the further development of globalization. National and regional media cultures outside the American aegis have become increasingly important, in particular in Asia, the Middle East and Latin America (Tunstall, *The Media were American*).

46 Giddens, 'Egalitarianism'.

47 Nightingale, *On the Edge*; Fitzgerald, Stockdale and Hale, *Young People and Street Crime*; Curran et al., *Street Crime in London*; Hayward, *City Limits*; Hallsworth, *Street Crime*.

48 Young, *The Exclusive Society*.

49 The term seems to have been coined by Weber's student Joseph Schumpeter in 1908–9, but to refer to Weber's viewpoint.

50 Weber, *Economy and Society*, p. 13.

51 Young, 'Voodoo criminology', p. 15.

52 Weber, *The Theory of Social and Economic Organisation*, pp. 99–100.

53 Indeed, the Talmudic sage Ben Azzai specifically relates the Golden Rule to the earlier statement in Genesis 1: 27 that all people were created in the image of God, i.e. that individuals share in a common basis for equal concern and respect.

54 Reiner, 'Beyond risk', pp. 11–21.

55 The remark, and its context, are discussed further in chapter 4, where it is shown that this perspective has become a core ingredient in the politics of law and order, frequently echoed by New Labour.

56 This is reminiscent of the old McCarthyite charge that 'premature anti-Fascism' was an indicator of secret communist affiliation.

57 This is the line consistently taken by such deterministic analyses as Barbara Wootton's (*Social Science and Social Pathology*).

58 Reiner, Livingstone and Allen, 'From law and order to lynch mobs'.

Chapter 2 An Inspector Calls

1 Some recent discussions of the problems of defining crime are Henry and Lanier, *What is Crime?*; Lacey, Wells and Quick, *Reconstructing Criminal Law*, ch. 1; Zedner, *Criminal Justice*, chs 1 and 2; Hillyard et al., *Beyond Criminology*; and Morrison, 'What is crime?'.

2 A television commercial some years ago captured the Durkheimian point perfectly. Monks who follow the rule of silence are pictured at a table eating a sparse evening meal. A young novice gets up, scraping his seat noisily, and questioning eyebrows are raised. He goes to a barrel of ale with the logo of the brand being advertised, every footfall attracting disapproving looks. He draws a pint, the gushing liquid gurgles, arousing ever more furious looks. Finally he downs the pint noisily, ending with a sigh of satisfaction, and is bundled out of the monastery for his deviance from their saintly cloister's norms.

3 Ashworth, 'Is the criminal law a lost cause?'.

4 Lea, *Crime and Modernity*, is a comprehensive recent analysis of the relationship between the emergence of modern concepts of crime and capitalism. See also Jeffery, 'The development of crime'; Kennedy, 'Beyond incrimination'; Sharpe, *Crime in Early Modern England*.

5 Lea, *Crime and Modernity*, chs 2–4.

6 Cohen, 'Crime and politics'.

7 Lacey, 'Legal constructions of crime', p. 281.

8 Farmer, 'The obsession with definition'; Ashworth, 'Is the criminal law a lost cause?'; Lacey, Wells and Quick, *Reconstructing Criminal Law*, pp. 1–15; Ramsay, 'The responsible subject as citizen'.
9 Cockburn, *Crime in England.*
10 Wrightson, 'Two concepts of order'.
11 Sharpe, *Crime in Early Modern England*, pp. 50–3.
12 Hart, *The Concept of Law*, pp. 189–94.
13 Lacey, 'Contingency and criminalisation'.
14 Williams, 'The definition of crime', p. 107.
15 Reviewed in detail in Emmerson and Ashworth, *Human Rights and Criminal Justice*, ch. 4; Treschel, *Human Rights in Criminal Proceedings*, ch. 2.
16 *Engel v. Netherlands* (1979–80) 1 European Human Rights Reports 647.
17 Emmerson and Ashworth, *Human Rights and Criminal Justice*, pp. 151–2.
18 Burney, *Making People Behave*, is a comprehensive analysis of the origins, operation and significance of ASBOs. Empirical assessments of their impact include Squires and Stephen, *Rougher Justice*; Hough, Millie and Jacobson, *Anti-social Behaviour Strategies.*
19 *Clingham v. Royal Borough of Kensington and Chelsea*; *R. v. Crown Court at Manchester ex.p. McCann and others* [2003] 1 A.C. 787. For discussion see Macdonald, 'The nature of the anti-social behaviour order'.
20 Ashworth, 'Social control and "anti-social behaviour"', p. 277.
21 Ramsay, 'What is anti-social behaviour?', p. 918.
22 Ashworth, 'Is the criminal law a lost cause?', pp. 253–4.
23 Ibid., p. 256.
24 Tadros and Tierney, 'The presumption of innocence'.
25 Nelken 'Critical criminal law' and 'Criminal law and criminal justice'; Dennis, *Criminal Law and Justice*; Loveland, *Frontiers of Criminality*; Norrie, *Crime, Reason and History.*
26 Lacey, 'Legal constructions of crime', p. 282.
27 Mill, *On Liberty*; Stephen, *Liberty, Equality, Fraternity*; Hart, *Law, Liberty and Morality*; Devlin, *The Enforcement*

of Morals; Feinberg, *The Moral Limits of the Criminal Law*; Lee, *Law and Morals*.

28 Sutherland, *White-Collar Crime*; Schwendinger and Schwendinger, 'Guardians of order?'; Slapper and Tombs, *Corporate Crime*; Tombs and Whyte, '"Two steps forward, one step back"'; Green and Ward, *State Crime*. For discussion of the problems of defining and regulating white-collar or corporate crime, see Gobert and Punch, *Rethinking Corporate Crime*; Nelken, 'Corporate and white-collar crime'.

29 Hillyard et al., *Beyond Criminology*.

30 Nelken 'White-collar crime', p. 846.

31 Ibid., pp. 846, 861.

32 Punch, *Dirty Business*; Slapper, *Blood in the Bank*.

33 Tombs, 'Death and work in Britain'.

34 Slapper, *Blood in the Bank*; Tombs, 'Death and work in Britain' and 'Workplace injury and death'; Slapper and Tombs, *Corporate Crime*; Wells, *Corporations and Criminal Responsibility*; Tombs and Whyte, *Safety Crimes*.

35 Priestley, *An Inspector Calls*, p. 172.

36 Ibid., p. 207.

37 Durkheim, *The Division of Labour in Society*, pp. 73, 80.

38 Lukes, *Liberals and Cannibals*.

39 Karstedt and Farrall, 'The moral maze of the middle class'.

40 Sykes and Matza, 'Techniques of neutralization'.

41 Tony Martin is a Norfolk farmer, who in 2000 received a life sentence for the manslaughter of a sixteen-year-old burglar. The case aroused a furious response, mainly in conservative circles, for supposedly punishing the 'real' victim. Ironically Martin was released in 2003 on the same day as the partner-in-crime of the boy he killed, who had also been wounded by the farmer ('A victim not a hero', leader, *Guardian*, 29 July 2003).

42 Karstedt and Farrall, 'The moral maze of the middle class', p. 65.

43 Priestley, *An Inspector Calls*, p. 179.

44 On ethnic minority imbalance see Bowling and Phillips, *Racism, Crime and Justice* and 'Policing ethnic minority

communities'; Phillips and Bowling, 'Racism, ethnicity, crime'; Morgan, 'Imprisonment', pp. 1132–9. On gender see Heidensohn, 'Gender and crime' and 'Gender and policing'; Gelsthorpe, 'Feminism and criminology'; Walklate, *Gender, Crime and Criminal Justice*. On economic class see Reiman, *The Rich Get Richer*, and Reiner, 'Political economy'. For the US see Beckett and Sasson, *The Politics of Injustice*; Western, *Punishment and Inequality in America*.

45 Hearndon and Hough, *Race and the Criminal Justice System*, p. vii.
46 Surette, *Media, Crime and Criminal Justice*.
47 For a summary of research on media representations of crime see Reiner, 'Media made criminality'.
48 Reiner, Livingstone and Allen, 'From law and order to lynch mobs', p. 18.
49 Allen, Livingstone and Reiner, 'True Lies'; Reiner, 'Media, crime, law and order'.
50 Reiner, Livingstone and Allen, 'From law and order to lynch mobs', p. 20.
51 Allen, Livingstone and Reiner, 'True Lies'; Reiner, Livingstone and Allen, 'No more happy endings?', 'Casino culture' and 'From law and order to lynch mobs'; Reiner, 'Media, crime, law and order'.
52 Tonry, *Punishment and Politics*, ch. 2.
53 An amusing example was reported in *Police Review* some years ago. A community meeting in Devon was addressed by the local Inspector, who reported on recent trends in burglary, car crime, and anti-social behaviour. 'That's all very well, young man,' interjected an old lady at the back, 'but what I want to know is what you are doing about the problem of terrorism in Torbay.'
54 J. Hall, *Theft, Law and Society*, ch. 1. In the Carrier's Case it was held that a carrier who legally had possession of bundles he was transporting for a client stole them when he 'broke' into them – an extension of the meaning of trespass – for his own use.
55 Nelken, 'White-collar crime', pp. 860–3.

56 Hoyle, *Negotiating Domestic Violence.*
57 Stinchcombe, 'Institutions of privacy'.
58 Nelken, 'White-collar crime', p. 855.
59 The classic sources are Wilson, *Thinking about Crime*, and Lea and Young, *What is to be Done?*.
60 S. Hall et al., *Policing the Crisis.*

Chapter 3 A Mephistophelean Calculus

1 The 1856 County and Borough Police Act required the establishment of police forces in all areas of England and Wales. These forces were obliged to compile records of 'crimes known to the police', and supply these to the Home Office (Hough and Mayhew, *The British Crime Survey*, pp. 1–2).
2 Victim surveys had been pioneered in the US in the 1960s, and annual surveys conducted and published by the Department of Justice from 1972. A pioneering British victim survey was Sparks, Genn and Dodd, *Surveying Victims* (1977). Important contributions were also made by other local victim surveys in the 1980s, notably Kinsey, *The Merseyside Crime Survey*, and Jones, MacLean and Young, *The Islington Crime Survey.*
3 The latest is Walker, Kershaw and Nicholas, *Crime in England and Wales 2005/06* (from which the third epigraph above was taken). The earlier annual publication *Criminal Statistics*, which contained only the police recorded figures, also gave data on subsequent stages of the criminal justice process, culminating in court proceedings and their outcomes. These are now published separately.
4 Early discussions are Morrison, 'The interpretation of criminal statistics' (1897), and Mannheim, *Social Aspects of Crime* (1940), part 1. See also McLintock and Avison, *Crime in England and Wales*; N. Walker, *Crimes, Courts and Figures*; Bottomley and Pease, *Crime and Punishment*; M. Walker, *Interpreting Crime Statistics*; Coleman and

Moynihan, *Understanding Crime Data*. The issues are explored fully in Maguire, 'Crime statistics'.

5 For recent examples see 'Crime up, convictions down', *Mirror*, 29 May 2006; 'Attacks in street up 10%', *Sun*, 17 July 2006.

6 Until 1892 the Home Office published the police figures under the title 'Crimes committed' (H. Taylor, 'Rising crime: the political economy of criminal statistics', p. 581). This was replaced by the more gnomic 'crimes known to the police' until the early 1980s, when this usage fell into abeyance as there was a growing realization that many crimes literally *known* to the police were not in fact recorded by them.

7 H. Taylor, 'Rising crime: the political economy of criminal statistics' and 'Rising crime: a crisis of "modernisation"'.

8 Walker, Kershaw and Nicholas, *Crime in England and Wales 2005/06*, p. 59.

9 Hough and Mayhew, *The British Crime Survey*, p. 12.

10 Walker, Kershaw and Nicholas, *Crime in England and Wales 2005/06*, pp. 53–4.

11 Burrows et al., *Review of Police Forces' Crime Recording Practices*, ch. 5.

12 A story I heard from a police source some years ago illustrates the difficulty of deciding whether a report is genuine, giving rise to legitimate discretion. An old lady appeared at a police station to report that her shed had been broken into by 'the men from Mars'. The station sergeant, in the classic avuncular Dixon mould, humoured her but did not make a crime report. Nor did he the next day, when she came back. It was only on her third visit that a lateral-thinking constable noticed her address – immediately opposite the factory where Mars chocolate bars were manufactured, and duly traced the thieves 'from Mars'.

13 Home Office, *Counting Rules*. McCabe and Sutcliffe, *Defining Crime*, Bottomley and Coleman, *Understanding Crime Rates*, and M. Young, *An Inside Job*, ch. 5, analyse how police have used their discretion to record offences in the past.

14 Burrows et al., *Review of Police Forces' Crime Recording Practices*, p. 36.
15 Simmons, Legg and Hosking, *National Crime Recording Standard.*
16 H. Taylor, 'Rising crime: the political economy of criminal statistics', p. 580.
17 A vivid insider's account of the various devices used as recently as the early 1990s can be found in a study by a former senior officer (M. Young, *An Inside Job*, ch. 5).
18 N. Davies, 'Watching the detectives', 'Fiddling the figures' and 'Exposing the myth of the falling crime rate'.
19 In 2001, leaked Home Office documents (they had been inadvertently left in a pub by a civil servant!) revealed plans to change definitions used to construct the statistics in order to ensure manifesto pledges were met (Thompson and Bright, 'Secret papers'). In December 2006 the Statistics Commission suggested the 'Home Office should be stripped of responsibility for publishing crime statistics because public trust in the figures has been eroded, partly by departmental manipulation of their timing and context' (Wintour: 'Restore trust in crime figures').
20 The same problem of before and after comparability applies to changes in the technical definition of a notifiable offence, for example when in 1977 the Home Office decided to include criminal damage offences where the value of property damaged was less than £20.
21 Walker, Kershaw and Nicholas, *Crime in England and Wales 2005/06*, p. 20.
22 Shepherd, 'Violent crime in Bristol'; Sivarajasingam et al., *Trends in Violence*. Insights can be gained into specific types of crime by indirect indices such as changing street prices for drugs. Oral histories, although qualitative, also shed light on the validity of the picture presented by statistical indicators (Hood and Joyce, 'Three generations').
23 For example 'Overall crime levels remain stable with a 1% rise recorded by the *authoritative* British Crime Survey', *Guardian*, 20 July 2006 (emphasis added).
24 Hough and Mayhew, *The British Crime Survey*, pp. 2–5.

25 Sparks, Genn and Dodd, *Surveying Victims*. There have also been victim surveys in other countries. Since 1989 there have been four sweeps of the International Crime Victimisation Survey (Van Kesteren, Mayhew and Nieuwbeerta, *Criminal Victimisation*).
26 Hough and Mayhew, *The British Crime Survey*, pp. 3–4.
27 Home Office, *Criminal Statistics* (2000), p. 38.
28 The Home Office has conducted surveys of crime against businesses that show some of this (Shury et al., *Crime against Retail and Manufacturing Premises*).
29 The Home Office has recently conducted a survey of experiences of crime among 10–16 year olds (Budd et al., *Young People and Crime*).
30 Newburn and Rock, *Living in Fear*.
31 Grant et al., *2004–5 British Crime Survey Technical Report*, p. 7.
32 The other alternative methodologies also have characteristic limitations even if impeccably conducted. Self-report studies, in which samples are asked about their offending behaviour, yield data that can be compared to official statistics to test whether the patterns of offending in these reflect discrimination in policing and other criminal justice processes. However, there are inevitable issues about the accuracy and honesty of respondents' accounts of their own behaviour (Maguire, 'Crime statistics', pp. 363–8, summarizes the findings and problems). In any event, such studies don't shed light on trends over time. The hospital A&E data can do this (Shepherd, 'Violent crime in Bristol'; Sivarajasingam et al., *Trends in Violence*). But again these are limited to a very specific kind of offence. As one of the basic findings of this data is that a very high proportion of such cases are not known to the police, there is also a conceptual issue: are the 'victims' of some injuries sustained in fights treated in hospital possibly those who would be seen as perpetrators by the police?
33 Walker, Kershaw and Nicholas, *Crime in England and Wales 2005/06*, p. 17.
34 Home Office, *Criminal Statistics* (1976), p. 22.

35 Barclay and Tavares, *Digest 4*, p. 4.
36 Although there are no figures for crimes that were not prosecuted prior to 1856, on the basis of the judicial statistics historians generally believe that the mid-Victorian levels represent a decline from much higher levels in the early nineteenth century (Gatrell, 'The decline of theft'; Emsley, 'The history of crime', pp. 204–7). There is some debate about whether the flat trend indicated in figure 3.2 is attributable to supply-side rationing of the figures driven both by fiscal parsimony and the wish to present an appearance of success for the new police forces and other nineteenth-century criminal justice reforms (H. Taylor, 'Rising crime: the political economy of criminal statistics' and 'Rising crime: a crisis of "modernisation"'; R. Morris, '"Lies, damned lies and criminal statistics"'; Emsley, 'The history of crime').
37 Walker, Kershaw and Nicholas, *Crime in England and Wales 2005/06*, p. 14.
38 Hough and Mayhew, *Taking Account of Crime*, p. 16.
39 Mayhew, Elliott and Dowds, *The 1988 British Crime Survey*, pp. 19–22.
40 Barclay, Tavares and Prout, *Digest 3*, p. 7.
41 Reiner, 'The case of the missing crimes'.
42 Weatheritt, 'Measuring police performance'; McLaughlin and Murji, 'Lost connections and new directions'; Long, 'Leadership and performance management'.
43 The 2003 introduction nationally of new police powers to issue Penalty Notices for Disorder, which have been used largely to deal with harassment offences, may have further boosted the police recorded violent rate relative to the BCS, by widening the net to include incidents that might not have attracted any formal action at all (Hough, Mirrlees-Black and Dale, *Trends in Violent Crimes*, pp. 29–30).
44 Beckett, *Making Crime Pay*; Hough and Roberts, *Understanding Public Attitudes*.
45 Dennis and Erdos, *Cultures and Crimes*; Green, Grove and Martin, *Crime and Civil Society*. The limitations of the BCS

have also been stressed by more sympathetic critics (e.g. Davies, 'Exposing the myth'; Garside, *Crime, Persistent Offenders, and the Justice Gap* and *Right for the Wrong Reasons*), and of course are frankly outlined in its reports.

Chapter 4 Permissiveness versus Political Economy

1 Wilson and Herrnstein, *Crime and Human Nature*, ch. 16, Green, Grove and Martin, *Crime and Civil Society*, and Dennis and Erdos, *Cultures and Crimes*, are elaborations of this argument. For comprehensive accounts of the complexities of social change in the 1960s see Donnelly, *Sixties Britain*; Sandbrook. *White Heat*.
2 Blair, 'A new consensus'.
3 Newburn, *Permission and Regulation*.
4 Downes, *Contrasts in Tolerance*; Tham, 'Crime and the welfare state' and 'Law and order as a leftist project'; Pakes, 'The politics of discontent'; Bondeson, 'Levels of punitiveness in Scandinavia'.
5 Currie, *Crime and Punishment in America*, p. 135. Currie, *Confronting Crime*, 'Market, crime and community', *Crime and Punishment in America* and 'Crime and market society' detail how neoliberalism undermines families.
6 James, *Juvenile Violence in a Winner–Loser Society*.
7 Giddens, *Modernity and Self-Identity*.
8 Miliband, 'A state of desubordination'.
9 Currie, *Confronting Crime*, 'Market, crime and community', *Crime and Punishment in America* and 'Crime and market society'; Taylor, 'The political economy of crime' and *Crime in Context*; S. Hall and Winlow, 'Rehabilitating Leviathan' and 'Barbarians at the gates'; Downes, 'New Labour'; Garside, 'Is it the economy?'; Hale, 'Economic marginalization'; Reiner, 'Beyond risk' and 'Political economy'.
10 Polanyi, *The Great Transformation*.
11 Currie, 'Market, crime and community', p. 150.

12 Vold, Bernard and Snipes, *Theoretical Criminology*, and Downes and Rock, *Understanding Deviance*, are comprehensive overviews of the main criminological theories.
13 Matza and Sykes, 'Juvenile delinquency and subterranean values'; Katz, *Seductions of Crime*; Jacobs and Wright, 'Stick-up, street culture, and offender motivation'.
14 Merton, 'Social structure and anomie'; J. Young, *The Exclusive Society*; Hallsworth, *Street Crime*; Messner and Rosenfeld, *Crime and the American Dream*.
15 Sykes and Matza, 'Techniques of neutralization'; Cohen, *States of Denial*.
16 Marris, *Survey of the Research Literature*; Fielding, Clarke and Witt, *The Economic Dimensions of Crime*; Grogger, 'An economic model'; Hale, 'Economic marginalization'; Reiner, 'Political economy'.
17 Merton, 'Social structure and anomie'; Reiner, 'Crime, law and deviance'; Messner and Rosenfeld, *Crime and the American Dream*.
18 Mann and Sutton, 'Netcrime', p. 201.
19 Wall, *Crime and the Internet*; Jewkes, *Dot.Cons*; Yar, *Cybercrime and Society*.
20 Sheptycki and Wardak, *Transnational and Comparative Criminology*.
21 Gill, 'Reducing the capacity to offend', pp. 311–12. See also Ekblom and Tilley, 'Going equipped'.
22 Mayhew, Sturan and Hough, *Crime as Opportunity*; Cohen and Felson, 'Social change and crime rate trends'; Cornish and Clarke, *The Reasoning Criminal*; Clarke, *Situational Crime Prevention*; Pease, 'Crime reduction'; Felson, *Crime and Everyday Life*; Tilley, *Handbook of Crime Prevention*.
23 Felson and Clarke, *Opportunity Makes the Thief*. Zedner, 'Opportunity makes the thief-taker' is a vigorous and insightful critique.
24 Clarke and Mayhew, 'The British gas suicide story'.
25 Curran et al., *Street Crime in London*, pp. 15–16.
26 Bratton, 'Crime is down: blame the police'; these claims will be evaluated in the next chapter.
27 Eysenck, *Crime and Personality*.

28 Malinowski, *Crime and Custom in Savage Society*; Innes, *Understanding Social Control*.
29 Hirschi, *Causes of Delinquency*.
30 Hirschi and Gottfredson, *The Generality of Deviance*. See also Wilson and Herrnstein, *Crime and Human Nature*; Gottfredson and Hirschi, *A General Theory of Crime*.
31 Sandbrook, *Never Had It So Good*, p. xxi.
32 Bottoms and Stevenson, 'What went wrong?'.
33 'Real incomes became the highest in history, slums were demolished one by one, educational attainment rose, social services expanded in order to provide extensive welfare provisions and safety nets, and yet the crime rate doggedly rose! All of the factors which should have led to a drop in delinquency if mainstream criminology were even half correct were being ameliorated and yet precisely the opposite effect was occurring. Such an aetiological crisis was an empirical anomaly' (J. Young, 'The failure of criminology', pp. 5–6). Similar arguments have been put strongly by Smith, 'Youth crime and conduct disorders', and, from a radical right-wing perspective, by Wilson, *Thinking about Crime*, pp. 3–4.
34 Galbraith's book *The Affluent Society* is frequently misrepresented (just as Macmillan's 'never had it so good' has been). Galbraith's main theme was the proliferation of 'public squalor' in an era of growing private affluence. Moreover, he was painfully aware of the substantial pockets of poverty that were hidden by the conspicuous consumption that dominated the media (*The Affluent Society*, ch. 22). Indeed Galbraith's book is one of the first examples of what came to be referred to in the 1960s as the 'rediscovery of poverty', and its originally planned title was to be *Why People are Poor*! (See Parker, *John Kenneth Galbraith*, p. 273.)
35 Bonger, *Criminality and Economic Conditions*.
36 Merton, 'Social structure and anomie'.
37 Downes, *The Delinquent Solution*, p. 269. In a prophetic anticipation of what was to happen twenty years later under Thatcherism he saw that if 'slump, unemployment

or redundancy' undermined the socioeconomic conditions permitting early marriage for working-class youth, which facilitated their growth out of adolescent delinquency, the effect would hoist the rates of adult criminality' (ibid., pp. 268–9).

38 Downes, 'Back to the future', p. 103. Also striking was the prediction by John Mays in 1964 that 'if inequality remained unchecked in the context of growing affluence, crime rates would double within 25 years' (*Crime and the Social Structure*). As Downes comments acerbically: 'He was wrong about the magnitude of the change – they trebled – but right about the direction' ('Back to the future', p. 108).

39 Longford Study Group, *Crime*, pp. 4–5.

40 A direct precursor of *Who Wants to be a Millionaire?*. The 'Guardian of the Questions' on this show (modelled on the American *$64,000 Question*) was ex-Superintendent Robert Fabian, a celebrated Scotland Yard detective whose exploits had inspired an eponymous BBC television series.

41 Harbord and Wright, *Forty Years of British Television*, pp. 8–11.

42 This was the title of a 1962 film, and a novel by Jack Trevor Story. 'The first cinematic dissection of modern consumerism, its very title seemed to capture the spirit of the age' (Sandbrook, *Never Had It So Good*, p. 487).

43 Access cards were the first commonly available credit cards in Britain, marketed under the slogan 'Take the waiting out of wanting'.

44 As hire purchase and other nascent forms of consumer credit were called.

45 Gottfredson and Hirschi, *A General Theory of Crime*, pp. 89–91.

46 J. Young, *The Exclusive Society*; Lea, *Crime and Modernity*, pp. 78–81; Fitzgerald, Stockdale and Hale, *Young People and Street Crime*; Hayward, *City Limits*; Hallsworth, *Street Crime*.

47 Sandbrook, *Never Had It So Good*, chs 12, 13. A homely yet striking illustration is suggested by Hennessy's

comments about photographs of crowds at football matches: 'In the early postwar years . . . [y]oung men dressed like their fathers and grandfathers – jackets, mackintoshes and caps . . . Not until the first glimmerings of affluence put money into young pockets in the mid-Fifties did the external expressions of a youth culture come to distinguish the generations in a sporting crowd' (*Never Again*, p. 307). Since then the differences have disappeared again as the attire of the fathers and grandfathers has become the jeans and denims of their teenage offspring, a reversal symbolizing the decline of deference.

48 Reiner, *The Politics of the Police*, ch. 2.

49 Box, *Recession, Crime and Punishment*. See also Chiricos, 'Rates of crime and unemployment', for a similar US review.

50 Of these, eighteen were time-series analyses, looking at the relationship between measures of crime and unemployment over a number of years; thirty-two were cross-sectional studies, assessing whether there are associations between crime and unemployment levels in different places at a given time.

51 Box cited with approval the conclusion of a slightly earlier literature review by an American economist: 'despite differences and weaknesses among the studies, a general finding emerges: namely that rises in unemployment . . . are connected with rises in the crime rate, but the effect tends to be modest and insufficient to explain the general upward trend of crime in the period studied' (Freeman, 'Crime and unemployment', p. 96). Box also looked at one American longitudinal study of a cohort of boys born in 1945. This found a clear link between periods of unemployment and greater levels of arrest for the boys. However, Box pointed out that this could be because the police were more likely to arrest them when they were unemployed. The boys' own self-reported offending was not clearly related to unemployment (Box, *Recession, Crime and Punishment*, pp. 93–5). This was a disappointing finding, because cohort studies offer the potential for overcoming

some of the problems of either time-series or cross-sectional aggregate studies: self-reported offending does not suffer from the reporting and recording issues bedevilling official statistics (though it has its own problems), and there is no need to control for other socioeconomic variables that could affect both crime and unemployment because the same people are being studied throughout. It is thus important to note that a study based on the British Cambridge Study of Delinquent Development was published shortly before Box's book, but too late to be included (Farrington et al., 'Unemployment, school leaving and crime'). This showed that the boys in the sample *did* admit to committing more offences while unemployed, providing support for the standard hypothesis that unemployment is linked to more crime.

52 Box, *Recession, Crime and Punishment*, p. 87.
53 Weber, *The Theory of Social and Economic Organisation*, pp. 99–100.
54 Which was what prompted him to write it: preface to Box, *Recession, Crime and Punishment*.
55 Campbell, *Goliath*; Currie, *Crime and Punishment in America* and 'Crime and market society'; Davies, *Dark Heart*.
56 Marris, *Survey of the Research Literature*; Witt, Clarke and Fielding, 'Crime and economic activity'; Fielding, Clarke and Witt, *The Economic Dimensions of Crime*, part 2; Kleck and Chiricos, 'Unemployment and property crime'; Deadman and Macdonald, 'Why has crime fallen?'; Hale, 'Economic marginalization'.
57 Marris, *Survey of the Research Literature*, pp. 73–4.
58 Pyle and Deadman, 'Crime and the business cycle'.
59 Hale, 'The labour market' and 'Economic marginalization', pp. 333–4.
60 Grogger, 'Market wages and youth crime' and 'An economic model'.
61 Machin and Meghir, 'Crime and economic incentives'.
62 Hansen and Machin, 'Spatial crime patterns'.
63 Cantor and Land, 'Unemployment and crime rates'; Kleck and Chiricos, 'Unemployment and property crime'.

64 Field, *Trends in Crime* and *Trends in Crime Revisited*; Dhiri et al., *Modelling and Predicting Property Crime*.
65 Field used the level of consumption expenditure as the main indicator of the business cycle. He found that unemployment was not associated with crime if consumption was taken into account (*Trends in Crime*, p. 7). This does not mean it was not associated with crime fluctuations, but that on his analysis it was only related to crime through its effects on consumption. Subsequent analyses of the time-series relationship between crime trends since the Second World War and economic variables, using different modelling techniques and assumptions, confirmed the link with consumption levels, but also found associations between crime and gross domestic product and unemployment (Pyle and Deadman, 'Crime and the business cycle'; Hale, 'Crime and the business cycle'). Altogether this is a powerful body of evidence confirming the negative relationship between fluctuations in prosperity and fluctuations in property (and overall) crime levels.
66 Field found a positive cyclical relationship between consumption and *violent* crime. He accounted for this by suggesting that in times of prosperity there is more socializing and alcohol consumption, leading to more fights between young men in pubs etc. (the association with beer consumption in particular indicated this).
67 Field, *Trends in Crime Revisited*, pp. 2–3.
68 Hills, *Inequality and the State*; Hills and Stewart, *A More Equal Society?*.
69 Hale, 'Economic marginalization', pp. 334–6.
70 Beckett and Sasson, *The Politics of Injustice*; Wilkinson, *The Impact of Inequality*, pp. 47–51 and ch. 5.
71 Dorling, 'Prime suspect', p. 191.
72 Downes, 'New Labour'; Garside, 'Is it the economy?'; Hale, 'Economic marginalization'.
73 Ehrlich, 'Participation in illegal activities' and 'The deterrent effect of capital punishment', pp. 409–13.
74 I. Taylor, 'The political economy of crime', p. 266 (emphasis in the original).

75 Nelken, 'Comparing criminal justice'.
76 Barclay and Tavares, *International Comparisons*, pp. 3–4.
77 Van Kesteren, Mayhew and Nieuwbeerta, *Criminal Victimisation*, ch. 2.
78 Ibid., pp. 91–2, 98–9.
79 Ibid., p. 48.
80 J. Young, 'Winning the fight against crime?', pp. 36–7, and 'Voodoo criminology'.
81 Messner and Rosenfeld, 'Market dominance, crime and globalisation' and *Crime and the American Dream*.
82 The typology is based on Cavadino and Dignan's analysis of comparative penal policy (*Penal Systems*). This was itself derived from Esping-Andersen's comparative analysis of types of capitalism in *The Three Worlds of Welfare Capitalism*.
83 Currie, *Confronting Crime*, 'Market, crime and community', *Crime and Punishment in America* and 'Crime and market society'; James, *Juvenile Violence in a Winner–Loser Society*; S. Hall, 'Visceral cultures and criminal practices'; Davies, *Dark Heart*; S. Hall and Winlow, 'Rehabilitating Leviathan'; Dorling, 'Prime suspect'; Hallsworth, *Street Crime*; S. Hall and McLean, 'A tale of two capitalisms'.
84 Currie, 'Market, crime and community', p. 154.
85 Eisner, 'Modernisation, self-control and lethal violence', p. 629.
86 Gurr, Grabosky and Hula, *The Politics of Crime*; Gurr, 'Historical trends in violent crime'. This cannot of course take into account the fall in crime rates after the early 1990s.
87 Gatrell, 'The decline of theft and violence'. As discussed in the previous chapter, the validity of the English statistics on which these analyses rely has been called into question by Howard Taylor, in a series of papers attempting to demonstrate that even the homicide figures are essentially driven by 'supply side' factors, the shifting exigencies and strategies of the authorities responsible for producing the data, primarily the Home Office and police forces (Taylor, 'Rising crime' and 'Forging the job'). Taylor's evidence and

arguments certainly offer a sharp and salutary reminder of the need for caution in interpreting all criminal statistics (they have been challenged in turn by other historians, notably R. Morris, '"Lies, damned lies and criminal statistics"'; for a review of the arguments see Emsley, 'Historical perspectives on crime').

88 Geary, *Policing Industrial Disputes*; Della Porta and Reiter, *Policing Protest.*

89 Elias, *The Civilizing Process.*

90 Fletcher, *Violence and Civilization*, pp. 36, 64.

91 Silver, 'The demand for order'; Bittner, *The Functions of the Police*; Reiner, *The Politics of the Police*, chs 1, 2.

92 Garland, *Punishment and Welfare* and *The Culture of Control*, ch. 2.

93 Punch, *Dirty Business*; Slapper and Tombs, *Corporate Crime*; Ruggiero, *Crime and Markets*; Gobert and Punch, *Rethinking Corporate Crime*; Green and Ward, *State Crime.*

94 O'Malley, *Risk, Uncertainty and Government.*

95 Garland, *The Culture of Control*, p. 199.

96 This does not, however, appear to have been accompanied by a decline in fear of crime, a puzzle in its own right (Hough, 'Modernization and public opinion').

97 Blumstein and Wallman, *The Crime Drop in America*; Tonry and Farrington, *Crime and Punishment in Western Countries*; Zimring, *The Great American Crime Decline.*

98 J. Young, 'Voodoo criminology', pp. 24–5.

99 Bowling, 'The rise and fall of New York murder'; Karmen, *New York Murder Mystery*; Eck and Maguire, 'Have changes in policing reduced violent crime?'; Dixon and Maher, 'Policing, crime and public health'.

100 Spelman, 'The limited importance of prison expansion' and 'Jobs or jails?'; Bottoms, Rex and Robinson, *Alternatives to Prison.*

101 Smith, 'Less crime without more punishment'; Tonry and Farrington, *Crime and Punishment in Western Countries.*

102 Downes, 'New Labour'.

103 Pissarides, 'Unemployment in Britain', p. 22, now also in Werding, *Structural Unemployment.*

104 In econometric studies inequality is usually measured by the 'Gini coefficient'. This is based on calculating the proportion of total income earned by particular percentages of earners. Equality is defined as the situation where each percentage of income receivers gets the corresponding percentage of income, which on a diagram would be represented by a straight diagonal line. The Gini coefficient measures the deviation of the actual distribution from this.

105 Brewer et al., *Poverty and Inequality in Britain*, p. 1.

106 One obvious temptation is to deny its reality, a line that has been taken particularly by some conservative commentators in Britain (Dennis and Erdos, *Cultures and Crimes*; Green, Grove and Martin, *Crime and Civil Society*), but also by others (Davies, 'Exposing the myth'). The recorded crime figures in Britain have indeed increased in most years since 1998, but this is primarily due to major changes in the Home Office counting rules, as the last chapter showed. The main reason most criminologists do not question the downward trend is because it is indicated by the British Crime Survey and similar victimization surveys elsewhere. While these are not subject to the same well-known problems as the police recorded figures, they are certainly not beyond dispute (Garside, *Crime, Persistent Offenders, and the Justice Gap*; J. Young, 'Voodoo criminology', pp. 17–22). It could be that trends in the nature of crime make the BCS increasingly unable to uncover the crimes it used to record, thus producing a spurious decline in victimization levels. For example several studies have suggested that one consequence of better domestic and car security is that potential thieves switch to robbery (Fitzgerald, Stockdale and Hale, *Young People and Street Crime*; Hallsworth, *Street Crime*), in particular of young people. As the BCS only samples people over sixteen, if there is a trend towards disproportionate victimization of younger people it could produce an increasing underestimate of crime. Perhaps there has been some displacement to other forms of crime not recorded by the BCS, such as

shoplifting (Davies, 'Exposing the myth'). It would be as premature to conclude that the apparent trend towards falling crime is spurious as to suggest that any of the array of possible contributing factors is *the* one 'whodunnit'. But it may be that at any rate a partial solution to the mystery of the falling crime rate is that it didn't happen to the extent suggested by the BCS.

107 Millie and Herrington, 'Bridging the gap'; Innes, 'Reassurance and the "new" community policing'; Hough, 'Policing'.

108 Innes and Fielding, 'From community to communicative policing'; Innes, '"Signal crimes"'.

109 Fitzgerald, Stockdale and Hale, *Young People and Street Crime*; Hallsworth, *Street Crime*; Curran et al., *Street Crime in London*; D. Rose, 'Violent crime'.

110 Currie, 'Reflections on crime'.

Chapter 5 A New Leviathan?

1 Matthews, 'The myth of punitiveness'.

2 Zedner, 'Dangers of dystopia'.

3 P. Hall and Soskice, *Varieties of Capitalism*.

4 Downes and Morgan, 'The skeletons in the cupboard'.

5 Ryan, *The Acceptable Pressure Group* and *The Politics of Penal Reform*; T. Morris, *Crime and Criminal Justice since 1945*.

6 Pearson, *Hooligan*.

7 Beckett, *Making Crime Pay*. 'Law and order' itself is an old phrase, traditionally invoked as if it represented some unproblematically linked perfect partnership, like Laurel and Hardy or sausage and mash. But as it came to be used as a political slogan it became impregnated with controversial meanings. Classical social theory of all kinds had been explicitly or implicitly sceptical about the law playing a significant part in social order (Reiner, 'Classical social theory and law'). Order was the product of complex processes of social interdependence and informal control

(Durkheim, *The Division of Labour in Society*), or of ruling class interests (Marx, *Capital Volume 1*, ch. 10), or of different types of power and authority (Weber, *Economy and Society*, pp. 217–20). In all these analyses, for all their differences, law was seen as the expression or product of order, not its source.

8 The seminal analysis of the tension between crime control and due process models of law is Packer, *The Limits of the Criminal Sanction*. For more recent debate about the applicability of these models see McBarnet, *Conviction*; McConville, Sanders and Leng, *The Case for the Prosecution* and 'Descriptive or Critical Sociology?'; Smith, 'Case construction' and 'Reform or moral outrage?'; Sanders and Young, 'From suspect to trial'; Ashworth and Redmayne, *The Criminal Process*.

9 Downes and Morgan, 'The skeletons in the cupboard', p. 288.

10 Reiner and Cross, *Beyond Law and Order*; Brake and Hale, *Public Order and Private Lives*; Freeman, 'Law and order in 1984'.

11 Reiner, 'Fuzzy thoughts'; McLaughlin and Murji, 'Resistance through representation'; Loader and Mulcahy, *Policing and the Condition of England*, ch. 7.

12 Butler and Kavanagh, *The British General Election of 1979*, p. 163.

13 Blair, 'Why crime is a socialist issue'; N. Cohen, 'How Blair put 30,000 more in jail' and *Pretty Straight Guys*; Downes and Morgan, 'The skeletons in the cupboard', pp. 296–7; Newburn, *Crime and Criminal Justice Policy*, pp. 206–7, and ' "Tough on crime" ', p. 11; Hale, 'The politics of law and order', pp. 439–41.

14 Lawson, 'Turbo-consumerism'.

15 Downes and Morgan, 'The skeletons in the cupboard', p. 287.

16 Downes, *Law and Order*.

17 Lea and Young, *What is to be Done?*.

18 I. Taylor, *Law and Order*.

19 Kinsey, Lea and Young, *Losing the Fight against Crime*; Matthews and Young, *Confronting Crime*.

20 Baker, *The Turbulent Years*, p. 450.
21 Resodihardjo, 'Discourse and funnelling'.
22 Downes and Morgan, 'The skeletons in the cupboard'.
23 This controversial formulation, with its notoriously 'know nothing' tone, appeared in an interview with John Major in the *Mail on Sunday* on 21 February 1993.
24 Tony Blair, 'Our citizens should not live in fear'.
25 Zimring, 'Imprisonment rates', pp. 163–4.
26 Tonry, *Thinking about Crime*, p. 137.
27 Garland, *The Culture of Control*, pp. 124–7.
28 Speech launching the Home Office five-year Strategy for Criminal Justice, 19 July 2004, at www.number-10.gov.uk/output/page6129.asp.
29 Garland, *The Culture of Control*, pp. 161–3.
30 Zedner, 'Too much security?', p. 165.
31 Rose, 'The death of the social?'
32 Beck, *Risk Society*.
33 Giddens, *The Third Way*; Leys, *Market-Driven Politics*; Bevir, *New Labour*.
34 Reiner, *The Politics of the Police*, ch. 6.
35 Carter, *Managing Offenders, Reducing Crime*; Hough, Jacobson and Millie, *The Decision to Imprison*; Farrington and Jolliffe, 'Crime and punishment'; Newburn, '"Tough on crime"'.
36 The probability of custody for serious violence has always been high (90–95 per cent for rape or homicide; around 70 per cent for robbery) throughout the last quarter of a century, but the average time served has gone up (Farrington and Jolliffe, 'Crime and punishment', pp. 57–63).
37 Shearing and Stenning, 'Private security'; South, *Policing For Profit*; Johnston, *The Rebirth of Private Policing* and *Policing Britain*; Bayley and Shearing, 'The future of policing'; Loader, 'Consumer culture' and 'Plural policing'; Jones and Newburn, *Private Security and Public Policing*, 'The transformation of policing?' and *Plural Policing*; Johnston and Shearing, *Governing Security*; Crawford, 'The pattern of policing'; Zedner, 'Too much security?' and

'Policing before the police'; Crawford, Lister and Blackburn, *Plural Policing*; Wood and Dupont, *Democracy, Society and the Governance of Security*.

38 Home Office, *Criminal Justice System Review*.

39 Pitts, *The New Politics of Youth Crime*; Newburn, 'Young people, crime and youth justice'; Matthews and Young, *The New Politics of Crime and Punishment*.

40 *Doli incapax* was a rebuttable presumption that children aged between ten and thirteen were not capable of differentiating right from wrong, a necessary element of criminal liability. Children below ten are not deemed criminally responsible. The abolition of *doli incapax* made children of ten to thirteen fully responsible for crime, with their age relevant only to sentencing.

41 Tonry, *Punishment and Politics*, pp. 41–7; Fitzgerald, Stockdale and Hale, *Young People and Street Crime*; Curran et al., *Street Crime in London*.

42 Morris, 'Blair's "frenzied law-making"', p. 1.

43 Blair, 'Foreword', p. 2.

44 Home Office, *Criminal Justice System Review*.

45 Radzinowicz, 'Penal regressions' and *Adventures in Criminology*; Simon, '"They died with their boots on"'; Pratt, 'The return of the wheelbarrow men' and 'Emotive and ostentatious punishment'; Wacquant, 'The new "peculiar institution"'; Pratt et al., *The New Punitiveness*.

46 Zedner, 'Policing before the police'.

47 Shearing and Stenning, 'Private security'.

48 Garland, *The Culture of Control*, p. 199.

49 Tonry, *Thinking about Crime*, p. 23. Tonry is certainly correct that the harshness of recent American penal trends makes the US an outlier among contemporary liberal democracies, but the trajectory towards tougher crime control policies can be found in all of them, in particular England and Wales (Cavadino and Dignan, *Penal Systems*).

50 Garland, *The Culture of Control*, pp. 154–6.

51 Kelling et al., *The Kansas City Preventive Patrol Experiment*. This and other research questioning police effectiveness in

crime control was given much publicity by several influential Home Office publications in the 1980s (Clarke and Hough, *The Effectiveness of Policing* and *Crime and Police Effectiveness*; P. Morris and Heal, *Crime Control and the Police*). The police effectiveness research is reviewed in Bayley, *Police for the Future* and *What Works in Policing?*; Morgan and Newburn, *The Future of Policing*; Reiner, *The Politics of the Police*, ch. 3.

52 Martinson, 'What works?'; Lipton, Martinson and Wilks, *The Effectiveness of Correctional Treatment*. Brody, *The Effectiveness of Sentencing*, was a Home Office study to the same effect.

53 Martinson, 'New findings, new views'.

54 Miller, 'The debate on rehabilitating criminals'.

55 Beckett, *Making Crime Pay*.

56 As anticipated by S. Hall et al., *Policing the Crisis*, at the dawn of these developments.

57 Reiner, Livingstone and Allen, 'No more happy endings?', 'Casino culture' and 'From law and order to lynch mobs'.

58 Reiner, 'Media made criminality', p. 391.

59 Reiner, Livingstone and Allen, 'From law and order to lynch mobs', pp. 25–6. The 1961 story was the first news story about the crime statistics to be found in a large sample of crime stories since the Second World War.

60 Ibid., pp. 26–30.

61 Reiner, Livingstone and Allen, 'No more happy endings?' and 'Casino culture'.

62 Grella, 'Murder and manners', p. 42.

63 This is also true of the *films noirs* that flourished in the late 1940s and early 1950s, which typically featured likable protagonists who were lured into murder and frequently faced execution at the denouement. Audience sympathies were with the murderer, not the victim or the law enforcers, although the necessity of the legal process taking its course was not questioned. The quintessential example is Billy Wilder's 1944 film *Double Indemnity*.

64 Fitzgerald et al., *Policing for London*, p. 80.
65 Livingstone, Reiner and Allen, 'Audiences for crime media'; Gillespie and McLaughlin, *Media and the Shaping of Public Knowledge*.
66 Sparks, *Television and the Drama of Crime*; Hale, 'Fear of crime'; Ditton and Farrall, *The Fear of Crime*; Jackson, 'An analysis of a construct'; Ditton et al., 'From imitation to intimidation'; Jewkes, *Media and Crime*, ch. 6; Chadee and Ditton, 'Fear of crime and the media'; Greer, 'Crime and media', pp. 171–3.
67 Sasson, *Crime Talk*; Beckett, *Making Crime Pay*; Cavender, 'Media and crime policy'; Hough and Roberts, *Understanding Public Attitudes*.
68 Leishman and Mason, *Policing and the Media*.
69 News and fiction stories depict police corruption and malpractice much more frequently (Reiner, Livingstone and Allen, 'No more happy endings?', 'Casino culture', p. 186, and 'From law and order to lynch mobs', pp. 22–4).
70 In a representative sample of cinema films between 1945 and 1964 the most frequent way the crime was cleared up (and almost all were) was by the offender being brought to justice; from the late 1960s this slipped to 10 per cent, and the most common method of clear-up became killing the criminal (Reiner, Livingstone and Allen, 'Casino culture'). In nearly all films before the mid-1960s (89 per cent) the police operated within the restrictions of legal due process; after that they only do so in less than a third. The police do not use any force at all in 54 per cent of films between 1945 and 1964, and in the rest of these they predominantly use only necessary and proportionate (i.e. legal) violence. After the late 1960s they frequently use illegitimate, excessive force.
71 Garland, *The Culture of Control*, pp. 124–31, 184–6.
72 Ibid., pp. 131–5.
73 Beckett and Western, 'Governing social marginality'; Downes and Hansen, 'Welfare and punishment'.
74 Cavadino and Dignan, *Penal Systems*.

75 Tham, 'Crime and the welfare state' and 'Law and order as a leftist project'; Bondeson, 'Levels of punitiveness in Scandinavia'.
76 Bratton, 'Crime is down'.
77 Dixon and Maher, 'Policing, crime and public health'; Jones and Newburn, *Policy Transfer and Criminal Justice*.
78 Bowling, 'The rise and fall of New York murder'; Karmen, *New York Murder Mystery*.
79 For a detailed discussion of these managerial changes see Weisburd et al., 'Reforming to preserve'; Moore, 'Sizing up Compstat'.
80 Levitt, 'Understanding why crime fell'; Levitt and Dubner, *Freakonomics*.
81 Hopkins Burke, *Hard Cop, Soft Cop*.
82 Levitt, 'Understanding why crime fell', pp. 176–7.
83 This is often buttressed by invoking the experience of police strikes, some of which were attended by notorious outbreaks of violence and disorder. But what is less well known is that on other occasions, even in large cities, the police have gone on strike with no discernible consequences for law-breaking (Reiner, *The Blue-Coated Worker*, pp. 5–6). This variability underlines the point that assuming constant elasticity between police numbers and crime, across time and space, is problematic.
84 Clarke and Hough, *Crime and Police Effectiveness*, pp. 6–7.
85 Audit Commission, *Streetwise*.
86 Spelman, 'The limited importance of prison expansion' and 'Jobs or jails?'; Bottoms, 'Empirical evidence'; Western, *Punishment and Inequality in America*.
87 There are, of course, also other purported justifications of punishment in non-utilitarian terms, notably the claim that penalties are proportionate measures of pain meted out to offenders as just desert for their wrongdoing.
88 Home Office, *Making Punishments Work*.
89 Bottoms, 'Empirical evidence', p. 62.
90 Contrast the inspiring record of more humane systems as in Scandinavian countries even today, described recently by Pearce, 'Danish prisons', p. 16.

91 For example the negative Home Office assessment of the 'short sharp shock detention centres' that were a centrepiece of early Thatcherite law and order strategy (Thornton et al., *Tougher Regimes in Detention Centres*).
92 Doob and Webster, 'Sentence severity and crime', p. 134.
93 Although the chances of being caught for a single offence are very small, a prolific offender does face a greater risk of being apprehended eventually.
94 Von Hirsch et al., *Criminal Deterrence and Sentence Severity*; Farrington and Jolliffe, 'Crime and punishment', pp. 70–3.
95 Home Office, *Making Punishments Work*, para. 1.66.
96 Spelman, 'The limited importance of prison expansion' and 'Jobs or jails?'; Bottoms, 'Empirical evidence'.
97 Spelman, 'Jobs or jails?'.
98 Blumstein and Wallman, *The Crime Drop in America*; Bernstein and Houston, *Crime and Work*; Spelman, 'The limited importance of prison expansion' and 'Jobs or jails?'; Karmen, *New York Murder Mystery*; Rosenfeld, 'The case of the unsolved crime decline'; Levitt, 'Understanding why crime fell'; Western, *Punishment and Inequality in America*; Zimring, *The Great American Crime Decline*.

Chapter 6 Conclusion

1 Garland, *The Culture of Control*, pp. 106–7.
2 Spelman, 'Jobs or jails?'. Western, *Punishment and Inequality in America*, ch. 7, confirms this conclusion.
3 O'Malley, 'Risk, power and crime prevention'; Garland, *The Culture of Control*, pp. 124–7.
4 Hacker, *The Great Risk Shift*.
5 Zedner, 'Too much security?'; Ericson, *Crime in an Insecure World*.
6 Shearing and Stenning, 'Private security'.
7 Newburn and Jones, 'Urban change and policing'; Blakely and Snyder, *Fortress America*; Von Hirsch, Garland and Wakefield, *Ethical and Social Perspectives*; Kempa, Stenning and Wood, 'Policing communal spaces'; Atkinson and

Flint, 'Fortress UK?'; Atkinson et al., *Gated Communities in England*; MacLeod, *Privatising the City?*.

8 Low, *Beyond the Gates*.

9 Shearing and Stenning, '"Say cheese!"'.

10 Wakefield, *Selling Security*; Button, *Security Officers and Policing*.

11 Currie, 'Reflections on crime', p. 6.

12 Luxemburg, *The Junius Pamphlet*. See also Lea, *Crime and Modernity*, p. 191.

13 Reiner, 'Beyond risk'.

14 Esping-Andersen, *The Three Worlds of Welfare Capitalism* and 'Inequality of incomes'; Goodin et al., *The Real Worlds of Welfare Capitalism*; P. Hall and Soskice, *Varieties of Capitalism*; Glyn, *Social Democracy in Neo-liberal Times*; Held, *Global Covenant*; R. Taylor, *Sweden's New Social Democratic Model*.

15 Beckett and Western, 'Governing social marginality'; Cavadino and Dignan, *Penal Systems*; Downes and Hansen, 'Welfare and punishment'.

16 Currie, 'Market, crime and community'; Wilkinson, *The Impact of Inequality*; S. Hall and Winlow, 'Barbarians at the gates'; S. Hall and Maclean, 'A tale of two capitalisms'; Reiner, 'Political economy'.

17 Davies, 'How the richest man in Britain avoids tax'. 'Defining deviancy down' was the title of an influential 1993 article by the late Senator Daniel Patrick Moynihan decrying a perceived trend to greater acceptance of 'minor' deviance, in effect advocating what would now be called zero tolerance (*American Scholar*, 62 (Winter 1993): 17–30).

18 Cook, *Criminal and Social Justice*.

19 Held, *Global Covenant*, p. 15; Harvey, *A Brief History of Neoliberalism*, ch. 7.

20 Hart Research, *Changing Public Attitudes*, pp. 1–2. See also Hough and Park, 'How malleable are attitudes to crime and punishment?'; Hough and Roberts, *Understanding Public Attitudes*; Allen, 'What works in changing public attitudes to prison'.

21 Wilby, 'Thatcherism's final triumph'.
22 Fones-Wolf, *Selling Free Enterprise*; Frank, *One Market under God*; Harvey, *A Brief History of Neoliberalism*, ch. 2.
23 Cohen, *If You're an Egalitarian.*
24 Lukes, *Marxism and Morality*, p. 70.
25 Harvey, *A Brief History of Neoliberalism*, p. 20.
26 Quoted in Jenkins, *Mrs Thatcher's Revolution*, p. 142.
27 In the words of the advertising slogan for Tesco, the largest UK supermarket chain – not best noted for social democratic philosophy.
28 Rabbi Tarphon, *Ethics of the Fathers*,. 2:21.

References

Allen, J., Livingstone, S. and Reiner, R., 'True lies: changing images of crime in British postwar cinema', *European Journal of Communication*, 13/1 (1998): 53–75.

Allen, R., 'What works in changing public attitudes to prison: lessons from rethinking crime and punishment', in P. Mason (ed.), *Captured by the Media*, Cullompton: Willan, 2006.

Ashworth, A., 'Is the criminal law a lost cause?' *Law Quarterly Review*, 116/2 (2000): 225–56.

Ashworth, A., 'Social control and "anti-social behaviour": the subversion of human rights', *Law Quarterly Review*, 120/2 (2004): 263–91.

Ashworth, A., 'Sentencing', in M. Maguire, R. Morgan and R. Reiner (eds), *The Oxford Handbook of Criminology*, 4th edn, Oxford: Oxford University Press, 2007.

Ashworth, A. and Redmayne, M., *The Criminal Process*, 3rd edn. Oxford: Oxford University Press, 2005.

Atkinson, R. and Flint, J., 'Fortress UK? Gated communities, the spatial revolt of the elites and time-space trajectories of segregation', *Housing Studies*, 19/6 (2004): 875–92.

Atkinson, R., Blandy, S., Flint, J. and Lister, D., *Gated Communities in England*. London: Office of the Deputy Prime Minister, 2003.

Audit Commission, *Streetwise: Effective Police Patrol*. London: Audit Commission, 1996.

Bakan, J., *The Corporation*. London: Constable, 2005.

Baker, K., *The Turbulent Years*. London: Faber, 1993.

Barclay, G. and Tavares, C., *Digest 4: Information on the Criminal Justice System in England and Wales*. London: Home Office, 1999.

Barclay, G. and Tavares, C., *International Comparisons of Criminal Justice Statistics 2001*. London: Home Office, 2003.

Barclay, G., Tavares, C. and Prout, A., *Digest 3: Information on the Criminal Justice System in England and Wales*. London: Home Office, 1995.

Bayley, D., *Police for the Future*. New York: Oxford University Press, 1994.

Bayley, D. (ed.), *What Works in Policing?* New York: Oxford University Press, 1998.

Bayley, D. and Shearing, C., 'The future of policing', *Law and Society Review*, 30/3 (1996): 586–606.

Beck, U., *Risk Society*. London: Sage, 1992.

Becker, G., 'Crime and punishment: an economic approach', *Journal of Political Economy*, 76 (1968): 175–209.

Becker, H., *Outsiders*. New York: Free Press, 1963.

Beckett, K., *Making Crime Pay*. New York: Oxford University Press, 1997.

Beckett, K. and Sasson, T., *The Politics of Injustice*, 2nd edn. Thousand Oaks: Pine Forge, 2003.

Beckett, K. and Western, B., 'Governing social marginality: welfare, incarceration and the transformation of state policy', *Punishment and Society*, 3 (2001): 43–59.

Beirne, P., *Inventing Criminology*. Albany: SUNY Press, 1993.

Bernstein, J. and Houston, E., *Crime and Work*. Washington DC: Economic Policy Institute, 2000.

Bevir, M., *New Labour: A Critique*. London: Routledge, 2005.

Bittner, E., *The Functions of the Police in Modern Society*. Chevy Chase, MD: National Institute of Mental Health, 1970.

Blair, T., 'Why crime is a socialist issue', *New Statesman*, 25 Jan. 1993.

Blair, T., 'A new consensus on law and order', speech 19 July 2004, At http://news.bbc.co.uk/1/hi/uk_politics/3907651.stm.

Blair, T., 'Our citizens should not live in fear', *Observer*, 11 Dec 2005, p. 30.

Blair, T., 'Foreword', in *Rebalancing the Criminal Justice System in Favour of the Law-Abiding Majority*, London: Home Office, 2006.

Blakely, E. J. and Snyder, M. G., *Fortress America: Gated Communities in the United States*. Washington DC: Brookings Institution, 1999.

Blumstein, A. and Wallman, J. (eds), *The Crime Drop in America*. Cambridge: Cambridge University Press, 2000.

Blyth, M., *Great Transformations: Economic Ideas and Institutional Change in the Twentieth Century*. Cambridge: Cambridge University Press, 2002.

Bondeson, U., 'Levels of punitiveness in Scandinavia: description and explanations', in J. Pratt et al. (eds), *The New Punitiveness*, Cullompton: Willan, 2005.

Bonger, W., *Criminality and Economic Conditions* (1916). Bloomington: Indiana University Press, 1969.

Bottomley, K. and Coleman, C., *Understanding Crime Rates*. Farnborough: Gower, 1981.

Bottomley, K. and Pease, K., *Crime and Punishment: Interpreting the Data*. Milton Keynes: Open University Press, 1986.

Bottoms, A., 'Empirical evidence relevant to sentencing frameworks', in A. Bottoms, S. Rex and G. Robinson (eds), *Alternatives to Prison*, Cullompton: Willan, 2004.

Bottoms, A. and Stevenson, S., 'What went wrong? Criminal justice policy in England and Wales 1945–70', in D. Downes (ed.), *Unravelling Criminal Justice*. London: Macmillan, 1992.

Bottoms, A., Rex, S. and Robinson, G. (eds), *Alternatives to Prison*. Cullompton: Willan, 2004.

Bowling, B., 'The rise and fall of New York murder', *British Journal of Criminology*, 39 (1999): 531–54.

Bowling, B. and Phillips, C., *Racism, Crime and Justice*. London: Longman, 2002.

Bowling, B. and Phillips, C., 'Policing ethnic minority communities', in T. Newburn (ed.), *Handbook of Policing*, Cullompton: Willan, 2003.

Box, S., *Recession, Crime and Punishment*. London: Macmillan, 1987.

Brake, M. and Hale, C., *Public Order and Private Lives: The Politics of Law and Order*. London: Routledge, 1991.
Bratton, W., 'Crime is down: blame the police', in N. Dennis (ed.), *Zero Tolerance: Policing a Free Society*, 2nd edn, London: Institute of Economic Affairs, 1998.
Brewer, M., Goodman, A., Shaw, J. and Sibieta, L., *Poverty and Inequality in Britain: 2006*. London: Institute for Fiscal Studies, 2006.
Brody, S. R., *The Effectiveness of Sentencing*. London: HMSO, 1975.
Budd, T., Sharp, C., Weir, G., Wilson, D. and Owen, N., *Young People and Crime (Appendix D)*. London: Home Office, 2005.
Burney, E., *Making People Behave: Anti-social Behaviour, Politics and Policy*. Cullompton: Willan, 2005.
Burrows, J., Tarling, R., Mackic, A., Lewis, R. and Taylor, G., *Review of Police Forces' Crime Recording Practices*. London: Home Office, 2000.
Butler, D. and Kavanagh, D., *The British General Election of 1979*. London: Macmillan, 1980.
Button, M., *Security Officers and Policing*. Aldershot: Ashgate, 2007.
Campbell, B., *Goliath: Britain's Dangerous Places*. London: Methuen, 1991.
Cantor, D. and Land, K. C., 'Unemployment and crime rates in post World War II United States: a theoretical and empirical analysis', *American Sociological Review*, 50 (1985): 317–32.
Carter, P., *Managing Offenders, Reducing Crime*. London: Home Office, 2003.
Cavadino, M. and Dignan, J., *Penal Systems: A Comparative Approach*. London: Sage, 2006.
Cavender, G., 'Media and crime policy', *Punishment and Society*, 6/3 (2004): 335–48.
Chadee, D. and Ditton, J., 'Fear of crime and the media: assessing the lack of relationship', *Crime, Media, Culture*, 1/3 (2005): 322–32.
Chiricos, T. G., 'Rates of crime and unemployment', *Social Problems*, 34 (1987): 187–211.

Clarke, R., *Situational Crime Prevention*, 2nd edn. New York: Harrow and Heston, 1997.
Clarke, R. and Hough, M. (eds), *The Effectiveness of Policing*. Farnborough: Gower, 1980.
Clarke, R. and Hough, M., *Crime and Police Effectiveness*. London: Home Office, 1984.
Clarke, R. and Mayhew, P. (eds), *Designing out Crime*. London: Home Office, 1980.
Clarke, R. and Mayhew, P., 'The British gas suicide story and its criminological implications', in M. Tonry and N. Morris (eds), *Crime and Justice 10*, Chicago: Chicago University Press, 1988.
Cockburn, J. S., *Crime in England 1550–1800*. London: Methuen, 1977.
Cohen, G., *If You're an Egalitarian, How Come You're So Rich?* Cambridge, MA.: Harvard University Press, 2001.
Cohen, L. and Felson, M., 'Social change and crime rate trends: a routine activities approach', *American Sociological Review*, 44/4 (1979): 588–608.
Cohen, N., 'How Blair put 30,000 more in jail', *New Statesman*, 16 Dec. 2002.
Cohen, N., *Pretty Straight Guys*. London: Faber, 2004.
Cohen, S., 'The revenge of the null hypothesis: evaluating crime control policies', *Critical Criminologist*, 8/1 (1997).
Cohen, S., 'Crime and politics: spot the difference', in R. Rawlings (ed.), *Law, Society and Economy*, Oxford: Oxford University Press, 1997.
Cohen, S., *States of Denial*. Cambridge: Polity, 2000.
Coleman, C. and Moynihan, J., *Understanding Crime Data*. Buckingham: Open University Press, 1996.
Cook, D., *Criminal and Social Justice*. London: Sage, 2006.
Cornish, D. and Clarke, R. (eds), *The Reasoning Criminal*. New York: Springer-Verlag, 1986.
Crawford, A., 'The pattern of policing in the UK: policing beyond the police', in T. Newburn (ed.), *Handbook of Policing*, Cullompton: Willan, 2003.
Crawford, A., Lister, S. and Blackburn, S., *Plural Policing*. Bristol: Policy Press, 2005.

Curran, K., Dale, M., Edmunds, M., Hough, M., Millie, A. and Wagstaff, M., *Street Crime in London*. London: Government Office for London, 2005.

Currie, E., *Confronting Crime*. New York: Pantheon, 1985.

Currie, E., 'Market, crime and community: toward a mid-range theory of post-industrial violence', *Theoretical Criminology*, 1 (1997): 147–72.

Currie, E., *Crime and Punishment in America*. New York: Holt, 1998.

Currie, E., 'Crime and market society: lessons from the United States', in P. Walton and J. Young (eds), *The New Criminology Revisited*, London: Macmillan, 1998.

Currie, E., 'Reflections on crime and criminology at the millennium', *Western Criminology Review*, 2/1 (2000): 1–15.

Davies, N., *Dark Heart*. London: Verso, 1998.

Davies, N., 'Watching the detectives: how the police cheat in the fight against crime', *Guardian*, 18 Mar. 1999.

Davies, N., 'How the richest man in Britain avoids tax', *Guardian*, 11 Apr. 2002.

Davies, N., 'Fiddling the figures', *Guardian*, 11 July 2003.

Davies, N., 'Exposing the myth of the falling crime rate', *Guardian*, 10 July 2003.

Deadman, D. and Macdonald, Z., 'Why has crime fallen? An economic perspective', *Economic Affairs*, 22 (2002): 5–14.

Della Porta, D. and Reiter, H. (eds), *Policing Protest*. Minneapolis: University of Minnesota Press, 1998.

Dennis, I. (ed.), *Criminal Law and Justice*. London: Sweet and Maxwell, 1987.

Dennis, N. and Erdos, G., *Cultures and Crimes: Policing in Four Nations*. London: Civitas, 2005.

Devlin, P., *The Enforcement of Morals*. Oxford: Oxford University Press, 1965.

Dhiri, S., Brand, S., Harries, R. and Price, R., *Modelling and Predicting Property Crime Trends in England and Wales*. London: Home Office, 1999.

Ditton, J. and Farrall, S. (eds), *The Fear of Crime*. Aldershot: Dartmouth, 2000.

Ditton, J., Chadee, D., Farrall, S., Gilchrist, E. and Bannister, J., 'From imitation to intimidation: a note on the curious and changing relationship between the media, crime and fear of crime', *British Journal of Criminology*, 44/4 (2004): 595–610.

Dixon, D. and Maher, L., 'Policing, crime and public health: lessons for Australia from the "New York miracle"', *Criminal Justice*, 5 (2005): 115–44.

Donnelly, M., *Sixties Britain: Culture, Society and Politics*. London: Longman, 2005.

Doob, A. and Webster, C., 'Sentence severity and crime: accepting the null hypothesis', in M. Tonry (ed.), *Crime and Justice 30*, Chicago: Chicago University Press, 2003.

Dorling, D., 'Prime suspect: murder in Britain', in P. Hillyard, C. Pantazis, S. Tombs and D. Gordon (eds), *Beyond Criminology*, London: Pluto, 2004.

Downes, D., *The Delinquent Solution*. London: Routledge, 1966.

Downes, D., *Law and Order: Theft of an Issue*. London: Fabian Society and Labour Campaign for Criminal Justice, 1983.

Downes, D., *Contrasts in Tolerance*. Oxford: Oxford University Press, 1988.

Downes, D., 'Back to the future: the predictive value of social theories of delinquency', in S. Holdaway and P. Rock (eds), *Thinking about Criminology*, London: UCL Press, 1998.

Downes, D., 'New Labour and the lost causes of crime', *Criminal Justice Matters*, 55 (2004): 4–5.

Downes, D. and Hansen, K., 'Welfare and punishment in comparative perspective', in S. Armstrong and L. McAra (eds), *Perspectives on Punishment*, Oxford: Oxford University Press, 2006.

Downes, D. and Morgan, R., 'The skeletons in the cupboard: the politics of law and order at the turn of the Millennium', in M. Maguire, R. Morgan and R. Reiner (eds), *The Oxford Handbook of Criminology*, 3rd edn, Oxford: Oxford University Press, 2002.

Downes, D. and Rock, P., *Understanding Deviance*, 4th edn. Oxford: Oxford University Press, 2003.

Dumenil, G. and Levy, D., *Capital Resurgent: Roots of the Neoliberal Revolution*. Cambridge, MA: Harvard University Press, 2004.

Durkheim, E., *The Division of Labour in Society* (1893). Glencoe: Free Press, 1973.

Durkheim, E., *Suicide* (1897). London: Routledge, 1951.

Eck, J. and Maguire, E., 'Have changes in policing reduced violent crime?', in A. Bloomstein and J. Wallman (eds), *The Crime Drop in America*, Cambridge: Cambridge University Press, 2000.

Ehrlich, I., 'Participation in illegal activities: a theoretical and empirical investigation', *Journal of Political Economy*, 81 (1973): 521–63.

Ehrlich, I., 'The deterrent effect of capital punishment', *American Economic Review*, 65 (1975): 397–447.

Eisner, M., 'Modernisation, self-control and lethal violence: the long-term dynamics of European homicide rates in theoretical perspective', *British Journal of Criminology*, 41 (2001): 618–38.

Ekblom, P. and Tilley, N., 'Going equipped: criminology, situational crime prevention and the resourceful offender', *British Journal of Criminology*, 40 (2000): 376–98.

Elias, N., *The Civilizing Process* (1939). Oxford: Blackwell, 1994.

Emmerson, B. and Ashworth, A., *Human Rights and Criminal Justice*. London: Sweet and Maxwell, 2001.

Emsley, C., 'The history of crime and crime control institutions', in M. Maguire, R. Morgan and R. Reiner (eds), *The Oxford Handbook of Criminology*, 3rd edn, Oxford: Oxford University Press, 2002.

Emsley, C., 'Historical perspectives on crime', in M. Maguire, R. Morgan and R. Reiner (eds), *The Oxford Handbook of Criminology*, 4th edn, Oxford: Oxford University Press, 2007.

Ericson, R., *Crime in an Insecure World*. Cambridge: Polity, 2006.

Esping-Andersen, G., *The Three Worlds of Welfare Capitalism*. Cambridge: Polity, 1990.

Esping-Andersen, G., 'Inequality of incomes and opportunities', in A. Giddens and P. Diamond (eds), *The New Egalitarianism*, Cambridge: Polity, 2005.

Eysenck, H., *Crime and Personality*. London: Flamingo, 1970.

Farmer, L., 'The obsession with definition', *Social and Legal Studies*, 5/1 (1996): 57–73.

Farrington, D. and Jolliffe, D., 'Crime and punishment in England and Wales 1981–99', in M. Tonry and D. Farrington (eds), *Crime and Punishment in Western Countries 1980–1999*, Chicago: Chicago University Press, 2005.

Farrington, D., Galagher, B., Morley, L., St Ledger, R. J. and West, D. J., 'Unemployment, school leaving and crime', *British Journal of Criminology*, 26/4 (1986): 335–56.

Feinberg, J., *The Moral Limits of the Criminal Law*, vols 1–4. New York: Oxford University Press, 1984–90.

Felson, M., *Crime and Everyday Life*. Thousand Oaks, CA: Pine Forge, 1994.

Felson, M. and Clarke, R., *Opportunity Makes the Thief*. London: Home Office, 1998.

Field, S., *Trends in Crime and their Interpretation: A Study of Recorded Crime in Post-war England and Wales*. London: Home Office, 1990.

Field, S., *Trends in Crime Revisited*. London: Home Office, 1999.

Fielding, N., Clarke, A. and Witt, R. (eds), *The Economic Dimensions of Crime*. London: Palgrave, 2000.

Fitzgerald, M., Stockdale, J. and Hale, C., *Young People and Street Crime*. London: Youth Justice Board, 2003.

Fitzgerald, M., Hough, M., Joseph, I. and Qureshi, T., *Policing for London*. Cullompton: Willan, 2002.

Fletcher, J., *Violence and Civilization*. Cambridge: Polity, 1997.

Fones-Wolf, E., *Selling Free Enterprise: The Business Assault on Labour and Liberalism, 1945–1960*. Urbana: University of Illinois Press, 1994.

Frank, T., *One Market under God*. London: Secker and Warburg, 2001.

Freeman, M., 'Law and order in 1984', *Current Legal Problems 1984* (1984): 175–231.

Freeman, R., 'Crime and unemployment', in J. Q. Wilson (ed.), *Crime and Public Policy*, San Francisco: Institute of Contemporary Studies, 1983.

Freud, S., *Civilisation and its Discontents* (1930). London: Penguin, 2004.

Galbraith, J. K., *The Affluent Society*. London: Penguin, 1958.

Gamble, A., *The Free Economy and the Strong State*. London: Macmillan, 1994.

Gamble, A., *Hayek: The Iron Cage of Liberty*. Cambridge: Polity, 1996.

Garland, D., *Punishment and Welfare*. Aldershot: Gower, 1985.

Garland, D., *The Culture of Control*. Oxford: Oxford University Press, 2001.

Garside, R., *Crime, Persistent Offenders, and the Justice Gap*. London: Crime and Society Foundation, 2004.

Garside, R., 'Is it the Economy?', *Criminal Justice Matters*, 55 (2004): 32–3.

Garside, R., *Right for the Wrong Reasons: Making Sense of Criminal Justice Failure*. London: Crime and Society Foundation, 2006.

Gatrell, V., 'The decline of theft and violence in Victorian and Edwardian England', in V. Gatrell, B. Lenman and G. Parker (eds), *Crime and the Law*, London: Europa, 1980.

Geary, R., *Policing Industrial Disputes*. Cambridge: Cambridge University Press, 1985.

Gelsthorpe, L., 'Feminism and criminology', in M. Maguire, R. Morgan and R. Reiner (eds), *The Oxford Handbook of Criminology*, 3rd edn, Oxford: Oxford University Press, 2002.

Giddens, A., *Modernity and Self Identity*. Cambridge: Polity, 1991.

Giddens, A., *The Third Way*. Cambridge: Polity, 1998.

Giddens, A., 'Egalitarianism: old and new', Miliband Lecture, London School of Economics, London, 7 Oct. 2004.

Gilbert, J., 'The second wave: the specificity of New Labour neo-liberalism', *Soundings*, 26 (Spring 2004): 25–45.

Gill, M., 'Reducing the capacity to offend', in N. Tilley (ed.), *Handbook of Crime Prevention and Community Safety*, Cullompton: Willan, 2005.

Gillespie, M. and McLaughlin, E., *Media and the Shaping of Public Knowledge and Attitudes towards Crime and Punishment*. London: Rethinking Crime and Punishment, 2003.

Glyn, A. (ed.), *Social Democracy in Neo-liberal Times*. Oxford: Oxford University Press, 2001.

Glyn, A., *Capitalism Unleashed*. Oxford: Oxford University Press, 2006.

Gobert, J. and Punch, M., *Rethinking Corporate Crime*. London: Butterworths, 2003.

Goodin, R., Headey, B., Muffels, R. and Dirven, H.-J., *The Real Worlds of Welfare Capitalism*. Cambridge: Cambridge University Press, 1999.

Goodman, A. and Webb, S., *For Richer, For Poorer: The Changing Distribution of Income in the United Kingdom, 1961–1991*. London: Institute for Fiscal Studies, 1994.

Gottfredson, M. and Hirschi, T., *A General Theory of Crime*. Stanford: Stanford University Press, 1990.

Grant, C., Harvey, A., Bolling, K. and Clemens, S., *2004–5 British Crime Survey Technical Report*. London: Home Office, 2006.

Green, D., Grove, E. and Martin, N., *Crime and Civil Society*. London: Civitas, 2005.

Green, P. and Ward, T., *State Crime*. London: Pluto, 2004.

Greer, C., *Sex Crime and the Media*. Cullompton: Willan, 2003.

Greer, C., 'Crime and media', in C. Hale et al. (eds), *Criminology*, Oxford: Oxford University Press, 2005.

Grella, G., 'Murder and manners: the formal detective story', *Novel*, 4/1 (1970): 30–48.

Grogger, J., 'Market wages and youth crime', *Journal of Labour Economics*, 16 (1998): 756–91.

Grogger, J., 'An economic model of recent trends in violence', in A. Bloomstein and J. Wallman (eds), *The Crime Drop in America*, Cambridge: Cambridge University Press, 2000.

Gurr, T. R., 'Historical trends in violent crime', in M. Tonry and N. Morris (eds), *Crime and Justice 3*, Chicago: Chicago University Press, 1981.

Gurr, T. R., Grabosky, P. and Hula, R., *The Politics of Crime and Conflict: A Comparative History of Four Cities*. Beverly Hills: Sage, 1977.

Hacker, J., *The Great Risk Shift: The Assault on American Jobs, Families, Health Care and Retirement and How You Can Fight Back*. New York: Oxford University Press, 2006.

Hale, C., 'Fear of crime: a review of the literature', *International Review of Victimology*, 4/1 (1996): 79–150.

Hale, C., 'Crime and the business cycle in post-war Britain revisited', *British Journal of Criminology*, 38 (1998): 681–98.

Hale, C., 'The labour market and post-war crime trends in England and Wales', in P. Carlen and R. Morgan (eds), *Crime Unlimited*, London: Macmillan, 1999.

Hale, C., 'Economic marginalization and social exclusion', in C. Hale, K. Hayward, A. Wahidin and E. Wincup (eds), *Criminology*, Oxford: Oxford University Press, 2005.

Hale, C., 'The politics of law and order', in C. Hale, K. Hayward, A. Wahidin and E. Wincup (eds), *Criminology*, Oxford: Oxford University Press, 2005.

Hall, J., *Theft, Law and Society* (1935), 2nd edn. Indianapolis: Bobbs-Merrill, 1952.

Hall, P. and Soskice, D. (eds), *Varieties of Capitalism*. Oxford: Oxford University Press, 2001.

Hall, S., 'Visceral cultures and criminal practices', *Theoretical Criminology*, 1 (1997): 453–78.

Hall, S. and McLean, C., 'A tale of two capitalisms: a preliminary comparison of violence rates in European and Anglo-American market societies', MS, Division of Sociology and Criminology, University of Northumbria, 2006.

Hall, S. and Winlow, S., 'Rehabilitating Leviathan: reflections on the state, economic regulation and violence reduction', *Theoretical Criminology*, 7 (2003): 139–62.

Hall, S. and Winlow, S., 'Barbarians at the gates: crime and violence in the breakdown of the pseudo-pacification process', in J. Ferrell, K. Hayward, W. Morrison and M. Presdee (eds), *Cultural Criminology Unleashed*, London: Glasshouse, 2004.

Hall, S., Critcher, C., Jefferson, T., Clarke, J. and Roberts, B., *Policing the Crisis*. London: Macmillan, 1978.

Hallsworth, S., *Street Crime*. Cullompton: Willan, 2005.

Hansen, K. and Machin, S., 'Spatial crime patterns and the introduction of the UK minimum wage', *Oxford Bulletin of Economics and Statistics*, 64 (2002): 677–97.

Harbord, J. and Wright, J., *Forty Years of British Television*. London: Boxtree, 1995.

Hart, H., *The Concept of Law*. Oxford: Oxford University Press, 1961.

Hart, H., *Law, Liberty and Morality*. Oxford: Oxford University Press, 1963.

Hart Research, *Changing Public Attitudes toward the Criminal Justice System*. Washington DC: Peter D. Hart Research Associates, 2002.

Harvey, D., *A Brief History of Neoliberalism*. Oxford: Oxford University Press, 2005.

Hayek, F., *The Road to Serfdom* (1944). London: Routledge, 2001.

Hayward, K., *City Limits: Crime, Consumer Culture and the Urban Experience*. London: Glasshouse, 2004.

Hearnden, I. and Hough, M., *Race and the Criminal Justice System: An Overview to the Complete Statistics 2002–3*. London: Kings College Institute for Criminal Policy Research, 2004.

Heidensohn, F., 'Gender and crime', in M. Maguire, R. Morgan and R. Reiner (eds), *The Oxford Handbook of Criminology*, 3rd edn, Oxford: Oxford University Press, 2002.

Heidensohn, F., 'Gender and policing', in T. Newburn (ed.), *Handbook of Policing*, Cullompton: Willan, 2003.

Held, D., *Global Covenant*. Cambridge: Polity, 2004.

Hennessy, P., *Never Again: Britain, 1945–1951*. London: Vintage, 1993.

Henry, S. and Lanier, M. (eds), *What is Crime?* Lanham, MD: Rowman and Littlefield, 2001.

Hills, J., *Inequality and the State*. Oxford: Oxford University Press, 2004.

Hills, J. and Stewart, K. (eds), *A More Equal Society?* Bristol: Policy Press, 2005.

Hillyard, P., Pantazis, C., Tombs, S. and Gordon, D. (eds), *Beyond Criminology: Taking Harm Seriously*. London: Pluto, 2004.

Hirschi, T., *Causes of Delinquency*. Berkeley: University of California Press, 1969.

Hirschi, T. and Gottfredson, M. (eds), *The Generality of Deviance*. Piscataway, NJ: Transaction, 1994.

Hobbs, D., *Bad Business: Professional Crime in Modern Britain*. Oxford: Oxford University Press, 1995.

Home Office, *Criminal Statistics, England and Wales*. London: Home Office, various years.

Home Office, *Making Punishments Work: Report of a Review of the Sentencing Framework for England and Wales*. London: Home Office, 2001.

Home Office, *Counting Rules for Recording Crime* (2006), General Rule A. At www.homeoffice.gov.uk/rds/countrules.html.

Home Office, *Criminal Justice System Review: Rebalancing the Criminal Justice System in Favour of the Law-Abiding Majority*. London: Home Office, 2006.

Hood, R. and Joyce, K., 'Three generations: oral testimonies on crime and social change in London's East End', *British Journal of Criminology*, 39/1 (1999): 136–60.

Hopkins Burke, R. (ed.), *Hard Cop, Soft Cop*. Cullompton: Willan, 2004.

Horton, J., 'The dehumanisation of anomie and alienation', *British Journal of Sociology*, 15/2 (1964): 283–300.

Hough, M., 'Modernization and public opinion: some criminal justice paradoxes', *Contemporary Politics*, 9 (2003): 143–55.

Hough, M., 'Policing, new public management and legitimacy in Britain', in J. Fagan and T. Tyler (eds), *Legitimacy, Criminal Justice, and the Law*, New York: Russell Sage Foundation Press, forthcoming.

Hough, M. and Mayhew, P., *The British Crime Survey*. London: Home Office, 1983.

Hough, M. and Mayhew, P., *Taking Account of Crime: Key Findings from the Second British Crime Survey*. London: Home Office, 1985.

Hough, M. and Park, A., 'How malleable are attitudes to crime and punishment? Findings from a British deliberative poll', in J. Roberts and M. Hough (eds), *Changing Attitudes to Punishment*, Cullompton: Willan, 2002.

Hough, M. and Roberts, J., *Understanding Public Attitudes to Criminal Justice*. Maidenhead: Open University Press, 2005.

Hough, M., Jacobson, J. and Millie, A., *The Decision to Imprison: Sentencing and the Prison Population*. London: Prison Reform Trust, 2003.

Hough, M., Millie, A. and Jacobson, J., *Anti-social Behaviour Strategies*. Bristol: Policy Press, 2005.

Hough, M., Mirrlees-Black, C. and Dale, M., *Trends in Violent Crimes since 1999/2000*. London: Institute for Criminal Policy Research, King's College London, 2005.

Hoyle, C., *Negotiating Domestic Violence: Police, Criminal Justice and Victims*. Oxford: Oxford University Press, 1998.

Innes, M., '"Signal crimes": detective work, mass media and constructing collective memory', in P. Mason (ed.), *Criminal Visions*, Cullompton: Willan, 2003.

Innes, M., *Understanding Social Control*. Maidenhead: Open University Press, 2003

Innes, M. (ed.), 'Reassurance and the "new" community policing', special issue of *Policing and Society*, 16/2 (2006).

Innes, M. and Fielding, N., 'From community to communicative policing: "signal crimes" and the problem of public reassurance', *Sociological Research Online*, 7/2 (2002), at www.socresonline.org.uk.

Jackson, J., 'An analysis of a construct and debate: the fear of crime', in H.-J. Albrecht, T. Serassis and H. Kania (eds), *Images of Crime II*, Freiburg: Max Planck Institute, 2004.

Jackson, T., *Chasing Progress: Beyond Economic Growth*. London: New Economics Foundation, 2004.

Jacobs, B. and Wright, R., 'Stick-up, street culture, and offender motivation', *Criminology*, 37/1 (1999): 149–73.

Jacobs, L. and Skocpol, T. (eds), *Inequality and American Democracy*. New York: Russell Sage Foundation, 2005.

James, O., *Juvenile Violence in a Winner–Loser Society*. London: Free Association Books, 1995.

Jeffery, C. R., 'The development of crime in early English society', *Journal of Criminal Law, Criminology and Police Science*, 47 (1957): 647–66; reprinted in W. Chambliss (ed.), *Crime and the Legal Process*, New York: McGraw-Hill, 1969.
Jenkins, P., *Mrs Thatcher's Revolution*. London: Pan, 1989.
Jewkes, Y. (ed.), *Dot.Cons: Crime, Deviance and Identity on the Internet*. Cullompton: Willan, 2003.
Jewkes, Y., *Media and Crime*. London: Sage, 2004.
Johnston, L., *The Rebirth of Private Policing*. London: Routledge, 1992.
Johnston, L., *Policing Britain*. London: Longman, 2000.
Johnston, L. and Shearing, C., *Governing Security*. London: Routledge, 2003.
Jones, T. and Newburn, T., *Private Security and Public Policing*. Oxford: Oxford University Press, 1998.
Jones, T. and Newburn, T., 'The transformation of policing? Understanding current trends in policing systems', *British Journal of Criminology*, 42/1 (2002): 129–46.
Jones, T. and Newburn, T., *Policy Transfer and Criminal Justice*. Maidenhead: Open University Press, 2006.
Jones, T. and Newburn, T. (eds), *Plural Policing: A Comparative Perspective*. London: Routledge, 2006.
Jones, T., MacLean, B. and Young, J., *The Islington Crime Survey*. Aldershot: Gower, 1986.
Karmen, A., *New York Murder Mystery*. New York: New York University Press, 2000.
Karstedt, S. and Farrall, S., 'The moral maze of the middle class', in H.-J. Albrecht, T. Serassis and H. Kania (eds), *Images of Crime II*, Freiburg: Max Planck Institute, 2004.
Katz, J., *Seductions of Crime*. New York: Basic Books, 1988.
Kay, J., *The Truth about Markets*. London: Penguin, 2004.
Kelling, G., Pate, T., Dieckman, D. and Brown, C., *The Kansas City Preventive Patrol Experiment*. Washington DC: Police Foundation, 1974.
Kempa, M., Stenning, P. and Wood, J., 'Policing communal spaces: a reconfiguration of the "mass private property" hypothesis', *British Journal of Criminology*, 44/4 (2004): 562–81.

Kennedy, M., 'Beyond incrimination', *Catalyst*, 5 (1970): 1–37; reprinted in W. Chambliss and M. Mankoff (eds), *Whose Law? What Order?* New York: Wiley, 1976.

Kinsey, R., *The Merseyside Crime Survey*. Liverpool: Merseyside County Council, 1984.

Kinsey, R., Lea, J. and Young, J., *Losing the Fight against Crime*. Oxford: Blackwell, 1986.

Kleck, G. and Chiricos, T., 'Unemployment and property crime: a target-specific assessment of opportunity and motivation as mediating factors', *Criminology*, 40 (2002): 649–79.

Krugman, P., 'Who was Milton Friedman?', *New York Review of Books*, 54/2 (15 Feb. 2007): 27–30.

Lacey, N., 'Contingency and criminalisation', in I. Loveland (ed.), *Frontiers of Criminality*, London: Sweet and Maxwell, 1995.

Lacey, N., 'Legal constructions of crime', in M. Maguire, R. Morgan and R. Reiner (eds), *The Oxford Handbook of Criminology*, 3rd edn, Oxford: Oxford University Press, 2002.

Lacey, N., Wells, C. and Quick, O., *Reconstructing Criminal Law*, 3rd edn. London: Butterworths, 2003.

Lawson, N., 'Turbo-consumerism is the driving force behind crime', *Guardian*, 29 June 2006.

Lea, J., *Crime and Modernity*. London: Sage, 2002.

Lea, J. and Young, J., *What is to be Done about Law and Order?* London: Penguin, 1984.

Lee, S., *Law and Morals*. Oxford: Oxford University Press, 1987.

Leishman, F. and Mason, P., *Policing and the Media*. Cullompton: Willan, 2003.

Levitas, R., 'Shuffling back to equality?' *Soundings*, 26 (Spring 2004): 59–72.

Levitt, S., 'Understanding why crime fell in the 1990s: four factors that explain the decline and six that do not', *Journal of Economic Perspectives*, 18/1 (2004): 163–90.

Levitt, S. and Dubner, S., *Freakonomics*. London: Penguin, 2006.

Leys, C., *Market-Driven Politics: Neoliberal Democracy and the Public Interest*. London: Verso, 2003.

Lipton, D. S., Martinson, R. and Wilks, J., *The Effectiveness of Correctional Treatment*. New York: Praeger, 1975.

Livingstone, S., Reiner, R. and Allen, J., 'Audiences for crime media 1946–91: a historical approach to reception studies', *Communication Review*, 4/2 (2001): 165–93.

Loader, I., 'Consumer culture and the commodification of policing and security', *Sociology*, 33/2 (1999): 373–92.

Loader, I., 'Plural policing and democratic governance', *Social and Legal Studies*, 9/3 (2000): 323–45.

Loader, I. and Mulcahy, A., *Policing and the Condition of England*. Oxford: Oxford University Press, 2003.

Long, M., 'Leadership and performance management', in T. Newburn (ed.), *Handbook of Policing*, Cullompton: Willan, 2003.

Longford Study Group, *Crime: A Challenge to Us All*. London: Labour Party, 1966.

Loveland, I. (ed.), *Frontiers of Criminality*. London: Sweet and Maxwell, 1995.

Low, S., *Beyond the Gates*. New York: Routledge, 2003.

Lukes, S., *Marxism and Morality*. Oxford: Oxford University Press, 1985.

Lukes, S., *Liberals and Cannibals: The Implications of Diversity*. London: Verso, 2003.

Luxemburg, R., *The Junius Pamphlet* (1915), reprinted in *The Mass Strike, the Political Party and the Trade Unions, and The Junius Pamphlet*, New York: Harper and Row, 1971.

Macdonald, S., 'The nature of the Anti-Social Behaviour Order', *Modern Law Review*, 66/4 (2003): 630–9.

Machin, S. and Meghir, C., 'Crime and economic incentives', *Journal of Human Resources*, 39/4 (2004): 958–79.

MacLeod, G., *Privatising the City? The Tentative Push towards Edge Urban Developments and Gated Communities in the United Kingdom*. Durham: International Centre for Regional Regeneration and Development Studies, University of Durham, 2004.

Maguire, M., 'Crime statistics: the "data explosion" and its implications', in M. Maguire, R. Morgan and R. Reiner (eds), *The Oxford Handbook of Criminology*, 3rd edn, Oxford: Oxford University Press, 2002.

Malinowski, B., *Crime and Custom in Savage Society*. London: Routledge, 1926.

Mann, D. and Sutton, M., 'Netcrime: more change in the organisation of thieving', *British Journal of Criminology*, 38/2 (1998): 210–29.

Mannheim, H., *Social Aspects of Crime in England between the Wars*. London: Allen and Unwin, 1940.

Marcuse, H, *Eros and Civilization*. Boston: Beacon Press, 1955.

Marris, R., *Survey of the Research Literature on the Economic and Criminological Factors Influencing Crime Trends*. London: Volterra Consulting, 2000.

Martinson, R., 'What works? Questions and answers about prison reform', *Public Interest*, 10/1 (1974): 22–54.

Martinson, R., 'New findings, new views: a note of caution regarding sentencing reform', *Hofstra Law Review*, 7/2 (1979): 243–58.

Marx, K., *Capital Volume 1* (1867). London: Penguin, 1976.

Matthews, R., 'The myth of punitiveness', *Theoretical Criminology*, 9/2 (2005): 175–201.

Matthews, R. and Young, J. (eds), *Confronting Crime*. London: Sage, 1986.

Matthews, R. and Young, J. (eds), *The New Politics of Crime and Punishment*. Cullompton: Willan, 2003.

Matza, D. and Sykes, G., 'Juvenile delinquency and subterranean values', *American Sociological Review*, 26/5 (1961): 712–19.

Mayhew, P., Elliott, D. and Dowds, L., *The 1988 British Crime Survey*. London: HMSO, 1989.

Mayhew, P., Sturan, A. and Hough, M., *Crime as Opportunity*. London: Home Office, 1976.

Mays, J. B., *Crime and the Social Structure*. London: Faber, 1964.

McBarnet, D., *Conviction*. London: Macmillan, 1981.

McCabe, S. and Sutcliffe, F., *Defining Crime*. Oxford: Blackwell, 1978.

McConville, M., Sanders, A. and Leng, R., *The Case for the Prosecution*. London: Routledge, 1991.

McConville, M., Sanders, A. and Leng, R., 'Descriptive or Critical Sociology?', *British Journal of Criminology*, 37/3 (1997): 347–58.

McLaughlin, E. and Murji, K., 'Resistance through representation: "storylines", advertising and Police Federation campaigns', *Policing and Society*, 8/4 (1998): 367–400.

McLaughlin, E. and Murji, K., 'Lost connections and new directions: neo-liberalism, new public managerialism and the "modernisation" of the British police', in K. Stenson and R. Sullivan (eds), *Crime, Risk and Justice*, Cullompton: Willan, 2000.

McLaughlin, E., Muncie, J. and Hughes, G., 'The permanent revolution: New Labour, new public management and the modernization of criminal justice', *Criminal Justice*, 1 (2001): 301–18.

McLintock, F. H. and Avison, N., *Crime in England and Wales*. London: Heinemann, 1968.

Merton, R. 'Social structure and anomie', *American Sociological Review*, 3 (1938): 672–82; revised in R. Merton, *Social Theory and Social Structure*, London: Free Press, 1997.

Messner, S. and Rosenfeld, R., 'Market dominance, crime and globalisation', in S. Karstedt and K.-D. Bussmann (eds), *Social Dynamics of Crime and Control*, Oxford: Hart, 2000.

Messner, S. and Rosenfeld, R., *Crime and the American Dream*, 4th edn. Belmont: Wadsworth, 2007.

Miliband, R., 'A state of desubordination', *British Journal of Sociology*, 29/4 (1978): 399–409.

Mill, J. S., *On Liberty* (1859). Oxford: Oxford University Press, 1998.

Miller, J., 'The debate on rehabilitating criminals: is it true that nothing works?', *Washington Post*, Mar. 1989. At www.prisonpolicy.org/scans/rehab.html.

Millie, A. and Herrington, V., 'Bridging the gap: understanding reassurance policing', *Howard Journal*, 44/1 (2005): 41–56.

Moore, M., 'Sizing up compstat: an important administrative innovation in policing', *Criminology and Public Policy*, 2 (2003): 469–94.

Morgan, R., 'Imprisonment', in M. Maguire, R. Morgan and R. Reiner (eds), *The Oxford Handbook of Criminology*, 3rd edn, Oxford: Oxford University Press, 2002.

Morgan, R. and Newburn, T., *The Future of Policing*. Oxford: Oxford University Press, 1997.

Morris, N., 'Blair's "frenzied law-making" ', *Independent*, 16 Aug. 2006.

Morris, P. and Heal, K., *Crime Control and the Police*. London: Home Office, 1981.

Morris, R., ' "Lies, damned lies and criminal statistics": reinterpreting the criminal statistics in England and Wales', *Crime, History and Societies*, 5 (2001): 111–27.

Morris, T., *Crime and Criminal Justice since 1945*. Oxford: Blackwell, 1989.

Morrison, W., 'What is crime?', in C. Hale, K. Hayward, A. Wahidin and E. Wincup (eds), *Criminology*, Oxford: Oxford University Press, 2005.

Morrison, W. D., 'The interpretation of criminal statistics', *Journal of the Royal Statistical Society*, 60 (1897): 1–24.

Nelken, D., 'Critical criminal law', *Journal of Law and Society*, 14/1 (1987): 105–17.

Nelken, D., 'Criminal law and criminal justice: some notes on their irrelation', in I. Dennis (ed.), *Criminal Law and Justice*, London: Sweet and Maxwell, 1987.

Nelken, D., 'White-collar crime', in M. Maguire, R. Morgan and R. Reiner (eds), *The Oxford Handbook of Criminology*, 3rd edn, Oxford: Oxford University Press, 2002.

Nelken, D., 'Comparing criminal justice', in M. Maguire, R. Morgan and R. Reiner (eds), *The Oxford Handbook of Criminology*, 4th edn, Oxford: Oxford University Press, 2007.

Nelken, D., 'Corporate and white-collar crime', in M. Maguire, R. Morgan and R. Reiner (eds), *The Oxford Handbook of Criminology*, 4th edn, Oxford: Oxford University Press, 2007.

Newburn, T., *Permission and Regulation*. London: Routledge, 1991.

Newburn, T., 'Young people, crime and youth justice', in M. Maguire, R. Morgan and R. Reiner (eds), *The Oxford Handbook of Criminology*, 3rd edn, Oxford: Oxford University Press, 2002.

Newburn, T., *Crime and Criminal Justice Policy*, 2nd edn. London: Longman, 2003.

Newburn, T., ' "Tough on crime": penal policy in England and Wales', in M. Tonry and A. Doob (eds), *Crime and Justice 36*, Chicago: University of Chicago Press, 2007.

Newburn, T. and Jones, T., 'Urban Change and policing: mass private property reconsidered', *European Journal of Criminal Policy and Research*, 7/2 (1999): 225–44.

Newburn, T. and Rock, P., *Living in Fear: Violence and Victimisation in the Lives of Single Homeless People*. London: Shelter, 2005.

Nightingale, C., *On the Edge: A History of Poor Black Kids and their American Dreams*. New York: Basic Books, 1995.

Norrie, A., *Crime, Reason and History*, 2nd edn. London: Butterworths, 2001.

O'Malley, P., 'Risk, power and crime prevention', *Economy and Society*, 21/3 (1992): 252–75.

O'Malley, P., *Risk, Uncertainty and Government*. London: Glasshouse, 2004.

Osborne, D. and Gaebler, T., *Reinventing Government*. New York: Perseus, 1992.

Packer, H., *The Limits of the Criminal Sanction*. Stanford: Stanford University Press, 1968.

Pakes, F. J., 'The politics of discontent: the emergence of a new criminal justice discourse in the Netherlands', *Howard Journal*, 43/3 (2004): 284–98.

Palast, G., *The Best Democracy Money Can Buy*. New York: Plume, 2004.

Parker, R., *John Kenneth Galbraith: His Life, His Politics, his Economics*. New York: Farrar, Straus and Giroux, 2005.

Pearce, N., 'Danish prisons: dinner for wife and kids', *New Statesman*, 4 Sept. 2006, p. 16.

Pearson, G., *Hooligan*. London: Macmillan, 1983.

Pease, K., 'Crime reduction', in M. Maguire, R. Morgan and R. Reiner (eds), *The Oxford Handbook of Criminology*, 3rd edn, Oxford: Oxford University Press, 2002.

Phillips, C. and Bowling, B., 'Racism, ethnicity, crime and criminal justice', in M. Maguire, R. Morgan and R. Reiner (eds), *The Oxford Handbook of Criminology*, 3rd edn, Oxford: Oxford University Press, 2002.

Pissarides, C., 'Unemployment in Britain: a European success story', London: Centre for Economic Performance, London School of Economics, 2003; now published in M. Werding (ed.), *Structural Unemployment in Western Europe*, Cambridge, Mass.: MIT Press, 2006.

Pitts, J., *The New Politics of Youth Crime: Discipline or Solidarity?* London: Macmillan, 2001.

Polanyi, K., *The Great Transformation* (1944). Boston: Beacon, 2001.

Pollock, A., *NHS plc*. London: Verso, 2005.

Pratt, J., 'The return of the wheelbarrow men; or, the arrival of postmodern penality?', *British Journal of Criminology*, 40/1 (2000): 127–46.

Pratt, J., 'Emotive and ostentatious punishment: its decline and resurgence in modern society', *Punishment and Society*, 2/4 (2000): 417–39.

Pratt, J., Brown, D., Brown, M., Hallsworth, S. and Morrison, W. (eds), *The New Punitiveness*. Cullompton: Willan, 2005.

Priestley, J. B., *An Inspector Calls* (1947). London: Penguin, 2001.

Prime, J., White, S., Lirjano, S. and Patel, K., *Criminal Careers of those Born between 1953 and 1978*. London: Home Office, 2001.

Punch, M., *Dirty Business: Exploring Corporate Misconduct*. London: Sage, 1996.

Pyle, D. and Deadman, D., 'Crime and the business cycle in post-war Britain', *British Journal of Criminology*, 34 (1994): 339–57.

Radzinowicz, L., 'Penal regressions', *Cambridge Law Journal*, 50/4 (1991): 422–44.

Radzinowicz, L., *Adventures in Criminology*. London: Routledge, 1999.

Ramsay, P., 'What is anti-social behaviour?', *Criminal Law Review* (Nov. 2004): 908–25.

Ramsay, P., 'The responsible subject as citizen: criminal law, democracy and the welfare state', *Modern Law Review*, 69/1 (2006): 29–58.

Reiman, J., *The Rich Get Richer and the Poor Get Prison*, 7th edn. Boston: Allyn and Bacon, 2004.

Reiner, R., *The Blue-Coated Worker*. Cambridge: Cambridge University Press, 1978.

Reiner, R., 'Fuzzy thoughts: the police and law and order politics', *Sociological Review*, 28/2 (1980): 377–413.

Reiner, R., 'Crime, law and Deviance: the Durkheim legacy', in S. Fenton, *Durkheim and Modern Sociology*, Cambridge: Cambridge University Press, 1984.

Reiner, R., 'The case of the missing crimes', in R. Levitas and W. Guy (eds), *Interpreting Official Statistics*, London: Routledge, 1996.

Reiner, R., *The Politics of the Police*, 3rd edn. Oxford: Oxford University Press, 2000.

Reiner, R., 'Classical social theory and law', in J. Penner, D. Schiff and R. Nobles (eds), *Jurisprudence*, London: Butterworths, 2002.

Reiner, R., 'Media made criminality', in M. Maguire, R. Morgan and R. Reiner (eds), *The Oxford Handbook of Criminology*, 3rd edn, Oxford: Oxford University Press, 2002.

Reiner, R., 'Beyond risk: a lament for social democratic criminology', in T. Newburn and P. Rock (eds), *The Politics of Crime Control*, Oxford: Oxford University Press, 2006.

Reiner, R., 'Media, crime, law and order', *Scottish Journal of Criminal Justice Studies*, 12 (2006): 5–21.

Reiner, R., 'Political economy, crime and criminal justice', in M. Maguire, R. Morgan and R. Reiner (eds), *The Oxford Handbook of Criminology*, 4th edn, Oxford: Oxford University Press, 2007.

Reiner, R. and Cross, M. (eds), *Beyond Law and Order*. London: Macmillan, 1991.

Reiner, R. and Spencer, S. (eds), *Accountable Policing: Effectiveness, Empowerment and Equity*. London: Institute for Public Policy Research, 1993.

Reiner, R., Livingstone, S. and Allen, J., 'No more happy endings? The media and popular concern about crime since the Second World War', in T. Hope and R. Sparks (eds), *Crime, Risk and Insecurity*, London: Routledge, 2000.

Reiner, R., Livingstone, S. and Allen, J., 'Casino culture: the media and crime in a winner–loser society', in K. Stenson and R. Sullivan (eds), *Crime and Risk Society*, Cullompton: Willan, 2001.

Reiner, R., Livingstone, S. and Allen, J., 'From law and order to lynch mobs: crime news since the Second World War', in P. Mason (ed.), *Criminal Visions*, Cullompton: Willan, 2003.

Resodihardjo, S., 'Discourse and funnelling: how discourse affected Howard's leeway during the 1994–5 crisis', *Journal for Crime, Conflict and the Media*, 1/3 (2004): 15–27.

Roberts, J. and Stalans, L., *Public Opinion, Crime and Criminal Justice*. Boulder: Westview, 2000.

Rose, D., 'Violent crime: the shocking truth', *Observer*, 28 May 2006.

Rose, N., 'The death of the social?', *Economy and Society*, 25/3 (1996): 327–56.

Rosenfeld, R., 'The case of the unsolved crime decline', *Scientific American* (Feb. 2004): 82–9.

Ruggiero, V., *Crime and Markets*. Oxford: Oxford University Press, 2000.

Ryan, M., *The Acceptable Pressure Group*. London: Dartmouth, 1978.

Ryan, M., *The Politics of Penal Reform*. London: Longman, 1983.

Ryan, M., *Penal Policy and Political Culture in England and Wales*. Winchester: Waterside, 2003.

Sandbrook, D., *Never Had It So Good: A History of Britain from Suez to the Beatles*. London: Little, Brown, 2005.

Sandbrook, D., *White Heat: A History of Britain in the Swinging Sixties*. London: Little, Brown, 2006.

Sanders, A. and Young, R., 'From suspect to trial', in M. Maguire, R. Morgan and R. Reiner (eds), *The Oxford Handbook of Criminology*, 3rd edn, Oxford: Oxford University Press, 2002.

Sanders, A. and Young, R., *Criminal Justice*, 3rd edn. London: Butterworths, 2006.

Sasson, T., *Crime Talk*. New York: Aldine de Gruyter, 1995.

Schwendinger, H. and Schwendinger, J., 'Guardians of order or defenders of human rights?', in I. Taylor, P. Walton and J. Young (eds), *Critical Criminology*, London: Routledge, 1975.

Sennett, R., *The Corrosion of Character*. New York: Norton, 1998.

Sennett, R., *The Culture of the New Capitalism*. New Haven: Yale University Press, 2006.

Sharpe, J. A., *Crime in Early Modern England, 1550–1750*. London: Longman, 1984.

Shearing, C. and Stenning, P., 'Private security: implications for social control', *Social Problems*, 30/5 (1983): 493–506.

Shearing, C. and Stenning, P., ' "Say cheese!" The Disney order that's not so Mickey Mouse', in C. Shearing and P. Stenning (eds), *Private Policing*, Beverly Hills: Sage, 1987.

Shepherd J., 'Violent crime in Bristol: an accident and emergency department perspective', *British Journal of Criminology*, 30/2 (1990): 289–305.

Sheptycki, J. and Wardak, A. (eds), *Transnational and Comparative Criminology*. London: Glasshouse, 2005.

Shury, J., Speed, M., Vivian, D., Keuchel, A. and Nicholas, S., *Crime against Retail and Manufacturing Premises: Findings from the 2002 Commercial Victimisation Survey*. London: Home Office, 2005.

Silver, A., 'The demand for order in civil society', in D. Bordua (ed.), *The Police*, New York: Wiley, 1967.

Simmons, J., Legg, C. and Hosking, R., *National Crime Recording Standard: An Analysis of the Impact on Recorded Crime*. London: Home Office, 2003.

Simon, J., ' "They died with their boots on": the boot camp and the limits of modern penality', *Social Justice*, 22 (1995): 25–48.

Simon, J., ' "Entitlement to Cruelty": neo-liberalism and the punitive mentality in the United States', in K. Stenson and R. Sullivan (eds), *Crime, Risk and Justice*, Cullompton: Willan, 2001.

Sivarajasingam, V., Shepherd, J. P., Walker, R., Walters, L. and Morgan, P., *Trends in Violence in England and Wales 2000–2004: An Accident and Emergency Perspective*. Cardiff: Violence and Society Research Group, Cardiff University, 2005.

Slapper, G., *Blood in the Bank*. Aldershot: Ashgate, 1999.

Slapper, G. and Tombs, S., *Corporate Crime*. London: Longman, 1999.

Smith, D., 'Youth crime and conduct disorders: trends, patterns and causal explanations', in M. Rutter and D. Smith (eds),

Psychosocial Disorders in Young People: Time-Trends and their Causes, London: Wiley, 1995.
Smith, D., 'Case construction and the goals of the criminal process', *British Journal of Criminology*, 37/3 (1997): 319–46.
Smith, D., 'Reform or moral outrage?', *British Journal of Criminology*, 38/4 (1998): 616–22.
Smith, D., 'Less crime without more punishment', *Edinburgh Law Review*, 3 (1999): 294–316.
Smith, D., 'Crime and punishment in Scotland, 1981–1999', in M. Tonry and D. Farrington (eds), *Crime and Punishment in Western Countries, 1980–1999*, Chicago: University of Chicago Press, 2005.
South, N., *Policing for Profit*. London: Sage, 1988.
Sparks, R., *Television and the Drama of Crime*. Milton Keynes: Open University Press, 1992.
Sparks, R., Genn, H. and Dodd, D., *Surveying Victims*. London: Wiley, 1977.
Spelman, W., 'The limited importance of prison expansion', in A. Blumstein and J. Wallman (eds), *The Crime Drop in America*, Cambridge: Cambridge University Press, 2000.
Spelman, W., 'Jobs or jails? The crime drop in Texas', *Journal of Policy Analysis and Management*, 24/1 (2005): 133–65.
Squires, P. and Stephen, D., *Rougher Justice: Anti-social Behaviour and Young People*. Cullompton: Willan, 2005.
Stephen, J. F., *Liberty, Equality, Fraternity* (1873). Chicago: Chicago University Press, 1992.
Stinchcombe, A., 'Institutions of privacy in the determination of police administrative practice', *American Journal of Sociology*, 69 (1963): 150–60.
Surette, R., *Media, Crime and Criminal Justice: Images and Realities*, 2nd edn. Belmont: Wadsworth, 1998.
Sutherland, E., *White-Collar Crime*. New York: Holt, Rinehart and Winston, 1949.
Sykes, G. and Matza, D., 'Techniques of neutralization', *American Sociological Review*, 33 (1957): 46–62.
Tadros, V. and Tierney, S., 'The presumption of innocence and the Human Rights Act', *Modern Law Review*, 67/3 (2004): 411.

Tawney, R. H., *The Acquisitive Society* (1921). London: Fontana, 1961.

Taylor, H., 'Rising crime: the political economy of criminal statistics since the 1850s', *Economic History Review* 51 (1998): 569–90.

Taylor, H., 'Forging the job: a crisis of "modernisation" or redundancy for the police in England and Wales 1900–39', *British Journal of Criminology*, 39 (1999): 113–35.

Taylor, I., *Law and Order: Arguments for Socialism*. London: Macmillan, 1981.

Taylor, I., 'The political economy of crime', in M. Maguire, R. Morgan and R. Reiner (eds), *The Oxford Handbook of Criminology*, 2nd edn, Oxford: Oxford University Press, 1997.

Taylor, I., *Crime in Context*. Cambridge: Polity, 1999.

Taylor, L., *In the Underworld*. Oxford: Blackwell, 1984.

Taylor, R., *Sweden's New Social Democratic Model*. London: Compass, 2005.

Tham, H., 'Crime and the welfare state: the case of the United Kingdom and Sweden', in V. Ruggiero, N. South and I. Taylor (eds), *The New European Criminology*, London: Routledge, 1998.

Tham, H., 'Law and order as a leftist project: the case of Sweden', *Punishment and Society*, 3 (2001): 409–26.

Thompson, T. and Bright, M., 'Secret papers reveal crime rate fiddle', *Observer*, 28 Oct. 2001.

Thornton, D., Curran, L., Grayson, D. and Holloway, V., *Tougher Regimes in Detention Centres*. London: HMSO, 1984.

Tilley, N. (ed.), *Handbook of Crime Prevention and Community Safety*. Cullompton: Willan, 2005.

Tombs, S., 'Death and work in Britain', *Sociological Review*, 47/2 (1999): 345–67.

Tombs, S., 'Workplace injury and death: social harm and the illusions of law', in P. Hillyard, C. Pantazis, S. Tombs and D. Gordon (eds), *Beyond Criminology*, London: Pluto, 2004.

Tombs, S. and Whyte, D., '"Two steps forward, one step back": towards corporate accountability for workplace deaths?', *Policy and Politics in Occupational Health and Safety*, 1/1 (2003): 9–30.

Tombs, S. and Whyte, D., *Safety Crimes*. Cullompton: Willan, 2006.

Tomlinson, J., *Hayek and the Market*. London: Pluto, 1990.

Tonry, M., *Punishment and Politics*. Cullompton: Willan, 2004.

Tonry, M., *Thinking about Crime*. New York: Oxford University Press, 2004.

Tonry, M. and Farrington, D. (eds), *Crime and Punishment in Western Countries, 1980–1999*. Chicago: Chicago University Press, 2005.

Towne, S., 'Crime displacement' (2001), at www.crimereduction.gov.uk.

Treschel, S., *Human Rights in Criminal Proceedings*. Oxford: Oxford University Press, 2005.

Tunstall, J., *The Media are American*. London: Constable, 1977.

Tunstall, J., *The Media were American*. New York: Oxford University Press, 2007.

Van Kesteren, J., Mayhew, P. and Nieuwbeerta, P., *Criminal Victimisation in Seventeen Industrialised Countries*. The Hague: Ministry of Justice, 2000.

Vold, G., Bernard, T. and Snipes, J., *Theoretical Criminology*, 4th edn. New York: Oxford University Press, 1998.

Von Hirsch, A., Garland, D. and Wakefield, A. (eds), *Ethical and Social Perspectives on Situational Crime Prevention*. Oxford: Hart, 2005.

Von Hirsch, A., Bottoms, A., Burney, E. and Wikstrom, P.-O., *Criminal Deterrence and Sentence Severity: An Analysis of Recent Research*. Oxford: Hart, 1999.

Wacquant, L., 'The new "peculiar institution": on the prison as surrogate ghetto', *Theoretical Criminology*, 4/3 (2000): 377–89.

Wakefield, A., *Selling Security: The Private Policing of Public Space*. Cullompton: Willan, 2003.

Walker, A., Kershaw, C. and Nicholas, S., *Crime in England and Wales 2005/06*. London: Home Office, 2006.

Walker, M., *Interpreting Crime Statistics*. Oxford: Oxford University Press, 1995.

Walker, N., *Crimes, Courts and Figures*. London: Penguin, 1971.

Walklate, S., *Gender, Crime and Criminal Justice*. Cullompton: Willan, 2004.

Wall, D. (ed.), *Crime and the Internet*. London: Routledge, 2001.

Walmsley, R., Howard, L. and White, S., *The National Prison Survey 1991*. London: HMSO, 1992.

Weatheritt, M., 'Measuring police performance: accounting or accountability?', in R. Reiner and S. Spencer (eds), *Accountable Policing*, London: Institute for Public Policy Research, 1993.

Weber, M., *Economy and Society* (1914). Berkeley: University of California Press, 1978.

Weber, M., *The Theory of Social and Economic Organization* (1947). Glencoe: Free Press, 1964.

Weisburd, D., Mastrofski, S., Mcnally, A., Greenspan, R. and Willis, J., 'Reforming to preserve: Compstat and strategic problem solving in American Policing', *Criminology and Public Policy*, 2/3 (2003): 421–56.

Wells, C., *Corporations and Criminal Responsibility*. Oxford: Oxford University Press, 2001.

Welsh, B. and Irving, M., 'Crime and punishment in Canada, 1981–1999', in M. Tonry and D. Farrington (eds), *Crime and Punishment in Western Countries, 1980–1999*, Chicago: Chicago University Press, 2005.

Werding, M. (ed.), *Structural Unemployment in Western Europe*. London: MIT Press, 2006.

Western, B., *Punishment and Inequality in America*. New York: Russell Sage, 2006.

Wilby, P., 'Thatcherism's final triumph', *Prospect*, 127 (Oct. 2006): 28–31.

Wilkinson, R., *The Impact of Inequality*. New York: New Press, 2005.

Williams, G., 'The definition of crime', in *Current Legal Problems 1955* (1955), p. 107.

Wilson, J. Q., *Thinking about Crime*. New York: Vintage, 1975.

Wilson, J. Q. and Herrnstein, R., *Crime and Human Nature*. New York: Simon and Schuster, 1985.

Winlow, S. and Hall, S., *Violent Night: Urban Leisure and Contemporary Culture*. London: Berg, 2006.

Wintour, P., 'Restore trust in crime figures, urges watchdog', *Guardian*, 30 Dec. 2005.

Witt, R., Clarke, A. and Fielding, N., 'Crime and economic activity: a panel data approach', *British Journal of Criminology*, 39 (1999): 391–400.

Wood, J. and Dupont, B., (eds), *Democracy, Society and the Governance of Security*. Cambridge: Cambridge University Press, 2006.

Wootton, B., *Social Science and Social Pathology*. London: Allen and Unwin, 1959.

Wright, R. and Decker, S., *Burglars on the Job*. Boston: Northeastern University Press, 1996.

Wright, R. and Decker, S., *Armed Robbers on the Job*. Boston: Northeastern University Press, 1998.

Wrightson, K., 'Two concepts of order: justices, constables and jurymen in seventeenth-century England', in J. Brewer and J. Styles (eds), *An Ungovernable People: The English and their Law in the Seventeenth and Eighteenth Centuries*, London: Hutchinson, 1980.

Yar, M., *Cybercrime and Society*. London: Sage, 2006.

Young, J., 'The failure of criminology: the need for a radical realism', in R. Matthews and J. Young (eds), *Confronting Crime*, London: Sage, 1986.

Young, J., *The Exclusive Society*. London: Sage, 1999.

Young, J., 'Merton with energy, Katz with structure: the sociology of vindictiveness and the criminology of transgression', *Theoretical Criminology*, 7 (2003): 389–414.

Young, J., 'Winning the fight against crime? New Labour, populism and lost opportunities', in R. Matthews and J. Young (eds), *The New Politics of Crime and Punishment*, Cullompton: Willan, 2003.

Young, J., 'Constructing the paradigm of violence: mass media, violence and youth', in H.-J. Albrecht, T. Serassis and H. Kania (eds), *Images of Crime II*, Freiburg: Max Planck Institute, 2004.

Young, J., 'Voodoo criminology and the numbers game', in J. Ferrell, K. Hayward, W. Morrison and M. Presdee (eds), *Cultural Criminology Unleashed*, London: Glasshouse, 2004.

Young, M., *An Inside Job*. Oxford: Oxford University Press, 1991.

Zedner, L., 'Dangers of dystopia', *Oxford Journal of Legal Studies*, 22 (2002): 341–66.

Zedner, L., 'Too much security?', *International Journal of the Sociology of Law*, 31/1 (2003): 155–84.

Zedner, L., *Criminal Justice*. Oxford University Press, 2004.

Zedner, L., 'Opportunity makes the thief-taker: the influence of economic analysis on crime control', in T. Newburn and P. Rock (eds), *The Politics of Crime Control*, Oxford: Oxford University Press, 2006.

Zedner, L., 'Policing before the police', *British Journal of Criminology*, 46/1 (2006): 78–96.

Zimring, F., 'Imprisonment rates and the new politics of criminal punishment', *Punishment and Society*, 3/1 (2001): 161–6.

Zimring, F., *The Great American Crime Decline*. New York: Oxford University Press, 2006.

Index

Law and Order